THE
SUICIDE
BRIDE

T0385263

THE SUICIDE BRIDE

TANYA BRETHERTON

hachette
AUSTRALIA

hachette
AUSTRALIA

Published in Australia and New Zealand in 2019
by Hachette Australia
(an imprint of Hachette Australia Pty Limited)
Level 17, 207 Kent Street, Sydney NSW 2000
www.hachette.com.au

10 9 8 7 6 5 4 3 2 1

A catalogue record for this
book is available from the
National Library of Australia

ISBN: 978 0 7336 4098 8

Cover design by Christabella Designs
Cover photographs courtesy of Trove/State Library Victoria
Typeset in 12/18.6 pt Sabon LT Pro by Bookhouse, Sydney
Printed and bound in Great Britain by Clays Ltd, Elcograf S.p.A.

The paper this book is printed on is certified against the
Forest Stewardship Council® Standards. McPherson's Printing
Group holds FSC® chain of custody certification SA-COC-005379.
FSC® promotes environmentally responsible, socially beneficial
and economically viable management of the world's forests.

CONTENTS

CONTENTS

1

TRAGEDY STRIKES

Strike [verb]
1 *to hit forcibly and deliberately with one's hand or other implement.*
2 *a disaster or other unwelcome phenomenon that occurs suddenly and has harmful or damaging effects.*
Merriam-Webster Dictionary

WHEN FOUR-YEAR-OLD MERVYN SLY WOKE ON THE MORNING of Tuesday, 12 January 1904 in the inner city of Sydney, he did not know how close he was to death. While he had been sleeping peacefully on the ground floor of his home, a two-storey terrace house at 49 Watkin Street, death had arrived, and stayed. It now lurked silently on the top floor.

Beyond the boy's bedroom window, the borough of Newtown was charged with the restless and noisy energy of a busy weekday morning in metropolitan Sydney. Trains rattled loudly on their approach to Newtown Station. The air was filled with the sweet and heady smell of yeast from the bakery across the street. The flat and dull strike of a forging hammer pealed out from the blacksmith with the rolling rhythm of an off-key church bell. Even the soft snorting of horses from the stable on Wilson Street could be heard from the Sly residence on the corner. None of it, however, had been enough to stir the young boy from slumber.

It was around 9.30 a.m. Long lancet-shaped windows, arched like those found in a church, cast pillars of warm light across Mervyn's face. Dust rose from the rag-filled mattress on which he slept and floated up in the air, then fell with the softness of light snow. An open window briefly swept a fresh cool breeze off the Pacific Ocean into the room.

The young boy had gone to bed without dinner, and the grumbling of his stomach finally shook him from sleep. As soon as he opened his eyes, he leapt from bed and ran outside to seek out his older brothers: Bedford, eight, and Basil, six. He found them at the home of Mrs Shaw, a neighbour.

The Sly family had lived on Watkin Street for less than a week, but in that time they had made an impression on their new neighbour. The Slys were Catholic, and this alone made them strange, according to Mrs Shaw. But other things struck her as odd. Mr Sly was a nervous man: he complained about the house, about rapping and tapping in the walls, wires on the roof and intruders at night. On occasion he even complained about his children. Bedford, the eldest son, also told tall tales about the goings-on in the house. He had told Mrs Shaw, in more detail than she would ever care to know, that he and his father had seen dark figures moving about the house at night.

Mrs Shaw had spent most of the past week chasing the boys off her property; she had also become unwillingly involved in the comings and goings of the Sly household. She had looked after the children when their parents went out – which was often. She had provided the address of a local doctor when the youngest child, Olive, had fallen ill – this too seemed a burden. It was lucky Mrs Shaw had been willing to help. Olive had almost died, and remained in hospital recuperating.

Mrs Shaw had even fed the Sly children. The three boys complained that the bread and butter in their home tasted grainy, that it was jagged and bitter on the tongue. It burnt them, they said. Bedford had taught his brothers how to steal bread from the pantry and sprinkle it with sugar to make breakfast. When they could not find fresh bread at home, Bedford taught his brothers how to beg. For the past week, this activity had almost always led straight to Mrs Shaw's door.

On 12 January, sometime around midmorning, discussion between the three boys turned to the issue of their parents. Bedford said he had seen their father that morning when he had woken up. Their father had been dressed in his suit, and Bedford had seen him stride through the house with razor and strop in hand, shoes on and laced up, vest buttoned. Bedford told his brothers their father must have been going to work.

For some reason, Mervyn decided to return to the house alone. The little boy, dressed in a loose-fitting romper styled like a sailor suit, ran exuberantly through the terrace house. Finding no one in the kitchen or sitting room on the ground floor, Mervyn sped towards the steep and narrow stairs that led up to his parents' bedroom. Mervyn most certainly would have gathered speed at the bottom to ensure his small feet and short legs could make the ascent.

Then, at the top of the staircase, the boy abruptly stopped, unable to comprehend the extraordinary scene that confronted him.

Perhaps he noticed the way the sunlight came streaming in through the curtainless windows. Perhaps he noticed that the sunlight reflected off the wooden floor and glowed red with the blood that saturated almost every surface in the room. Or perhaps the young boy was fascinated by the sticky sensation and sound of his feet as they tracked across the red liquid that surrounded his mother's body.

Mervyn went in for a closer look. His mother was lying across a mattress on the floor. A spongy and slippery coil of muscle and connective cartilage lay in the space where the smooth skin of her neck had once been. The blood had pooled, soaked into the mattress and surrounded her head in a perfectly round congealed crimson aura. This must have been a terrifying scene for a young Catholic boy, familiar with sculptures and reliefs of the Virgin Mary and her sacred halo. He looked at a horrifying re-imagining of his mother: not Our Lady the Virgin, but a bloody Mary lying half naked on the bedroom floor.

Not able to fully understand what he saw but believing his mother desperately needed help, Mervyn ran back downstairs and outside to the comfort and safety of his brothers. He tugged at Bedford's sleeve. 'Come and see, there is something wrong with Mammy,' he said urgently.

Bedford, taking his responsibility as an older brother very seriously and being the closest thing to an adult, went to see for himself. Basil took Mervyn's hand. The two boys waited patiently, and fearfully, in the lane outside their home. Inside, Bedford made the second terrible discovery of that morning. He found not just their mother but also their father, in a similar condition on the bedroom floor. Somehow, little Mervyn had not noticed that his mother was not alone.

It took longer than it should have for the boys to get help. This was not because Bedford hesitated – he ran as fast as he could to Mrs Shaw's front door. But she did not believe him. When he opened with, 'Mammy and Daddy are dead', she quickly drew what she believed to be the only logical conclusion: he was lying. *Just another strange story from this strange boy*, she thought.

But Bedford did not give up. He insisted his parents needed help.

Mrs Shaw did not enter the terrace house to investigate Bedford Sly's claims. Instead she grabbed the arm of a passing stranger in the street, asking them to send word to the police.

She allowed the three boys to play nearer to her yard, and she told them not to worry. This was the extent of the comfort she showed them.

The three young brothers waited at the crossroad of Watkin and Wilson. Bedford stood in the shadow of the towering two-storey family home. Mervyn was bathed in sunlight. Basil waited between the two, flanked by light on one side and shadow on the other.

2

THE CALL-OUT

LATER THAT MORNING, POLICE SERGEANT MATTHEW AGNEW arrived at 49 Watkin Street looking for a dead body.

The front door was wide open, but from the doorstep he could not see what was on the other side. The bright midday sun obscured his vision, and the interior of the house lay in shadow.

He knocked. 'Is there anyone home?' he called. 'It is the police.' He did not expect an answer.

An hour before, Sergeant Agnew had been on foot patrol in north Newtown, walking down the main thoroughfare of King Street. Before private household phones, the individual uniformed officer on foot or bike represented the next best thing to an emergency police hotline for the general public. Foot patrols were an important part of a policeman's job.

Throughout his thirty years in the force, Agnew had spent a lot of time 'on the beat' in the streets of Newtown.

The sergeant was accustomed to being approached by anyone, about anything, at any time. On this morning, he was being swept along by the last of the morning commuters; already late for work, they were headed southward towards the tram stop and train station near the Enmore Road junction. For this reason, Agnew did not see the figure approach. A well-dressed gentleman was crossing King Street while waving his arm in the manner of hailing a cab, but he was clearly attempting to hail the man in the distinctive dark blue heavy wool police tunic. It was not until Agnew heard, 'Excuse me, Officer!' that he realised he was needed.

Agnew broke off from the shoal of commuters and steered the gentleman to the ridge of dirt in the gutter, clear of the jostling crowd.

'A woman has just asked me to fetch the police,' the gentleman said. 'I believe there's been a death, down on Watkin Street.' There was no suggestion of fear or distress in his voice, and he had no additional information to offer except an address.

At fifty-nine years old, and with the better part of his working life spent in the Newtown police force, Agnew knew that while no two cases were ever the same there were recognisable patterns. He had dealt with just about anything a Sydney policeman might come across: murders, suicides, assaults and thefts. He had seen grief and greed, rage and madness. As a constable, he had collared vagrants. He had pummelled belligerent drunks and brought them into custody. Agnew was willing to put his own life at risk if it meant keeping the public safe. Five years earlier when a pontoon collapsed suddenly on a harbour picnic and grown men were drowning, Agnew had managed to drag those who were twice his weight and half his age from the water. He had directly intervened in scraps between young thugs brawling outside Newtown pubs, a common event on a Saturday night. He had always been unafraid to throw punches if they were needed.

In his job, Agnew had come to know about both civic strife and civic life in the borough. Police had responsibility for frontline administrative Births, Deaths and Marriages work, and so handled the hatch, match and dispatch of local residents. They also took complaints about everything from blocked drains to noisy neighbours, and from sheep theft to dangerous dogs. In a single working day police might be required to register the birth of one child then inspect the death of another; chase a shoplifter; calm and release a distressed horse ensnared in a wire fence; and even test the scales at the local slaughterhouse to ensure the weights and measures were accurate. The police had also, just a week earlier, been made responsible for the labour-intensive task of compiling the Commonwealth electoral roll for the newly formed Federation of Australia. They were the frontline of a public health patrol too, monitoring possible outbreaks of typhoid, cholera and plague. There was very little about the borough that police hadn't seen, hand printed, typed, stamped and prepared in triplicate for government.

Although Sergeant Agnew did not know exactly what he was about to face, he could calculate probabilities based on the location of the reported incident and the time of day. Police work had given him an intimate knowledge of death and an understanding of all the ways people could die. As a man who had seen his wife die, he knew death as a personal event. He also understood death as a map: an accumulation of details, data and demography across the borough in which he lived and worked.

On this mid-January morning he guessed that someone elderly or very young had passed away overnight, as they were more likely to do in the warmer months. The heat increased the risk of milk and other highly perishable food becoming contaminated, and children in particular were in danger of being poisoned this way. Typhoid was a possibility too, as was plague. Since 1900 Sydney had suffered several contagion scares, and although the Board of Health claimed the city was now plague free, police were required by the state to remain vigilant. Any new cases of high fevers, significant lethargy and/or diarrhoea required mandatory reporting to a health official.

While Agnew was calm as he walked to Watkin Street, he was also an experienced officer who understood the need to be prepared for any contingency. He took a quick mental inventory of his duty gear: a large leather baton in his belt, a six-shot Colt Navy revolver in his holster, and a shrill police whistle fastened to his tunic with a chain. He felt the heavy reassurance of the D-shaped iron handcuffs in his jacket. He was armed for almost anything, from subduing an offender with a truncheon strike to the back of the neck to shooting a nuisance animal in the street.

When he arrived at the address, he did not enter immediately; he waited for his eyes to adjust to the dark interior of the home. His vision was obscured even further by the odd shape of the residence. On a corner block positioned at the end of a long row of terraces, it curved crookedly to the right and out of his line of sight, as though unwilling to give up its secrets.

Peering inside, the first thing Agnew noticed was an oilcloth rug, large enough that it covered the floor in the front room. This immediately struck him as odd. Front rooms were sitting rooms and places to receive guests. Even the poorest of residents usually tried to decorate the space with arts and crafts, to make it more welcoming. This room, however, was bare.

Slowly the busy pattern on the mat became visible as his eyesight adapted. It was as if the hardwood floor was coming to life with a garden of chestnut-coloured roses – oversized flowers in bold symmetry. Though the lack of furniture was odd, the rug was not. Varnished oilcloths were common in homes in the area, with darker tawny and russet-coloured designs favoured by working-class families because they better concealed dirt marks from labouring boots.

In the front doorway, Agnew called out loudly so he might be heard upstairs. He listened briefly for any response. Silence.

Reassured there was no immediate danger, he entered the front room holding no particular concerns about what he might find.

The high-set position of the property and the steep downward gradient of Watkin Street allowed the sergeant to see the entire road and all of the neighbouring homes through elongated windows.

The Sly home faced onto Wilson Street, a long road populated with an eclectic mix of family and business interests, often blended together in the same premises. Coach builders, blacksmiths, bootmakers, bakers and embalmers could all be found near this corner.

Nineteenth-century Newtown is often described as 'gritty' because of the dirty streetscapes that typified an industrialising Sydney, but this is an apt descriptor for another reason entirely. Unlike nearby Glebe, Surry Hills and Haymarket, which had reputations for crime and graft, Newtown was known for craft. The air of the borough in the late nineteenth century was periodically filled with smoke and soot, the sweet smell of sawdust, the heady scent of baking bread, the sourness of leather and glue, or perhaps the occasional gust of a blocked drain or the shuddering stink of a water closet in need of emptying. As one historical account of Newtown at the turn of the twentieth century notes, 'shops were the very foundation of the suburb'. The busy strip of shopfronts on King Street that ran through its centre was akin to a main artery that fed the families and businesses connected to it. Aspirational working-class families were positively drawn to the suburb and to houses like the one Agnew was now standing in. People came to create something new and become something new – and they hoped to make a little profit in the process.

On entering the second ground-floor room, Agnew's actuarial and analytical senses were truly awoken. Almost unconsciously he gathered data, weighing his observations and calculating probabilities as he drew on his bank of knowledge.

A single boot.

A tailor's pressing iron.

A piano in the corner.

The wall, half finished in a dirty wash of paint. Chalky to the touch.

Agnew stepped over a Bible in the middle of the floor.

Then the scene began to change. What was unfolding before his eyes seemed dramatically at odds with an industrious Newtown family home.

As he turned into the next room, he was confronted with a much more complex scene. Unlike the empty front room, this one was packed with goods. Mattresses were tossed in a shambolic jumble. A cooking pot suitable for boiling big joints of meat sat atop bedcovers twisted in a knot on the floor, and atop that were several loaves of mouldy bread. A dripping pan was in the corner as if thrown. A lamp lay on its side, as did a blanket box, kicked or dropped and simply left that way. Clothing was scattered from one end of the room to the other.

The dining table was set, with the remnants of a spoilt meal still on the plates. Pieces of buttered bread were discarded on the table and floor. More loaves of bread were mixed up in the maelstrom of clothing.

Cutlery scattered, as if dropped like fiddlesticks from a great height.

A kettle, upturned.

The sergeant's sense of unease grew.

Within this chaotic scene were pockets of order. On the floor, neatly labelled, stacked and tied, were small towers of sheet music, pins securing their corners. In all this disarray someone had sorted these pieces, carefully separating the bagatelles from the nocturnes. It only added to the eeriness of the scene.

Oil paintings were arranged on the floor, dozens of them. The placement of some seemed purposeful, as if they were leaning against the wall to mark where they should be hung above.

A scene of farming life.

A view of dry plains.

Still life of flowers and fruit.

Very quickly, the sergeant drew a conclusion: dark and light, the graceful and the grotesque, had dwelled together within this home.

A triangular three-tiered whatnot shelf, designed for placement in a corner, stood awkwardly in the middle of the hallway. A brass plate sat on the top shelf; screws had never been sunk into its polished face, indicating that it had never been hung. It was engraved with an inscription: *Mrs E G Sly, Teacher of music and dancing.* The sergeant made note of the name Sly. At the bottom of the whatnot shelf was more rotting food.

Agnew had seen enough to make an educated guess: he had not been called here because of a crime, but because of the public health hazard the property posed. During epidemics of typhoid and diphtheria, houses in the district had been doused with Lysol, a state-enforced attempt to contain the spread of disease to neighbouring properties. If houses were considered to be beyond cleaning, they were demolished. Agnew had overseen this process during one of the bubonic plague outbreaks. The gentleman on King Street had mentioned death in this home, and Agnew was now pretty sure it must have been due to disease.

If that proved correct, he knew what would happen from here. First, he would find the body; second, the home owner. Agnew had a high degree of certainty that they would not be the same person. Most of the borough was leased to working-class families, with over 90 per cent of Newtown owned by a small cartel of landlords. Agnew may not have known this as a statistical fact, or read the long lines of numbers being slowly tallied by public servants to build trend data for the city, but he knew it as a fact of foot-patrol policing. Leases turned over quickly. Working-class families came and went. From Sergeant Agnew's standpoint, a clear protocol would probably apply from this point forward. He would need to find the landlord and ensure he assumed responsibility for cleaning his property. The health inspector would also need to be contacted, and soon – this, too, was mandatory.

Agnew had seen just about enough. He abandoned his reconnaissance of the ground floor and decided to take a cursory look upstairs to assess the damage. As he circled the banister and began to climb, he stopped.

There were red puddles on the stairs. Blood dangled in a heavy droplet from the top step and had pooled on each one leading down. In a reflex action, Agnew rested his hand atop his revolver and proceeded cautiously up the stairs.

At the top, he stopped again. For a moment he thought these hardwood floors were also covered with a decorative oilcloth rug. A red one.

There was so much blood it coloured the floor with a macabre design. It was dark brown in thinner patches where the warm air had dried it more rapidly, while deeper plum and currant tones were present where the pools remained thick and wet.

Then Agnew noticed them. When he did, he was shocked at himself for overlooking them.

One man. One woman. Face up on the floor, a short distance from each other. Both completely soaked in blood. Their throats had been cut, though the woman had been subjected to far more savagery than the man.

In Agnew's long career he had seen blood, and plenty of it. He had seen murder. He had even seen suicide, both failed and successful attempts. Some fourteen years before, down the street from where the sergeant now stood, thirty-year-old William Carlton had attempted to end his life by cutting his throat with scissors. His housemate found him passed out on the floor. Agnew's quick dispatch of Carlton to the hospital had seemed to save the man's life, but he had lost too much blood and died the next morning.

Agnew believed he knew what had happened here. A cutthroat razor was still grasped in the man's coiled right hand. The two arms of the device were folded out like a pair of compasses about to take measurement. The cuts on the man's neck were short and jagged, just as they had been with William Carlton.

The woman's condition was a very different matter. A deep swipe of a cut, right across the neck, had created a most bizarre sight. The spooling thread of her windpipe looked like the thick string of a torn necklace, with her head resembling a threaded bead on the brink of breaking loose and rolling away.

Agnew believed he knew what he was looking at, because he had seen something like it before. Almost twenty years earlier in Newtown, a mathematics teacher at the elite Newington College, Arthur Blyth, had killed his wife, Edith, with a razor, and then himself. When Agnew had arrived at the Blyths' home that day, the scene had been one of absolute mayhem. Neighbours were out on the street, eager to hail anyone for help. Edith's mother wailed while she cradled her dead adult daughter in her arms. That scene had made sense to Agnew. It had been loud, chaotic and unholy, screaming at him in a way that seemed in perfect proportion to the crime. But there was a quietude here, in this home on Watkin Street, that made his skin prickle like gooseflesh.

Agnew worked hard to suppress his horror, returning to the observation and collection of facts. In a manner of speaking the woman was still in bed, lying on a mattress. However, the mattress was on the floor beneath the window; the bed frame sat empty in the middle of the room.

The woman was in her underwear. In the early twentieth century this was a very modest, full-length calico chemise that ran from the chest to the toes, with lacing in the front. Her boots were on, and these too were tied up. Whether Agnew as a male police officer derived any conclusions from that observation is unclear, but it was consistent with the custom many women used to dress at the time. They usually put on and laced up their boots before they slid into cumbersome skirts and blouses. Once a woman was dressed, it was difficult for her to bend over to tie laces or clasp buckles. At the time of her death, this woman had been getting dressed or undressed.

The man, on the other hand, had prepared himself for a grand outing. Shoes were shined. Waistcoat and suit had been neatly buttoned. His hair was slicked down. The only thing missing was his hat.

At first glance the position of his body seemed awkward, but on closer examination it was purposeful, almost ingeniously arranged. A long workbox, similar to those used by craftsmen to carry their tools of trade, had been placed beneath his neck so that his head remained sharply tilted backwards and at an obtuse angle. Agnew recognised the position: he had seen bodies posed by doctors and morgue keepers in the same way. This technique was routinely used to keep the neck and head of a corpse rigid on a slab, while doctors picked through chest cavities. It appeared the dead man had been precise and methodical in carrying out this act.

Agnew collected only two pieces of physical evidence from the scene. One was a sealed envelope on the floor near the woman, addressed to Mr J. J. O'Leary. The other was a piece of paper, roughly folded, on the floor near the man. As Agnew picked it up, he took a closer look at the corpse's face.

Even under the mask of blood and despite the contortion of the features, Agnew recognised him.

In the past few days, other members of the Newtown police had come to know him quite well. Very early on Saturday morning, he had complained to the local police station about intruders in his home. Agnew had not handled the matter directly, but he had heard workplace mumblings about an odd man on Watkin Street who had ranted about telephone wires that emitted bad smells, of invisible adversaries that knocked on walls, and things that thumped and bumped through the house. Police had dismissed it all as nonsense, largely because of the man's erratic manner.

Pieces of seemingly disconnected information slowly began to assemble in Agnew's head. On Sunday, at Prince Alfred Hospital in Newtown, the sergeant had interviewed a husband and wife about their sick toddler. The incident at the hospital had been the kind of call-out that officers dreaded: ambiguous, involving difficult conversations with parents, and often ending with no clear sense that a crime had been committed. A couple had presented with a gravely ill toddler, her symptoms gastroenteritis-like. One doctor said they could be signs of a contagious outbreak; another said they were consistent with ptomaine (food) poisoning. To add further confusion, the parents claimed their child was ill because a stranger had fed her white lollies. But as of Sunday night, in the absence of any evidence to the contrary, food poisoning appeared to be the final diagnosis. The toddler appeared to be slowly recovering, so the doctors concluded that her illness could not be anything too serious. To his horror, Agnew now realised that the two bodies sprawled on the floor in front of him were the very same couple he had spoken to only a few days before.

•

Sergeant Agnew exited the house and took a deep breath. He closed his eyes, trying to clear his head. As he calculated his next steps, he heard a woman calling from across the street. Then a figure emerged from behind a fence, bouncing forward with a determined step. Her long gored skirt almost touched the ground and was pulled in tight at the waist; the length and breadth of the hemline gave her an uncanny resemblance to a bell, as if she was clanging out a warning with every step. She had clearly been watching and waiting for Agnew to walk out of the house and was now very eager to peal out the information she had, loudly, like a church bell chiming across the rooftops of the borough.

'Officer!' she said. 'I'm the one who called for you. I'm Mrs Shaw.'

Agnew looked a little perplexed. He knew so many businesses in the borough, and Shaw was a common name.

'I'm the blacksmith's wife,' she added, 'the one up on King Street.'

Agnew nodded. He tried again to shake the heavy smell of blood that was trapped in his nostrils.

The woman continued talking. 'I am sorry I did not see you arrive. I was out the back, trying to settle the children,' she said, then quickly followed up with, 'Are the man Sly and his wife all right in there?'

'Their name was Sly, then?' asked Agnew. 'You can confirm that?'

Mrs Shaw nodded.

'And no, they are definitely not all right. They are dead,' the sergeant added matter-of-factly. 'And I will need to speak to you shortly, Mrs Shaw, and get a full account of what you know of them.'

She seemed eager to continue talking. 'They hadn't lived here long. He is . . .' She paused, then rephrased. 'He was a strange one from the beginning . . .' She paused again, as if unsure how best to explain things that could not easily be explained. 'Day and night the place never seemed quite right. The doors always seemed to be open, and the lamps seemed to burn in the house all night long.'

Agnew was not interested in gossip, only in facts pertinent to the investigation. He had much to do, in a short space of time. 'You will need to keep any children you may have indoors,' he said. 'There will be quite a lot of activity around the house for the next few hours.'

'But what am I to do with them?' she asked.

'Mrs Shaw, surely you are capable of looking after your children and keeping them off the streets for a few hours?' His voice was stern. His patience was clearly running thin.

'You misunderstand me, Sergeant. I don't mean my children, I mean *their* children.' She jerked her thumb towards the open door of the house where Agnew had just been.

'The little girl?' he asked. 'The one who was in hospital?'

'No. Not that one. They came home without the child days ago. I haven't seen her since. They also have boys. The three brothers are out the back of my place now. I can't look after them.'

The sergeant steadied himself. It would fall to him to tell the boys about their parents. 'Mrs Shaw, would you mind if I come in? I need to know the situation with the children more fully, and they need to be told very definitely not to go home.'

Mrs Shaw was quick to respond to this as well. 'Too late for that. The boys know they can't go home. They're the ones that found their parents.' She added, 'The boys can't stay here. And as far as I know it, they haven't got family.'

Agnew had not thought it possible, but the scale of this tragedy had just grown much larger.

Mrs Shaw's revelations had added a new burden to the already heavy task ahead of Agnew. He knew that if relatives could not be found for the children, they would be sent to what some locals colloquially called the Home of Hope. The official name of this institution was the Sydney Rescue Society Home of Hope for Friendless and Fallen Women. For those women who found themselves in the unfortunate position of being pregnant, unmarried and turned out by family, there were few options. The founder and owner, G. E. Ardill, said of these women and their children: 'our work is with the wrecked, but rescued'. One less kind commentator noted of those who resided in 'the Hope': 'not all were deserving, but all were in need'.

In modern social welfare jargon, people living in a residential care home might be called clients, boarders or residents. In 1904, the monikers for people in charitable institutions were far more brutal. Those at the Hope were called inmates. Sergeant Agnew had lived and worked in Newtown long enough to shudder at the thought of children going there. If the Sly brothers were placed at the Hope, it would be akin to a custodial sentence. Although the institution was called a Home, it bore no resemblance to one, and Agnew knew that very little hope was to be found there.

3

THE DEADLINE

IN 1904, SYDNEYSIDERS WHO SUFFERED VIOLENT DEATHS RECEIVED three visitations. Police arrived first to process evidence, and arrest any suspects. Next, doctors were called to declare the dead. Then the undertakers came.

The order of these visitations was disrupted when it came to the dead husband and wife in the house on Watkin Street. The next person to visit the bodies was not a doctor but a reporter. A journalist, not a judge, was the first major pivotal force in shaping societal judgements about the Slys.

Middle-aged journalist Ebenezer Furley might have been described by his colleagues as seasoned or experienced, but as he woke late on Tuesday, 12 January, all he felt was tired and jaded. He had been up late to observe and report on the bureaucratic morass of the city council.

In 1904, Sydney as a city was at many critical turning points. It needed more energy, better communication and faster transport. Technological advancements offered the promise of transitions from post and telegraph to telephone, gas to electricity, and horse to motorised vehicle. The cost and responsibility for negotiating these transitions fell heavily on local councils. Civic concerns included electricity, gas lighting, telephone exchanges, sanitation, dust containment, transport, traffic management and horse manure collection. These vital services were expensive and burdensome to provide.

Furley, like many journalists at the time, found himself writing about boring but important matters. At the local level reporters read council minutes, sought interviews with aldermen, and studied statistics in an effort to identify prevailing trends and perhaps predict impending dangers. Sometimes this generated exciting news stories; for instance, the 640 convictions for drunkenness and vagrancy in the Newtown borough in 1903 were great news fodder, providing a clear sign that the suburb was on the brink of moral decay. Less successful were articles on the many permit applications to fish, pawn and hawk – ninety-six, to be exact.

Like all good journalists, Furley was in search of a story with real meat – not the actual meat that had formed the basis of many stories about Newtown and its surrounds in the years leading up to 1904. Hundreds of sheep and cattle, making their final commute to the Glebe slaughterhouse, were driven through the streets of Newtown and Leichhardt each night, right past the doorways and windows of sleeping residents. This created havoc for locals, yet the council had done little about it. Petitions to remove the abattoir from Glebe Island had been raised many times over the previous two decades, but despite a general consensus that its foul miasma was a health hazard, its relocation seemed no closer to being actioned. It made a profit and provided jobs; the fact that the predominantly working-class residents had to live and raise their children in this noxious environment seemed a small price for the city to pay.

City newspapers had even featured stories on Newtown butcher etiquette. Aldermen had debated long and hard whether King Street butchers should be permitted to continue hanging sawn carcasses from shop awnings, where they dangled like mistletoe over pedestrians. Some interests saw this practice as meat curing, while others argued it was better described as meat rotting. Furley sometimes felt as if all he ever did was monitor meetings, along with the 'meatings' of Newtown and Glebe.

On this Tuesday morning, after slowly finishing his cup of tea, he gathered his notebooks and satchel with no sense of urgency. It was late morning before he emerged from his house on 67 Watkin Street and began to slouch his way uphill towards King Street and the tram.

What he saw on the intersection of Wilson and Watkin stopped him dead in his tracks.

The streets were packed. He heard the word 'murder', then 'suicide'. People were pointing at the second storey of the terrace that towered over the street corner. Eyewitness accounts suggest the crowd was composed almost entirely of women, and photographs taken of the street scene at the time confirm this.

Furley walked past 49 Watkin Street every day, but it was as if he was seeing it for the first time. A glint returned to the journalist's eye. Here was a great story only five doors from his home. He could hardly believe an opportunity of this magnitude had just been handed to him.

He inched closer to the action. Out front of a nearby terrace he saw Mrs Shaw, well known to many locals as the wife of a local blacksmith. She was talking to a group of onlookers, some of whom he also recognised – rival reporters. She was scattering leads to them freely, like seed on the ground.

'I know the landlord of the place personally,' she said with some pride. 'He is a coach builder called Lownds who actually lives right next door to my father.

'The couple seemed respectable enough. She impressed me as being a woman who had been better off. They were very odd, though, and they seemed to have more than their fair share of trouble on their minds.

'The man, the father, asked me to take his sons off his hands many times. The little one was sick, I think – the girl. She is in hospital. They never seemed to be home with the children at all. Bedford, the oldest one, always seemed to be begging at my door for food.

'Only last night the man knocked on my door and asked me for the name of a doctor, for his wife.'

Furley could barely keep up with her, scratching his pencil as fast as he could in his notepad. He felt he was being handed a story that was slipping through his fingers. Everyone within earshot had the same information. He knew two things for certain: he needed an angle – a different story from what would be offered by other newspapers – and he needed it fast. It was already well after lunch; he had to draft a story quickly to make the early print run.

Furley's mind raced. He tuned his ears carefully to Mrs Shaw's tales, but also quietly observed the actions of the policemen on the corner.

The police did not consider this a 'crime scene' in the modern sense of the word. Frontline Sydney police work of 1904 was meticulous and thorough, but not forensic by today's standards. To law enforcement, the notion simply did not exist that a space might need to be quarantined for the collection and preservation of physical evidence; the term 'crime scene' was confined to fictional murder mysteries. On rare occasions, police officers took photographs of a body or an object. They also sometimes made impressions of fingerprints, but usually in the controlled environment of a morgue or prison with a view to classifying and cataloguing the physical and genetic characteristics of people deemed criminals. Another thirty years passed before the notion of a crime scene became part of police vernacular, and only after celluloid film recordings were used regularly as evidence to support prosecutions in the United Kingdom.

Occasionally, the NSW constabulary even invited journalists to tromp right through crime scenes. In the Edwardian era, police often cultivated relationships with news media in order to maintain good standing with the public. Police supported the media in sharing what they had seen first hand. Haia Shpayer-Makov, a history professor at University of Haifa, undertook a comprehensive study of the evolution of British policing in the Victorian and Edwardian eras. She found that 'the detective departments and the police as a whole depended heavily on the press for their reputation. Journalists thus played a major role in shaping opinion about detectives in Britain . . . the relationship between members of the two occupations was unique as well as complex.' At the time, police practice in the United Kingdom was greatly influential in shaping NSW frontline law enforcement.

However, police were reticent to allow anyone into 49 Watkin Street. The Sly deaths had been discovered during the day beside a main thoroughfare, across the street from one of the largest bakeries in the area. Word had spread quickly throughout the borough, and Sergeant Agnew now needed to prevent looting while managing the traffic problems created by the crowd. Horses with delivery carts required a wide clearway, particularly when turning, but people were clustered in the middle of the crossroad because this offered the best view into both levels of the house. The rabble refused to move until they had seen the grand finale: the procession of bodies. One woman had even brought an upturned wooden crate to sit on, as if she was patiently waiting for the Newtown brass band to turn up and give a stirring rendition of 'God Save the King'.

Around the time that Furley arrived on the corner, Agnew was preparing to leave. He posted two senior constables, Carter and Payne, outside the premises, and instructed them to manage the crowd and prevent members of the public from promenading through the house.

Agnew had to set the next legal wheels in motion. An inquest would be held as soon as possible; for this, a doctor needed to sign a declaration of death. A morgue was also needed without delay, as the combination of heat, humidity and the dead would soon create a public health concern. The sergeant set off to the closest medical practice: Dr Alfred Lewis Levy's rooms on Church Street.

Furley joined the back of the crowd long enough to observe the activity directly around the house, and to check that the two constables were now the only police nearby. As the journalist watched Agnew walk away, he proceeded directly up Watkin Street as if hurrying to catch a tram on King. Both men moved with a sense of urgency, driven by their very different professional deadlines; the word 'deadline' now assuming an evocative and new meaning for each of them on that morning.

Being local, Furley knew just about every short cut. As he walked briskly up the street, he slipped into an alley used by the night-soil collectors, which led into the back of number 49. He was out of sight of the constables, in the yard where the three Sly boys had been playing only a few hours before.

Looking around, the journalist felt confused. The terrace was a large property for Newtown, and he had expected to see evidence of a fairly grand family home. Instead the yard was strewn with building materials, alongside furniture that appeared to have been abandoned. A large pile of sand and another of dirt almost obscured the back door, while bricks, broken roof shingles, twisted tin pieces and little iron nails were scattered across the ground. This was hardly the place for a family, he thought. Yet, a quite grand perambulator was parked just outside the back door.

Furley tried the door. It opened. He held his breath and listened carefully for any signs of life. He needed to gather information quickly – the sergeant could return at any time.

Furley noted the scent first. He was accustomed to houses in this part of Newtown having a somewhat stagnant smell. Outbreaks of typhoid fever had been linked to the suburb's rapidly constructed rows of terraces; built very close to the ground, they had little to no subfloor space. With most properties leased, and with landlords unwilling to pay for courtyards or kerbside drainage, Newtown had a background stench of rot. When it rained, as it had that month, water pooled in the thick clay soil under the houses; when it rained heavily, this heady soup backwashed into the streets and yards. In late summer and spring, when the heaviest rains fell, Newtown was known for miasmic moats that sometimes surrounded homes in Watkin and Wilson streets up to a foot deep.

But the smell at 49 Watkin Street seemed different. It was something that Furley, even as a local, could not fully explain.

As he walked inside, he noticed the Bible in the middle of the floor and snatched it up. Bibles often stored precious family artefacts, including locks of hair, carefully pressed flowers, notes or samples of embroidery. This edition was large, black and heavily bound with a Celtic cross on the front, popular with Irish Catholic families in particular. He flicked straight to what were known as the family pages: blank sheets bound into the Bible for the reader to transcribe psalms or verses of special significance. What Furley found there exceeded his expectations: the sketch of a genealogical tree. At its apex was the Irish name O'Leary. On the next line, in a very pretty and almost filigree form of looped script, was 'Ellen Sly'. The same hand had written five children's names, the darkness of the ink varying as the letters streaked down the page. From top to bottom Furley read: 'John Bedford, Basil Cornelius, Mervyn James, Norman Bede, Olive Clotilde'. The journalist now knew this was a mother's Bible; she had written the names of each newborn child at different times. If the gossip he had heard in the street was true and a murder had occurred in this home, he now held in the palm of his hand the beginnings of a newsworthy and tragic personal story. He felt the weight of the object in his hands, before placing it back down on the floor.

Furley moved forward to the main part of the ground floor. Just as Agnew had made careful observations, so too did the journalist – but, driven by different sensibilities and disciplines, the men viewed the scene with very different eyes. Furley jotted down descriptions in his notebook. Pots and bedcovers, loaves of bread and kitchen utensils in towers of disorder were described as a 'veritable jumble'. It was not enough that it was chaos; it was 'strewn' and 'inextricable' as well. He quickly formed an impression of the family as being part of the dirty underclass. He scrawled 'very poor and very eccentric'. Just as Agnew had done, Furley noted the great number of oil paintings on the floor.

In the dining room he observed the remnants of a moment that had passed but also seemed frozen in time. The unrefined 'coverless table', as he described it, was set with utensils, cups and plates, but they were chaotically arranged. It was as if someone could re-enter the room at any time, resume their seat, and continue eating their meal of rotten bread. Bedclothes, tossed on the floor, were 'scanty, ragged and dirty'. Furley's heartbeat quickened – this had the makings of a scandalous and gritty tale.

He headed upstairs. At the top, he could scarcely believe his eyes. His note-taking could not keep pace with his thoughts. There was 'blood everywhere, on everything', a 'crimson stream'. His words flowed easily. The 'thick congealing pool of blood half an inch deep covered a patch of the floor . . . the bed clothing was saturated with it'. Perhaps reflecting his own sense of malaise, the blood was noted to 'drop with a doleful monotony'.

Furley's eyes were drawn to the woman before the man – perhaps because the state of her body was more shocking, or because the Bible had given her a name, Ellen. He saw her semi-severed head for a second, then directed his gaze to other details. With an astonishingly cold focus, he noticed three rings on the middle finger of her left hand.

Next he turned to the man, who was fully dressed. The coat was moth-eaten. A razor lay in one hand. Furley scribbled 'hole in shoe', then 'moth'. He steered his eyes from the gash on the man's neck, but could not draw them away from that blank stare.

Time was running out. Soon the police would come in to remove the bodies. Still, Furley wanted more. He riffled through the dead man's pockets. Could he find a pocket watch with an inscription, or an initialled handkerchief or perhaps a flask? He wanted something of great personal significance that told a story about the man's true nature. Had he been a drinker? Had he been sentimental, carrying heirlooms and keepsakes? To what kind of family had he been born? Furley found an item that must have affected the seasoned journalist and touched him more than any other part of the pitiful scene – a bill from a loan company. It felt as if it was coated in glue; the blood had soaked into the pocket. This bill was an important find, providing the dead man's name: Alexander William Bedford Sly. Furley also found a pair of spectacles, a tailor's tape measure, and four pence. He shoved these items back into the pockets.

A picture of the dead man began to form in Furley's mind. The tape measure revealed the man's profession, while the pitiful number of coins gave insight to his financial state. Even the lowly rat catchers who combed the streets of Newtown were paid sixpence for each head of vermin.

The words did not come to Furley as fragments now, but as sentences that sprang forth from his mind. His hand trembled as he kept scratching out the skeleton of what would become his story: 'From the surroundings it appeared that Sly had attacked his wife as she lay in the bed and that she had been powerless to resist him. Her wound was of such a fearful character that death must have been <u>almost</u> instantaneous.' He underlined 'almost' – an important inclusion. This word would remind readers that the wife may have had time to truly feel terror and anticipate her awful fate. Furley continued to write obsessively: 'After killing his wife, there is no doubt that from the position in which his body was found that Sly had stood up a few feet away and had drawn the keen razor blade across his own throat.'

Furley jotted down possible titles for the article: 'A Ghastly Sight', 'Walls of Blood in a Family Home', 'Tragedy in Newtown'. This was not even melodrama; it was not sensationalist. This was a straightforward retelling of what he had seen with his own eyes.

Beside the dead man's hand lay the broken end of what Furley initially thought was a child's red pencil, but it was unlike any pencil he had ever seen. It looked more like a tool of trade. The strangeness of this did not sit well with him, and a series of questions niggled at him. Was it a marker of some kind, perhaps? Had children been casually playing near the bodies? He shuddered. Had the man tried to commit some final words to paper? The journalist could find no evidence of any letter.

Of all the horror he had just seen, it was not the bloodshed that haunted him, nor the razor. As he hurried off, the oddest of things stuck with him: the sight of that neat and tightly coiled tape measure seemed entirely out of place. Even more than the razor, it seemed to cut to the crux of the tragedy. It was as if at the very moment of his death, the man had a trouble so overwhelming that he struggled even to take its measure.

When Sergeant Agnew arrived at the front door, he had Dr Levy in tow. In the same instant, Furley slipped out the back door and into the lane. He soon rejoined the crowd at the crossroad. Their attention was now fixed with great fascination on a photographer, who fussed with his unwieldy bellow-bellied camera for some time. When finally satisfied with the depth of field, the light and the position, he fired his shot. It was unclear to Furley if the photographer had captured the house or the mayhem in the street. Furley was also unsure which newspaper had ordered the photograph. It was a bold move in 1904, as pictures were rarely used and newspaper copy was defined by long thin columns of text. Furley stepped back to assess the scene again, trying to imagine what the photographer had captured. Rows of terraces were on either side, and the severe angle of the tall roof at number 49 must have been the dead centre of the image.

It was then that Furley noticed an unusual decoration on the house. He walked past it every day, but somehow he had never seen it before. Right at the corner of the roof was a large, round jet-black pot with two curved handles on each side. There was nothing like it on any of the hundreds of rooftops within his line of sight. After he stared at it for some time, its shape became clear – and in the context of what had just transpired in the house, its significance was sibylline. It was unmistakably a funereal urn, with the distinctive barrel shape fashioned to a needle-like point. It cast a dark silhouette against the bright blue summer sky. To the journalist, it was as if the house had been stabbed with a push pin, marking its place on a map: a final destination that someone had set a course for long ago.

4

BLACK AND WHITE AND READ ALL OVER

IN LESS THAN TWENTY-FOUR HOURS, THE HEADLINE 'NEWTOWN Tragedy' was splashed across papers nationwide. In an eerie way, the tragedy echoed a well-known early twentieth-century riddle, popular among schoolchildren at the time: what is black, white and red all over? Newspapers served up the tragedy in black, white and bloody red detail, and it was certainly read all over Australia.

The tagline 'tragedy' was used on the story almost universally across news media. Editors had drawn one common conclusion: the most tragic part of it all was Alexander William Bedford Sly. Journalists set the scene using an almost artistic arrangement of facts concerning the man they called 'Alicks'. A strong sense of composition was presented in the stories, with background and foreground, shades of light and dark. Readers were left with an overall impression of the Sly family home as a richly detailed still life known as a Vanitas, which unsettles the viewer with symbolic reminders of death's nearness. Journalists described a backdrop crammed with objects signifying the transient nature of life: musical instruments, wilted flowers, food ready to perish. In this context Ellie Sly assumed a specific place, featuring as a motionless slab of meat. The other victims – the four Sly orphans – were painted into the scene to create chiaroscuro, amounting to short brushstrokes of muted colour in the shadows. In this macabre and artful depiction of the family tragedy, Alicks was positioned front and centre, like a skull amid the chaos and clutter. Journalists seemed most interested in casting light on this skull – and the mind that it contained.

By the standards of their time, the articles about the Sly murder-suicide are psychological reflections on death, madness and mortality. Journalists claimed that three main factors had played a role in this tragic affair: the brutality, spirituality and eccentricity of the man known as Alicks Sly.

BRUTALITY

The Sly family had lived in the neighbouring suburb of Glebe for two years, and the police there knew all about Alicks. Only a week before the Newtown Tragedy, he had kicked a youth almost to death. This incident had occurred outside the Sly family home on Mitchell Street, Glebe. The unconscious boy was transferred to Prince Alfred Hospital; for a time it was believed he would not wake up.

Alicks was held by police, and usually an assault of this kind would lead to a charge, but in this case it did not. To understand why he walked free, it is important to understand what life was like in Glebe, and why police showed such leniency towards a man who had displayed such immense brutality.

For two years, the Slys had lived in the middle of a gang war. Just as contemporary Los Angeles has the rival gangs of the Bloods and Crips, turn-of-the-century Sydney was divided along gang lines. The Slys' neighbourhood was controlled by the Liver Push, which occupied a large territory south-west of Liverpool Street and down towards Glebe. Like today's gangs, the Push used colours, hand symbols, verbal cues and fashion accoutrement to brand and demonstrate their affiliation. The Rocks Push were known for bell-bottom trousers, high-heeled boots and colourful neckerchiefs, while the Stanmore Push wore straw hats. Braids, pearls, velvet collars, enamel toecaps and long hair were associated with specific factions. For some, the boots were reportedly so high and the toes so pointed that wearers were said to 'mince with their knees thrust forward'. The activities attributed to the Push reflect the stereotypes of troubled young men from poorer Australian suburbs and towns that persist today. They nicked private transport in order to hoon – though the Push stole horses, not cars. They accessorised buggies, personalising them and giving them street cred. They also had a reputation for getting drunk and generally mucking up. The Push had little respect for the police, and these feelings were reciprocated.

Like many Glebe residents at the time, the Slys were aware of the Push and their activities. These included robbery, destruction of property, harassment and assault. Within Glebe alone, battlelines were drawn between rival factions of the Ferry Road Push, the Bay Street Push, the Bridge Road Push and the Forsyth Street Push. Street fighting and territorial warfare were part of daily life for the boys of the Push.

Local folklore surrounding the origin of the Glebe Liver Push's name provides insight on the type of social movement it was and the type of young men within it. One theory is that the gang was named after the large abattoir on Glebe Island, which handed out pluck – heart, liver and lungs – for free to locals (more an act of economy than generosity, as it reduced the amount of rotting material on site). Another theory posits that the Liver Push and a group known as the Blood Reds were so named because their members worked as butcher's apprentices. The third theory is a far darker one. Some claim the Liver Push targeted old people for robberies with the purpose of kicking them in the vicinity of the liver until they were dead. There is certainly some evidence of that. Larrikin slang of the time used the term 'jumping their livers out'. At the turn of the century, Sydney was in the midst of a kind of civic civil war being waged, and not just sticks and stones but liver and bones had also played a role.

On the street outside his home, Alicks Sly had attacked a young man who belonged to the notorious Liver Push. To police, this was important.

Gangs were dangerously unpredictable. Their mobs could comprise just a few people or grow quickly to a few hundred. The Push targeted individuals but were also known for stealing alcohol from hoteliers. The gang smashed shop windows, and harassed locals for money with bats and sticks. They gathered the bluestones used throughout the city to build stable road surfaces on heavy traffic intersections. The stones fitted nicely in the palm of the hand, and could be scooped up quickly and hidden in pockets, jackets or sacks: the perfect ammunition. Victims and witnesses of assaults often described Push boys 'pummelling' homes and shopfronts, or showering trams in a 'volley of stones'. One journalist called the boys 'an infestation'.

Though the Push spent a lot of time fighting each other, they also spent a good portion of it fighting the police. Officers were often dismayed to find themselves outnumbered. Glebe station, in particular, was dramatically understaffed, with only two permanent officers rostered on. More than once, officers were set upon opportunistically by Push gang members.

In 1897, the tension between the police and the Push had culminated in a full-blown riot. Thousands had turned up at Wentworth Park to watch a local first-grade cricket match between Glebe and the University team. What started with pushing, shoving, taunting and hooting escalated into a scuffle between several members of the Push and off-duty policemen. The scuffle became a skirmish. Within a very short period, hundreds of people were involved in a punch-on during what was meant to be a civilised game of English cricket. The fight was only resolved when some police drew their revolvers.

By 1904, police had begun to show a lenient attitude towards citizen vigilantism when it came to the Push. Alicks told them he had good reasons for the attack: the Push boy had harassed Alicks's children as they played in the street, and the Push had thrown stones on his roof until he could no longer stand the noise. So when the young man was alone, Alicks had set upon him and beaten him senseless.

After Alicks died, newspapers described him as a brutal figure. In establishing this, journalists made no reference to his marital relationship; they simply discussed the violent tendencies he had recently displayed. But plenty of men in his borough were brutal – the kind of behaviour towards which police turned a blind eye and the general public showed acceptance. Law-abiding Sydneysiders had a right to defend their families, and to take action against criminal gangs, wrote a number of editorials in this period.

ECCENTRICITY

According to newspapers, Alexander Sly was feeble-minded and eccentric. Glebe police happily supplied journalists with plenty of information about this. Alicks had been a regular visitor to their station – as frequently as three times a week.

He came to complain about the Push, but he also complained about far more outrageous things. Someone had assaulted his children by driving invisible hairpins into their abdomens, though he could not identify who or understand how. He heard noises in his home: knocking and rapping he could not explain. Vile smells, he said, were piped in through wires laid over the roof. He vehemently declared that someone or something was tormenting his family. At night, intruders came into their home and walked around in their boots. Alicks knew this, he said, because he had heard them and so had his son.

In order to quiet this persistent man, police inspected the property. They found nothing. They asked a doctor to inspect the children. Their bodies were unmarked. Police dismissed Alicks as a nuisance, an imbecile, and a waste of precious time and resources.

In modern-day vernacular, the word 'feeble' might be used to describe someone weak or sickly. In 1904, to be labelled 'feeble' implied mental illness that was the product of an inherent genealogical weakness. Today, calling someone 'eccentric' could be construed as a compliment, implying free-spiritedness and a desire to live unconventionally. In 1904, 'eccentric' was a grave slur; it suggested that someone had a poor ability to reason, and could even infer a predisposition for criminality.

Newspaper reports about Alicks Sly reflected and were informed by prevailing views on biology. At the turn of the century, it was believed that inborn tendencies shaped whether or not a man was feeble or eccentric.

A 1908 British Royal Commission provides some insights into how rigid attitudes to mental illness could be. Established in 1904, the reflections of the 'Royal Commission on the Care and Control of the Feeble-Minded' provide remarkable snapshots of social and medical understandings of crime and insanity. 'I certainly think there is such a thing as moral insanity. It is a distinct mental abnormality,' stated Dr Mercier, a London physician and specialist in mental health. Dr Clouston, who held the prestigious role of physician superintendent at the internationally renowned Royal Edinburgh Asylum, concurred: 'bad brain heredity' created the basis for the worst criminal behaviour, and it was 'often mixed up with it in the same individual and the same family'. A century later, the historian Hugh Freeman from the University of Oxford noted that at the turn of the twentieth century, terminology around mental illness was 'uncertain' with fluid categories of moral and mental afflictions. It was believed that people could be born mad or bad, and these conditions were often considered so deeply linked as to be interchangeable.

When discussing the Newtown Tragedy, journalists were quick to note what everyone else was thinking: Alicks Sly was born from weak stock. Interviews with neighbours revealed he was blind in one eye. He suffered headaches. He was not afraid to humiliate himself in front of others, even women. Neighbours reported that he had been known to get down on his knees and beg them to take his children. He had also shown himself to be poor at keeping employment; this was taken to be another indication of his failure to provide for his family. It all suggested a pattern of imbecility and inadequacy, or so newspapers wrote.

Prevailing views on criminality, insanity and heredity affected the public's expectations of how police should handle crimes of the type committed by Alicks Sly. Across the Western world, practitioners in psychological and neurological medicine agreed that there were links between immorality and criminal inheritance; understandings of right and wrong, it seemed, were passed from parent to child as surely as eye colour. Newspapers argued that potential criminals should be identified, classified and managed – and because police had failed to do this, they had failed to stop the Newtown Tragedy from happening in the first place.

Editorials from this era offer important insights on the ways in which the concept of inescapable moral inheritance was understood. One editor and commentator described this legacy as a 'child's deep laid plot', conjuring images of a garden bed in which children were raised like seedlings – but also images of a child buried in a deep grave with little hope of climbing out.

Only a decade before, policymakers in Sydney had debated whether steps should be taken to curb the 'propagation of lunatics'. As one editor wrote, 'men or women who have an insane taint in their constitutions, or marked insane charac-teristics ought to be prevented marrying and bringing into existence embryo lunatics'. As the legal and political historian Tom Butler noted, attitudes in Britain and Australia up to

World War I reflect 'rigid beliefs of the eugenic theorists on the association of moral weakness, social class and insanity'. In 1904, one conclusion was clearly drawn about the Sly tragedy: deviant behaviour could sometimes emerge quite late in life, but it always sprouted from a seed that was already buried deep within, waiting to grow.

Alicks Sly was a feeble man. According to commonly held views in the early twentieth century, this didn't make him weak or meek – it made him dangerous. Worse still, argued journalists, police had known he was dangerous long before the events of 12 January 1904.

A number of newspapers investigated the Sly family by interviewing Bedford, the eldest son. Like his father, he made claims about bizarre happenings in their home. He also described how his father had fed him and his siblings strange white powder. These interviews only further confirmed the general assumption surrounding mental illness: criminal insanity ran in families, so if the father was feeble then the children should be viewed with a deep level of suspicion.

SPIRITUALITY

Alicks Sly was not a religious man, but he was spiritual. In 1904, this was newsworthy. Through interviews with ex-neighbours, journalists quickly discovered that Alicks was a follower of spiritualism: an alternative to traditional Christianity that had swept through Britain, Germany, the United States and Australia in the second half of the 1800s.

At the turn of the century in Sydney, the spiritualist movement was not a registered nor recognised church, but more of an underground movement. Spiritualist leaders coordinated meetings in private homes and community halls. The movement published material and printed circulars to educate and help others explore and understand the spiritual realm. Services often commenced like any other Christian church service – with prayers, recitations from the Bible, or with the singing of hymns. Spiritualist services, however, differed in one key respect. Like-minded people gathered, forming a spiritual circle or seance, led by a charismatic medium who could act as a conduit in communications with the spiritual realm. Sometimes this involved connecting directly or seeking to make an overture to a specific person who had already passed, in other cases not. It is not possible to know how big the spiritualist movement was in Sydney at the time. What is known is that the movement was gathering in size and momentum. The history of the spiritualist church is deeply connected to the Enmore and Newtown area. In 1904, Alicks Sly made a conscious decision to live in close proximity to the movement's absolute ground zero and birthplace, in Sydney.

Spiritualists based their daily religious practice on the belief that regular communication could be established with spirits in the afterlife. Dr Alfred Gabay, one of the few historians of the spiritualist movement in Australia, has noted that at the turn of the twentieth century spiritualists considered themselves to be scientific explorers of a new frontier. According to Gabay, 'the opening of this channel was itself a gift from the higher spheres, for in sufficiently prepared and faithful persons mediumship would blossom, enabling higher beings residing within sublime spheres to communicate esoteric teachings concerning human existence, its purposes and relationship with the supernal worlds'. Henry Melville, a nineteenth-century Australian journalist who investigated spiritualism and occultism, wrote in his sermon on the subject: 'The visible world and the invisible are in very close contact: there is, indeed, a veil on our eyes, preventing our gazing on spiritual beings and things . . .'

People who claimed to have the gift of mediumship held a special place in the spiritualist movement. Some of the most powerful agents in spiritualism were trance mediums, because the movement believed they could lift the veil between this world and the next while in a trance. Journalists discovered that Alicks Sly had identified himself as a trance medium; he believed he could channel messages from the spirit realm. Alpheus, a turn-of-the-century writer who claimed to have first-hand observations of spirits and sought to chronicle them, described trance and hypnosis as the 'the power of sight'. He argued that the 'perfect medium' was one who was 'not a professional'. Alicks had sought to master the technique of mediumship, but there was no evidence he had done so for financial gain. This, according to newspapers, deepened the mystery surrounding the man. On one hand, Alicks had apparently not been a fraudster who financially exploited people; on the other, according to some journalists, the idea that he had undertaken mediumship gave weight to the assumption that he had been insane.

No one could be sure of the rituals Alicks had used to try to establish a connection with the other side. Some mediums used objects; others used human billets (bodies temporarily occupied by another consciousness) to open a channel. A clairvoyant saw, a clairaudient heard, and vapourists claimed to be able to smell the unseen world. Some vapourists were even documented returning from their trance state with the smell of tobacco, cigars or coffee lingering on them as they resumed consciousness in our world. Other mediums used the flute of a trumpet to communicate with those beyond, others wrote the words of spirits on a piece of slate, and still others read messages in bowls of water. Some argued that an astral hand could tap out messages on a tin sheet using a code decipherable only by the medium. The techniques were as varied as the mediums, and their equipment often reflected pre-existing skill sets in their terrestrial lives. Edward Power, a Newtown accountant, adapted the tools of his trade for his professional spiritualist work. He wound copper wire around an office spike – normally used to stab receipts and dockets – so it might transmit spiritual signals.

Committed trance mediums recorded their experiences and the names of spirits. Some kept what was called a blue book: a mix of logbook, personal diary and address book, in which they also transcribed what were known as their automatic writings. They would surrender directly to an unseen force, go into a trance, and draw or write whatever was transmitted to them. Not all mediums claimed to be able to comprehend the messages they received, and most said they did not retain memories of being in trances, so the blue book was often the only record of what had occurred for the medium while in this state. If a blue book was found at the Sly house, police did not document it anywhere; however, they found assorted letters described as incomprehensible ramblings and 'non-sensical'. The unusual pencil or marker found near Alicks's body was most likely a piece of tailor's chalk or crayon, which might have played a role in his channelling process.

Victorian and Edwardian society tolerated spiritualistic activities, but only just, and only if parishioners assembled quietly. The placement of religious advertisements in the paper reveals much about the status of a movement striving to be recognised as a formal religion. In the long column of advertised church services for the week, Catholic came first, then Church of England, followed by Presbyterian, Congregational, Methodist and Baptist. Then, in the subsection titled 'other', came the listings of services for the Australian Unitarians and the Christadelphians. Right at the bottom of the list were spiritualist advertisements; mainstream papers were happy to advertise their church services, if they were paid to do so.

What society did not tolerate were displays of erratic and unstable behaviour, and an overt commitment to spiritualism. Alicks's devotion to the movement was, according to the majority of mainstream press, a reflection of the mental instability and fragility that appeared to have played a role in the crime. Police had failed in one of their most important responsibilities: they had neglected to lock Alicks in an asylum when they knew he was unstable. They must therefore share some culpability in the crime. *Truth* newspaper, in particular, was scathing in its attack on Newtown police. This must have been mortifying for Sergeant Agnew, who had maintained a lifelong reputation for dedication and service to the community. 'There must be a vacuum where the average flat-footed police-man's brain should be or he suffers with the national tired feeling to an alarming extent,' wrote *Truth* in its commentary on the management of the Newtown Tragedy. Agnew was not the only bobby in the firing line, as Glebe police were identified as well: '. . . and yet the local Robert lacked sufficient nous or authority to detain them [Mr and Mrs Sly] on some pretext and hand them over for medical inspection'.

Newspapers did not seek to quell hysteria that might arise due to the crime. Instead, some papers seemed keen to stoke fear. An article written two days after the tragedy states: 'In our issue of today appear the details of the affair at Newtown where a tailor kills his wife and cutting his own throat converts the place to a perfect shambles.' Dramatically titled 'A Baptism of Blood', the article goes on to note: 'the white robes of innocence have upon them a crimson stain . . . The veneer upon our boasted enlightenment is wearing off, and the destroying and lustful animal appears beneath. It is not a good omen with which to begin the new year.'

When discussing the Newtown Tragedy, *Truth* subscribed to what it called 'the mysticide theory' and postulated that Alicks's commitment to spiritualism was the key to his madness. As *Truth* wrote in the days after the crime: 'the unfortunate man dabbled in spiritualism and became insane . . . The madness affected the weak mind of his wife to such an extent that they resolved to die together to escape the persecutions of their imaginary enemies.' Some papers seemed to suggest that Ellie had done the unthinkable and somehow participated in this act of mysticide. Perhaps she had not fought, they conjectured; perhaps she had been mad as well. Perhaps, as one newspaper suggested, the act had not just been premeditated by the husband but the wife had been complicit in this arrangement too.

In a strange way, Alicks Sly achieved in death what he had sought to achieve in life: he had proven that information could be transmitted from the dead to the living. In the week after his death, his presence was felt and his words were heard across the country. But it was journalists not mediums who shared his violent and dramatic final message. And there was just one problem – no one seemed able to understand what it meant.

5

BAD APPLE

Newspaper editorials identified that three factors had played a role in the terrible event on Watkin Street – brutality, eccentricity and spirituality. There was a fourth factor, however, which was also implied to have played a role: heredity. In the post-Victorian, early Edwardian world of 1904, newspapers used the theory of heredity to unite explanations of the Newtown Tragedy. Men who showed a capability for murder were born that way, or so it was believed at the time. But does an exploration of the family history of Alicks Sly bear this theory out? Was he a bad seed? And, if so, how had a 'woman who had been better off' – in the words of Mrs Shaw – become mixed up with him? If the values of his culture and society were borne out, his psychological and genealogical profiles would align.

The genealogical story of the Sly family in Australia begins with two brothers, and it is fair to say it also begins with a seed. In the early to mid-1800s, John and James Sly laid down roots in Van Diemen's Land. It was a parallel planting of sorts: two brothers living in the same town, employed in the same ventures on the island known colloquially as the Apple Isle. Like their neighbours at the time, they cultivated fruit – apples, in particular – while working as local craftsmen. Historians note the importance of the small orchard or garden orchard economy in this period and describe the blurring of home and commercial activities on the land. Families grew and sold apples to supplement income, and the cumulative impact of these small-scale farms contributed significantly to the macroeconomy of Van Diemen's Land.

Van Diemen's Land was remote, and colonists suffered the isolation and hardship associated with living on a frontier. Henry Reynolds, a professor of history at the University of Tasmania, notes that by the mid-1860s 'the colony had more lunatics, more orphaned and abandoned children, more prisoners, more invalids and paupers than South Australia and Queensland together although their combined population was two and a half times greater than that of Tasmania'. In the mid-1800s a boat trip from Sydney to Hobart Town took about ten days. Crossing from the island to the nearest mainland city, Melbourne, ships had to contend with the notoriously choppy and unpredictable Bass Strait.

The Sly brothers, however, were shrewd and dreamt beyond apple farming. They were resourceful and learnt to capitalise on their isolation. John and James were bootmakers, and everyone in the colony – rich or poor, young or old – needed boots. John was a skilled craftsman, described in the *Tasmanian Morning Herald* as capable of 'the most elaborate workmanship'. His boots were so impressive they were exhibited in mainland craft shows and sold in the lucrative Melbourne market. One newspaper article describes the work of the Sly brothers as 'anatomical and surgical boot making' because of their careful attention to achieving a streamlined fit. The two craftsmen were also crafty. They anticipated shifts in the market, such as the growing number of mass-produced boots coming out of England. John and James did not price themselves out of the market by solely selling higher-cost handmade units that could never compete with cheap ready-to-wear equivalents. For a time, the brothers were not just significant producers of customised boots in Van Diemen's Land, but also the biggest importers of factory-produced shoes to the island.

The brothers did not discriminate, supplying to the lowest and highest in the community. John was commissioned by the surveyor general's office to provide beautifully hand-crafted wellington boots to the men charged with planning and mapping the expanding town. But James and John knew how to exploit other markets as well. They sold Indian rubber 'goloshes' to outdoorsmen working parcels of land, leather boots to maids (lace and button available), bluchers (a hard-wearing working boot for men), and French clogs to women and children.

The island was known for the roaring forties, a wild weather pattern that blew heavy rain and icy drops in from the sea. The Slys sought out and offered the latest technology: gutta-percha. A latex extracted from the gutta-percha plant, it was used in a range of different manufacturing processes to insulate and seal. In shoes, gutta-percha was a breakthrough innovation because it gave the wearer the reassurance of a waterproof sole, which was difficult to achieve using leather alone.

The brothers also imported any accessories that would sell. Scarves, silks, fringes, dress trimmings and ribbons could be packed around bulkier items shipped from England. Lightweight items such as Holland jackets conformed to Victorian standards of modesty and practicality because they could be worn as a top: the double row of buttons running all the way down the front was designed to remained fastened at all times. Loose jackets known as mantles were ideal for an astute importer. They were lightweight and could be flattened easily for transport. The loose-fitting cape or shawl-like design made them popular with residents seeking to cope with the changeable weather of Van Diemen's Land because they could be thrown easily over indoor clothing.

John, Alicks's great-uncle, married Mary. This branch of the Sly tree produced fourteen children over twenty-four years. In a pattern of childhood mortality astonishingly at odds with probabilities of the time, John and Mary only lost one child.

James, Alicks's grandfather, married Sarah. Fruitful too, they had eleven children. Four died before they turned two.

These deaths were harrowing, even by nineteenth-century standards. During Christmas 1862, James and Sarah were blessed with twin sons; both were lost within seven weeks. One was noted by doctors to have suffered forty-four days of diarrhoea, which caused severe dehydration and malnourishment.

Both John and James named sons after their father, William.

•

The early years of the settlement in the wilds of Van Diemen's Land presented triumphs and setbacks for the Sly brothers – just as they did for every other European colonist. At the beginning of 1859, the Slys were well situated with a shopfront and workshop on busy Liverpool Street, Hobart Town. On a night in May 1859, the brothers lost their shopfront when a row of seven businesses caught fire. Five buildings were completely destroyed, including the Slys' boot, shoe and draper store. For reasons that cannot be known to us now, the buildings burnt to the ground yet all of the stock was saved. By October the brothers were back in business, and the shopfront reopened with more stock than ever.

At around the same time, the Slys found themselves at the centre of a crisis that threatened the security of their world. Whole crops of apples were ruined by the tiny codling moth, which grew to only a centimetre in length. This was disastrous for the local economy, as the island relied on the export sales of apples. The moth's breeding behaviour imperilled every apple tree on Van Diemen's Land. The adult insect lays its eggs directly onto the tree; the grub then burrows into the growing fruit. It gorges, silent and undetected, encased safely inside. Meanwhile, the growing apple appears completely normal on the outside. The tendency of apples to never fall far from the tree helps to complete the parasitic moth's life cycle; after the contaminated apple drops to the ground, the grub crawls back to the tree and begins the cycle again. Settlers were surprised by the speed of this reproduction. Three generations of codling moths were found living on one tree within one season.

Local farming families were distressed by their inability to combat the insidious and silent threat. An Act of Parliament was introduced to unleash a 'vigorous crusade against the moth and its progeny'. But while many Hobart Town families faced financial ruin, the Slys did not. Their diversified business portfolio made them less vulnerable to economic troughs. Cleverly, the brothers had not placed all of their apples in one basket. Workers still needed boots, and the shoe business grew. The Sly empire expanded to the north of the island, and the brothers also travelled frequently to offer custom fits for those in remote areas.

Over a twenty-year period, John and James Sly established their reputations as good men. When travelling, they stayed at temperance hotels. They were law abiding. As far as Hobart Town society was concerned, they were the very furthest thing from bad seeds. This good reputation was solidified even further when James helped police solve one of the most violent crimes ever to occur on the island: the brutal murder of Alice Hughes.

In March 1859, in the farming region of Bridgewater, young Alice was found dead in a field. The settlement was about twenty kilometres out of Hobart Town, on the other side of the bay. The community was shocked that a crime so violent could occur in such a small place, where everyone knew one another so well. Alice's parents had sent her to fetch her brother, who was working on an outlying field on the family farm. She never came home.

It was not just where Alice died that shocked the community, but also how. Her body was found only about a hundred metres from the family hut. She had been slashed across the throat so savagely that her windpipe and gullet were severed, and the cartilage of the third and fourth vertebrae had been cut. The jagged gash had most likely been made with a work tool, an all-purpose blade called a pointed clasp, or a pocketknife. Police concluded that the murderer had pinned down the girl, placing a hand over her mouth while her throat was cut. This, they argued, would explain why no one had heard a thing. During the post-mortem, the doctor took carefully worded notes: 'the interior of both thighs was covered with dirty blood . . . though I do not think deceased had been violated'. Alice was only eight years old.

Thomas Hughes, the girl's father, noticed boot marks in the soft sand near the body. During the inquest it was noted that the tracks had not been made by ordinary work boots, but seemed to be formed by a carefully fashioned and superior boot. Hughes said of the tracks, 'The nails in the centre of the boot formed what is called a diamond.'

Local police, who assumed an astonishingly modern sensibility in their investigation of the crime, carefully recorded the placement of the boot marks and the pattern of impressions leading away from the body. They organised a line-up of possible suspects, too, and Alice's mother pointed out a man who had visited their property that day. There was, however, no real physical evidence linking him to Alice's death. The key suspect was a drifter and did not appear to own boots that matched the impressions.

It was Alicks's grandfather, James Sly, bootmaker, who made the evidentiary link for police. James not only claimed that the prime suspect had purchased boots from him, but he also said he could prove it. He produced workshop drawings. Police compared the distinctive diamond-shaped pattern of nails used by the Sly bootmaker to the impressions – a perfect match.

•

Within twenty short years, the Sly brothers had suffered periods of bankruptcy and economic turmoil but had always bounced back. Both had built successful businesses and held positions of respect within their community. Any descendants could have traded on this for years to come. However, for reasons that cannot now be known, their heirs – both named William – turned heel on their bootmaking pedigree and walked away.

William Charles, son of John, married Agnes Bayley in Hobart in a very cold winter wedding in June 1881. He left for Melbourne soon after, and did not return to Van Diemen's Land. His son, Frederick Charles, was born in Melbourne and never returned to his ancestral home of the Apple Isle.

William, son of James, headed for Dunedin, but then moved on to Sydney. Like his cousin William, he would not resettle in Hobart. In New Zealand he met his wife, Alicks's mother, Barbara McGashan. The couple quickly started a family – very quickly. Alicks was born in April 1869, less than eight months after his parents married.

Alicks was William and Barbara's only son. Eight sisters followed, five of whom survived: Rosabella, Alice Virginia, Florence Barbara, Isabella Jane and Ada Isobel.

Alicks's father was not a labourer, worker or craftsman. He described himself as a trader and deal-maker, and his occupations throughout this time are variously described in historical documents (migration, census and BDM records) as trader, merchant and accountant. In historical research, occupation is often considered the most important piece of evidence a researcher might discover about someone's life; it can provide information about status, wealth, living conditions, aspirations and even life expectancy. An occupation is usually akin to an oracle affording the social history researcher the power of prophecy. In William Sly's case, however, it was not his job but what he chose to do in his spare time that revealed the most about his character.

William was a bird breeder – but not just any birds. He bred the magnificent golden duckwing leghorn rooster. This was an ambitious undertaking because the pattern and intensity of its gold colouring were achieved through a careful blending of an Italian fowl and an old English game bird. In the 1800s the leghorn breed was an exotic curiosity in Britain, the Americas and the Australian colonies. The bird's gold is vibrant and should appear only on the saddle, collar and wing tips. In trying to breed the golden duckwing leghorn rooster, William was engaged in the dark and elusive art of what can only be described as the equivalent of poultry alchemy.

By all accounts, William was an excellent chook alchemist. His hobby seems to have assumed the status of an obsession. To succeed, he needed to artfully pair the right red-breasted black duckwing leghorn with the right silver (white) partner; the gold and the silver colourings reflect the 'two different branches of ancestry' that laid the foundation of what it means to be a leghorn. Only the right genetic combination can produce the rare gold which contains enough red to produce gold but not turn orange, and remains white enough to throw yellow but not evolve all the way to cream. Because of its pure colouring, the leghorn embodied the values of good breeding extolled in the Victorian era: bloodline is undeniably and inescapably important.

In this most Victorian of pastimes, William was determined to breed the ideal, and his efforts were considered very impressive. He sold poultry throughout Tasmania, to breeders and poultry show families in Melbourne, and in New Zealand. His birds won best in show at exhibitions in both countries.

William's connections to his family in Hobart remained strong. He travelled home regularly to collect what he believed to be the purer bird stock available on the island. Local newspapers were proud of him: 'Tasmania . . . has set the example to her colonial sisters of establishing the Poultry and Canary shows . . . The association principally owes its existence to the energy of one of our Tasmanian youths, Mr William Sly, son of James Sly and nephew of Mr John Sly of Liverpool Street . . . By the prize list of the Dunedin Show we perceive that his birds and their progeny, in his or others hands, have been the successful prize takers.'

When William left New Zealand and moved his family to Sydney, his interests in breeding expanded to new fields. As with his efforts in poultry breeding, he received press coverage – now, however, it was in the police gazette.

William Sly committed many criminal offences in the late 1800s. In July 1885, when Alicks was sixteen, his father was thrown into gaol for being drunk, then again in October for using indecent language. From 1885 to 1887, William was charged three times for breach of the 1880 NSW *Public Instruction Act* for not ensuring his children attended school for at least the minimum 70 days per half year; on each occasion he served twenty-four hours in gaol. In the late 1800s, desertion of one's family was considered a serious and stigmatising criminal charge; William was charged with this as well.

He disappeared for long periods. Barbara had no idea where he was, and he left her without any money to feed their brood of children. Only when she had scratched together the last of the pennies to pay rent and buy food did she contact the police. William was convicted of desertion in both June and July 1880. On each occasion he was sentenced to serve a few days in gaol. On his release he would disappear again.

When his father began disappearing from home, Alicks was eleven years old. By the time he turned seventeen, a set of records suggests he had drawn some firm conclusions about what his father had been doing during his absences from the family.

In September 1891, Alicks Sly walked into the offices of the Mutual Life Assurance Society on the corner of Pitt and Hunter streets in Sydney. The society had a reputation as a reliable and trustworthy insurance company. This impression was reinforced to customers by the building in which it was located: a grand and very dignified structure considered to be one of the most impressive pieces of architecture in the city at the time. The solid façade must have offered reassurance to a young Alicks as he walked through the door to discuss matters of life and death.

He signed up for a policy. A premium had to be paid once a year. If he died, the policy would yield around 350 pounds (300 pounds sterling) to the beneficiary.

The terms of the policy suggest some extraordinarily complex family dynamics. While a deep distrust and resentment of his father are certainly present, the wording also hints at something else: 'Alexander William Bedford Sly desire that in the event of my death my mother Barbara Sly receive full benefit of my Life Assurance Policy . . . To be delivered over to her without the control of my father William Sly. In the event of her death to be equally divided amongst my sisters.' Alicks was angry at his father for leaving, that much is clear. It also seems Alicks had formed an impression of his father as an intractable and bad man. This type of policy is usually only drawn up to protect a family against infidelity. Alicks apparently believed his father had left to make a new family and feared that his own family bloodline would be disinherited.

Even taking into account a vastly different labour market, and the different expectations and aspirations of young adulthood in the late nineteenth century, Alicks's decision was still a remarkable one for a youth of seventeen. He was not married and had no children. The value of the policy was sufficient to set up his mother and sisters for life. For four years Alicks paid the huge premiums of four pounds, fourteen shillings and sixpence. Then, when he could no longer afford it, the policy lapsed.

The existence of this policy raises big questions. It presents a perplexing and conflicted portrait of Alicks Sly. Whatever else he became by 1904, at one time he had been a son and brother who tried to protect his mother and five sisters from a man he perceived to be rotten to the core.

6

COLD COMFORT

AS THE LONG SUMMER TWILIGHT FINALLY DIMMED ON TUESDAY, 12 January 1904, and the last vestiges of orange faded from the sky, each member of the Sly family found themselves in a similar predicament. All were now in the care of strangers. One Sly daughter slept soundly in a ward, watched with cool austerity by the nurses at the Royal Prince Alfred Hospital. Two Sly parents were spread on examination tables under the cold guardianship of a morgue attendant. Three Sly boys crossed the threshold of the Home of Hope into the care of an even colder matron; a single conversation between two women had led to the transfer of the boys into this place.

All day, two men, agents of the state, had worked diligently to bring legal closure to the event that had occurred that morning at 49 Watkin Street. At Newtown police station, Sergeant Agnew coordinated the investigation. He completed paperwork and conducted his analysis of the evidence in preparation for the coronial inquest scheduled for the following day. He dispatched constables in search of relatives of the dead. Meanwhile, at the city morgue Dr Jamieson hunched over a huge and elaborately bound entry book in preparation for the double post-mortem, then set about to count and measure the cuts on the bodies.

Around this time, two women were also drawn into the tragedy, carried forward by a similar devotion to duty to their community. It was not just men who would have a hands-on role in investigating the reasons for the Sly deaths; women, too, would be reckoners of this process. Their efforts, however, would remain hidden.

Mrs Shaw looked from her window towards the now empty home at 49 Watkin Street. She could see the second-floor bedroom window quite clearly. Before it had seemed unremarkable, but she now looked at it with the knowledge that just beyond that pane, Ellie Sly had died.

Only a few streets away, another local woman headed towards Watkin Street. Mrs Beth Bowden's boots kicked up dust as she wove through the back streets, trying to navigate the shortest possible route from her home in Rose Street, Darlington. She walked quickly because she had her own family to return to, and she would soon need to prepare a meal for them. It was a long walk on a warm summer afternoon, and she was sweating beneath her long skirt and voluminous pleated blouse. She was grateful for her wide-brimmed hat; it was not the shade she needed, but rather the band that tightly held the hat in place, as she stopped periodically to tuck her hair firmly beneath it. Securing her hair off her neck was the only thing keeping her cool.

During her time as a resident of Watkin Street, Mrs Shaw had seen many tenants come and go from number 49. Dressmakers, milliners, waitresses, even a fortune-reading palmist had operated a business there. They had all been wives and mothers, just like Ellie Sly. But she had never seen a woman depart a home in the way that Ellie had done. And no woman had ever left behind four children. Mrs Shaw could feel herself being unwillingly drawn into something bigger. The tragedy had crept into her home. Three of the Sly children still waited in her yard while police tried to locate any extended family members.

Mrs Shaw noted that the terrace house did not look as it should at a time like this. There were no lengths of black cloth hanging in the windows. The drapes were not drawn. The house displayed no signs of grief and none of the frenetic activity typical of a home in mourning. While much has since been written about the very public way in which Victorian families embraced grief through ornate funeral and burial rituals, there was another side to displays of grief in this era: bereaved homes were busy.

Death may have filled houses with sadness in 1904, but it also filled them with a cleaning catharsis. Bed coverlets were shaken out. Rugs were emptied of dust with a sound beating. Fireplaces were swept. Floors and walls were scrubbed, and curtains cleaned. Every room required a fresh bucket of water, and a different soap was used for each job – including the preparation of the bodies. Sunlight Soap was used to launder cloth. Because it was cheap, Monkey Brand soap was used for general cleaning and scrubbing surfaces. Detective Soap, an off-the-shelf grocery store product, was popular among housewives for cleaning the dead because it was good for preserving the skin; it was 'the perfect cleanser' for any corpse. Dirty pans of water were tipped into public drains on the street in the hope of removing anything contagious associated with the death. Sadness may well have filled the streets when a neighbour died, but so too did soap suds.

Without a woman to guide the mourning process at 49 Watkin Street, the house seemed uniquely alone. This thought occupied not only Mrs Shaw on that Tuesday afternoon but also Mrs Bowden as she walked towards the Sly home.

Victorian and Edwardian women prepared and kept house for the dead. Throughout the home, reflective surfaces were covered with sheets or cloths; mirrors were turned to walls. The pendulum of the household clock would be caught in the hand and brought to a stop. Gender roles in 1904 defined a woman's place to be in the home as a cleaner and carer, but also as a curator of corpses. Women undressed, bathed, clothed and arranged loved ones after they had passed. It was women who fossicked for coins suitable to weigh down the lids of dead eyes. Women also prepared and set the dead, binding limbs and digits, and bandaging mouths to ensure the jaw did not gape in an unsightly way. Needlework was used to stop contortions: a toe stitched to a hand, or an elbow to an elbow, then knotted off neatly. This was all done with careful thought to posture, and to ensure the bodies looked peaceful when visitors paid their final respects. Small interventions made by sisters, mothers and daughters while preparing the dead served another important practical function: women laid out the bodies mindful of the coffin. Christian rituals and prayers focused on the ascendance of the soul, but on Earth the dead had to fit in boxes. The quick intervention of women was essential before decomposition began to set their relatives to stone. But it seemed there was no female relative to care for Ellie Sly. This surely weighed on Mrs Shaw while she considered what to do next.

As Beth Bowden arrived at Watkin Street, and the large home on the corner came into view, a heaviness fell upon her too. Everything she looked at was at odds with what she understood a grieving home to be. For one thing, the front door was closed. Just as modern households leave a door or side gate open when celebrating a birthday, Victorian homes in grief left the door ajar; this allowed visitors to pay respects quietly.

On the front steps of number 49, there were no small arrangements of the pale and pastel flowers traditionally used in funerals. No offering of fruitcake. No bottles of homemade cider. No calling cards, printed neatly with formal messages of condolence. The steps of this house were bare.

Mrs Bowden took a moment to collect herself. She smoothed down her skirt and adjusted it back into position. She fixed her hair, and balanced her blouse so it sat symmetrically, with the puffed sleeves neat and upright. As she moved decisively towards the door, something stopped her: a woman quickly exited a house on the right and walked over to her.

The women introduced themselves and soon realised how much they shared. Their commentaries on the Sly family mirrored each other. Two women, with experiences two years apart, had eerily similar things to say.

In 1901, Beth Bowden had been a neighbour to the Sly family. Before Alicks and Ellie had moved, their family had lived for a brief time in Rose Street, Darlington. Mrs Bowden ran the grocery shop on the corner of that street, a family business, and like Mrs Shaw she had become intimately aware of the strangeness of the Sly household.

Mrs Bowden was well known in the area. Clever and resourceful, she exhibited the kind of domestic entrepreneurialism typical of women trying to make ends meet in 1904. She entered competitions, wrote to companies for free samples, and provided paid testimonials proclaiming the health benefits of products from eczema cream to Milk Arrowroot biscuits.

Along with six thousand other women, Mrs Bowden had participated in an advertising campaign for the biscuit company Arnott's. She provided them with a photograph, name, address and testimonial of her confidence in Milk Arrowroots. At the time these were branded not as a tea biscuit but as a kind of health food, to be served as a sloppy breakfast cereal. Arnott's had at first recommended the biscuits be soaked in milk or water and fed to small children, as young as two weeks old, as their staple food. In 1890, however, the credibility of this advertising campaign crumbled when a baby died. Loving parents Thomas and Annie Edwards of Prospect Creek, Western Sydney, faced a coronial inquest. Their claims represented a public relations disaster for Arnott's. The Edwards had followed the company's recommendations, they said, and fed their four-month-old son exclusively on a diet of Milk Arrowroots and condensed milk (diluted to a teaspoon per pint of water), three times a day. The coroner ruled the child had died of inanition (a severe form of malnutrition) and 'want of proper food'.

More than ten years later, Arnott's were still trying to restore consumer confidence and were prepared to go to extreme lengths to do so. In return for free product, members of the public were invited to write glowing testimonials of the Milk Arrowroot. Broadsheet-sized advertisements printed these long testimonials, accompanied by sketches of plump children who had been fed exclusively on Milk Arrowroots. Beth Bowden had been quick to sign up to the scheme and offer her personal details for publication.

Mrs Bowden was also an enthusiastic advocate for miracle cure Zam-Buk: a mix of paraffin, resin and eucalyptus oil with an approximately 5000 per cent mark-up. She was an ambassador for the product because it had saved her son's life, she said. Before Zam-Buk, she had helplessly watched him be crippled by 'running eczema', which reduced him to a 'red raw' state of 'watery discharge'. After Zam-Buk, she watched him return to a healthy and rambunctious little boy. Her detailed five-paragraph testimonials were printed in newspapers nationally. To maintain the economic security of her family, she believed it necessary for everyone in Australia to know that her son, Georgie Bowden of 62 Rose Street, Darlington, was a pathetic and weeping sore of a boy – before Zam-Buk, of course.

As a grocer, Mrs Bowden was not afraid to bend or even break the trading law. If you needed potatoes for a Sunday family dinner, she would sell them to you although it was illegal to trade on that day. If you needed a late-night smoke, she sold tobacco too. On two occasions she had been hauled before Redfern's local court charged with illegal trading and failing to register with the local police court to trade in tobacco and cigars; each time she had been issued with a fine, or the option of serving a few days in gaol. Of all the people charged with illegally selling tobacco around this time, only 10 per cent were women – most businesses were run by men. Mrs Bowden was known not just as a local grocer but a shrewd one at that.

On Watkin Street that Tuesday afternoon, Mrs Shaw and Mrs Bowden exchanged pleasantries.

'I heard about what had happened from a neighbour,' said Mrs Bowden. 'I hadn't seen the Slys for some time. I had to come. A terrible, terrible thing.' She paused as if the heaviness of the moment had overcome her, then added with a sense of resignation, 'Although I can't say I was surprised.'

'I was surprised,' said Mrs Shaw. 'I did not expect anything like this to happen. Although I hadn't known them for long.'

Mrs Bowden began to unload the burden of her thoughts on the Slys. It was as if she had carried it long enough, and she had decided that here and now, on the doorstep of their deaths, it would all be set down. When it was released, it rolled out as a stream-of-consciousness narrative.

'She suffered the pinch of poverty more than he,' said Mrs Bowden. 'She was very proud. She tried to hide it from me, but I knew. They were destitute. She booked anything and everything with me, and she did pay up all that she owed me. I can't say she didn't. But it was so slow and I could tell she was suffering to do it. It took them months and months to pay off the funeral of their boy, Norman. She was ashamed. She paid it off in instalments of sixpence at a time. Pitiful, pitiful thing.'

Mrs Shaw too had sensed a disparity between Ellie and her husband. The woman had seemed better born – Mrs Shaw had mentioned that to journalists.

Known for her gossip and colourful exaggerations, Mrs Shaw seemed to have met her match. Mrs Bowden continued before Mrs Shaw could offer her own evaluation. 'They constantly begged me to have my children learn music with her. She was proud. She didn't want to admit she couldn't pay me. She tried to make it sound like she was doing me a favour. She wanted to teach my children piano and violin, and for that she would clear her book-up at the store, she said. Desperate, really desperate, she was.'

At this Mrs Shaw nodded in agreement and interjected. 'Yes, he begged me too. He said he could pay me for looking after the children. He begged his landlord too. The coach builder, that fellow Lownds on King Street. I saw the men talking, the night before, as it happens. Sly said his wife had a number of paintings to sell. "You need not be afraid of losing your money, sir," he said. He was pleading with the landlord right in the middle of the street. "She is going to commence teaching music, we have the finest of pianos," he said. It was all very undignified.'

Mrs Shaw continued. 'I know Lownds. He's a hard man. He was disgusted with the state of the place and berated Sly for it. He said, "I would have thought you'd be glad to be leaving, Sly, on account of the bad smell you seem so fond of complaining about in the house anyway." It didn't look to me like Sly had enough money for anything, let alone paying neighbours like me to care for his children.'

With this comment, Mrs Bowden heartily concurred. 'They asked me and my husband to take their children too. They offered to pay other neighbours in Rose Street to take the children as well.'

A funereal stillness fell between the women. A horse and cart ground slowly past them, the road stones rhythmically popping beneath the wheels as it headed up the street. A plume of smoke spiralled out of the bakery chimney, carrying its powdery dust with the lightness of air. The two women knew better than to look up at it; they faced downwards. They waited for a moment, letting the soft ash settle across their hats.

It was a while before Mrs Bowden broke the silence. 'They had a vacant and faraway look about them. The father was queer. There was mental trouble there. That much was clear.'

This statement did not shock Mrs Shaw in the least. She nodded firmly.

Then came a summation: the confident delivery of a verdict that Mrs Shaw did not expect. 'They wanted the children out of the way and cared for, so they could be alone,' Mrs Bowden said. 'They had been planning this together for some time, I think.'

To this, Mrs Shaw did not nod. She just looked stunned.

Mrs Bowden again assumed the lead. 'I told my husband, neither of them was right in the head. There was something wild about his eyes. Though both of them had something of an insane and feeble look about them. When they left, the last time I saw them, I said to my husband, "I don't want anything to do with them, or their children."' Mrs Bowden had come to offer her condolences, but she reserved the right to offer up judgement as well, like a covered pot of cold stew, right on the front doorstep.

Something about this last comment shook Mrs Shaw to her core. It was not the notion that the Slys were deranged that shocked her – she had come to that conclusion on her own. It was the notion that their children were on her property, with her family. She had been uncomfortable with the police proposition that she could care for them while their relatives were located. This now sat even more uneasily with her.

Mrs Bowden's words confirmed what Mrs Shaw had felt from the very beginning: she could not allow the boys to stay with her any longer. If what Mrs Bowden had said was true, the Sly boys were bad seeds, just as bad as their father.

For the second time that Tuesday, Mrs Shaw called for the police. The first time had been for the Sly parents – this time was for the Sly children. We cannot know what she felt as the boys were led away from her home late that evening, only that it was she who insisted they be taken away. As a gesture of respect and in remembrance of their mother, she gave each of them a strip of black crepe so they might tie armbands around their sleeves.

Mrs Bowden's visit had helped Mrs Shaw realise how much she might have misunderstood about what had occurred in the Sly home. What she had tried to dismiss as a freak incident was perhaps something different entirely. Perhaps her assumption that Ellie had been better born and Alicks worse born had been wrong, and perhaps the vow of 'for better or for worse' had been their undoing. Had the Slys been inexorably moving towards this point of destruction all along?

7

LOW-HANGING FRUIT

NEWSPAPERS HAD DRAWN SOME FIRM CONCLUSIONS ABOUT Alicks Sly and the innate criminal tendencies that were assumed to dwell within him. Their descriptions of Ellie Sly, however, were underdeveloped and still forming.

Today the word 'criminology' is often defined narrowly to include only the study of the criminal. Usually the focus is placed on the perpetrator through documenting their deviant behaviour that led up to the crime, and/or developing a portrait of their psyche. In contrast, the victimology of a crime is not typically an area of focus. The impact of the crime on victims, the complex relationship of the victim to the criminal event and to the justice system all receive much less attention relative to the perpetrator. This was also true a century ago.

Alicks was profiled by newspapers because a focus on the perpetrator was an easy story. Dramatic headlines that laid bare the cruelty and brutality of human nature sold papers, just as they do today. Such stories were considered a kind of low-hanging fruit – easy pickings. Understanding and positioning Ellie as a victim was a much more involved and difficult task. Was her family history very different to Alicks's, as Mrs Bowden and Mrs Shaw had surmised?

While the Sly brothers were settling in remote Hobart Town, in remote New South Wales two Irish brothers were doing the same. And both family trees involved two brothers planting seed.

In the mid-1800s, Cornelius and Timothy O'Leary migrated from the county of Cork to the town of Goulburn. They chose to settle in an alienating and hostile habitat that was vastly different from what they knew. Cork was wet, flood prone and cold; Goulburn was dry, drought prone and hot.

Cornelius migrated first and worked a lease on a 383-acre farm with apple trees, pear trees and sheep. He ran the Union Inn at Currawang, just outside of Goulburn, before keeping a general store in the town. He paid the four-pound passage for his brother Timothy to migrate and join him. Both men then married: Cornelius to Ellen McCarthy, also from Cork, and Timothy to Mary Hennessey.

While the natural environment certainly presented challenges, the brothers and their wives were nestled within the support of a tight-knit Irish community. As one newspaper wrote of Goulburn at the end of the nineteenth century, 'The

Roman Catholics are very strong in the town, and in the region round about.'

Each of the brothers had six children. Timothy (Ellie's uncle) and Mary had Honora, Ellie Cecily, Sonny, Michael, Minnie and Timmy. Cornelius and Ellen (Ellie's mother and father) had Timmy, Cornelius Jr, James, Jeremiah and John James (J. J.). In 1872, Ellie Gertrude was born: the sixth and last child, and the only daughter.

Cornelius worked hard to achieve economic security for his family. The O'Leary store sold an immense variety of product. Suits, curtains and zephyrs (bolts) of gingham were available in all the most fashionable colours. Three varieties of sugar were sold to suit all budgets: brown, good yellow, and best white. Two classes of tea were available: common and best. Cornelius brought in luxury items as well. Sperm candles were particularly popular; made of oil extracted from the head cavity of the sperm whale, they were the whitest candles available, burning brighter and cleaner than those made from animal tallow. The cumbersome and rather impractical parasols known as silk and satin parachutes sold well to Irish colonists seeking shade in the unrelenting heat of the Australian summer.

The peculiar contradictions of Goulburn weather must have been difficult for Irish migrants to ignore. While the region was drought prone, it was also subject to harsh and chaotic storm fronts. The horizon could sear with white-hot heat in summer, yet it could be blanketed in white frost come winter. In her 1901 novel, *My Brilliant Career*, Stella Miles

Franklin described Goulburn as stagnant and barren, where wind and dirt and dry grass 'darkened the air with dust' while covered by 'the cruel dazzling brilliance of the metal sky'. At other times, however, the land roared with a fury that surely terrified its migrant residents. Gale-force winds swept through with the change of seasons. In the June before Ellie was born, the town was rocked by several earthquakes.

Just like in Van Diemen's Land, apples were important to the early NSW colonists: 'Almost every resident who possesses garden ground desires to have two or three apple trees in it in preference to any other fruit tree.' The O'Learys, like all their compatriot families, were trying to adapt to their hostile environment, prepare garden beds and create favourable breeding conditions for resilient varieties. Hundreds of different apples were tested to see which could endure the austere landscape. At every Goulburn Horticultural Society Show, which convened regularly in the Mechanics Institute hall, locals shared their expertise and the results of their own breeding experiments.

The Catholic Church sought to support good breeding too, by providing proper growing conditions for children in the Goulburn area. The town prided itself on its culture and refinement. Private tutors ran classes in everything from Greek and Latin to drawing, music, painting, singing and dancing. Boys were typically taught the classics and mathematics, but also more commercial skills such as mercantile bookkeeping. For young women, lessons in French, piano, organ, harmonium and harp were strongly encouraged, and since there were so many teachers, these classes remained affordable for many families.

Despite the best efforts of the colonists to re-create a gentrified Anglo-Celtic country life, there were daily reminders that they were living at odds with their environment. Tea was served each afternoon and pianos were played in parlours, but carpet snakes were still regularly found in linen closets. Settlers sought to change their alien surrounds by planting their own horticulture, including small evergreens contained as shrubs or clipped to hedgerows in manicured gardens. European plants grew, however, in ways the colonists did not expect. Blackberry bushes became bramble. Irish strawberry trees became forest tall. Laurel bays thrived, exhibiting growth never observed in cold climates.

The O'Leary women carried on their domestic traditions from Ireland, with needlework being a favourite of Ellen and Mary. Both were fond of embroidery in the Mountmellick style: white thread on a white cotton fabric. Although it originated in Laois, further north than the O'Learys' home county of Cork, the style was popular with Irish women in general. Mountmellick remains the only form of embroidery that can claim to be distinctively Irish. The embroidery was inspired by the Irish countryside and was developed by an Irish woman (its invention is attributed to a teacher called Johanna Carter), and the technique was shared and taught throughout Ireland during the Victorian era.

Mountmellick is practical and durable, designed to adorn everyday items and withstand washing and general use.

Tablecloths, tray covers, and pillow and bedcovers often feature Mountmellick motifs.

The technique appears to be controlled, meticulous, careful and modest, but creatively it is an untamed and unrestrained celebration of the natural world. The dog rose is a common motif; though pretty and delicate, in Ireland it is known for climbing and strangling. Clover, a wild weed, is another common feature, and shamrocks are sometimes depicted. Acorns are a reminder that the smallest seeds can become mighty oaks. Intricately stitched blackberries, comprised of tiny coils and knots, are positioned against the wild and thorny bramble in which the sweet fruit grows.

The embroidery stitched by the O'Leary women was a remembrance of home, but it was also an homage to the struggle of life and death happening right outside the windows of their antipodean homes. In their own way, the women were stitching their history and uniquely conveying their own survival-of-the-fittest struggle with the Australian landscape. Alongside a climbing dog rose from the homeland, a cluster of a native boronia might also be sewn. Next to a switch of pippin apple blossom, there might be a stitch of local native daisies. Mountmellick seemed to embody the relationship evolving between an Irish family and the foreign land they now called home: things that could not be tamed had to be honoured and memorialised. Because Mountmellick is the only white-on-white form of embroidery, its ornateness is often hidden. What appears on the surface to be simple and uncomplicated is, in fact, complex.

•

The O'Leary brothers had large families, and this was certainly not unusual for the time, but the losses experienced by Cornelius and Ellen were. One by one they lost four of their six children, and not all in infancy as most parents did in the Victorian era. As one newspaper wrote around the time, Cornelius and Ellen atypically lost sons 'on reaching manhood'. Cornelius Jr died very early, for reasons that to this day remain unclear. However, Timmy, the eldest, and the namesake of Cornelius's dear brother, died at twenty-seven. James died of a mysterious liver condition which could not be explained because he had a reputation for a wholesome and clean-living lifestyle. Even by Victorian standards, it seems a devastating series of improbable tragedies. For Cornelius and Ellen, these events must have been almost impossible to come to terms with. They had successfully nursed their offspring through the most hazardous period of life, only to watch helplessly as they died in their prime. Only J. J. and Ellie lived past their twenties.

Perhaps even more perplexing for Cornelius was the luck that his brother Timothy seemed to have. The brothers lived and worked side by side, but while one branch of the family tree thrived, the other withered. Timothy's children lived long (at least for the time) – with the exception of Sonny, who died at six years old – and the majority led successful lives.

The year 1891 began a particularly prolonged and severe period of bad luck for Cornelius and his family. The first half of the year was filled with hope. J. J. was working with his father to expand the drapery business. Ellie was nineteen and working in the family shop. Although she had completed formal schooling, it was considered important for her to refine her accomplishments as a young woman, so she continued to receive tuition in piano and violin. Jeremiah, who was known as Jerry, applied for and won a job in Sydney with a successful trader and importer; by late July, preparations for his new life in the city had begun.

The young man decided to stop over in Batemans Bay for a holiday before knuckling down to a career in the big smoke. Using Victorian vernacular, he planned to 'go on a spree', which usually involved a lot of binge drinking and passing out. Along with friends, Jerry tried to navigate a boat out from the bay into the Pacific. Their inexperience, the choppy sea and inebriation soon got the better of them. The boat capsized. All on board were lost except for one man, found by a local fisherman in the freezing water as he clung to the upturned boat. Somehow, miraculously, Jerry had survived. But it was midwinter and he was submerged up to his neck, dog paddling to keep himself alive.

Word was sent to the O'Leary family, and this took considerable time. The trip by coach from Goulburn to the rest stop in Braidwood was eighty-five kilometres, a journey of more than nine hours. Batemans Bay was roughly this distance again. When Cornelius received the news he rushed to be at his son's side, but it took the better part of a day to get there over rough roads and across the treacherous Clyde

Mountain. Cornelius finally arrived – just in time to see his son pass away.

Bringing Jerry home to Kenmore Cemetery near Goulburn was another ordeal. The body had to be brought by cart, bumping along sixty kilometres of rough road from the bay to the nearest mail train; from there, the body could travel by rail to Goulburn. The road was dirt and slippery stone, and if this was not enough the journey also required crossing Clyde Mountain again, only this time at night and while towing a corpse.

Late in the evening, as Cornelius walked up the steepest part of the road, he accidentally stepped right off the mountainside. To the horror of those around him, the old man disappeared, plunging into the dark abyss. Everyone in the party believed they now had a double tragedy on their hands. But somehow Cornelius had grabbed hold of a broken tree stump and clung on. Only a few days before, his son had hung perilously in the water, clinging on for dear life as he awaited rescue; now Cornelius found himself in an uncannily similar predicament. Ropes were quickly knotted and anchored to winch him to safety, but it was a slow and clumsy affair as the rescue party fumbled in the dark. Cornelius was finally dragged to the top, but he was battered, bruised and scared.

The funeral for Jerry was at Saints Peter and Paul's Old Cathedral in Goulburn. The church was crowded. Handel's 'Dead March' played as the congregation filed out. A pure white marble tombstone was erected – the most elaborate memorial that Cornelius and Ellen ever arranged for one of their children. Jerry was also the only child they ever acknowledged on the shared family tombstone. While it was a beautiful tribute to their most adored son, it offered little comfort to the couple. Nothing could stave off the grief that was about to consume Ellen. She and Cornelius had now lost their favourite son and 'the general favourite', and this would deeply affect the two siblings who remained.

Almost immediately after Jerry's death, his mother was overcome by a mystery illness. A local doctor eventually diagnosed it as 'brain fever'. Though the term was sometimes used to describe inflammations such as encephalitis and meningitis, it also euphemistically described a range of emotional disturbances, hallucinations, delusions and any behaviours considered 'unusual'. Medical historians have described brain fever as a uniquely Victorian disease because it did not exist as a diagnostic label before or extensively after the nineteenth century. It is most likely that Ellen's condition was not a bacterial infection like meningitis, because her death would have occurred within hours, or a few days at most. It is much more likely that the term was applied to mask a shameful and deeply stigmatising illness in the nineteenth century – a serious mental collapse which meant she would require full-time care. As Ellie was the only daughter, this responsibility would have fallen to her.

The few remaining family members tried to pull together. Cornelius ran the general store, and J. J. ran the drapery. They all spent more time in town, eventually deciding to live permanently in the residence behind the shop. It was a cosy place and had the most modern conveniences available. There was a balcony on top, a parlour at the back, a sitting room, four bedrooms, a laundry, and water and gas. It was certainly better than the family's residence at Currawang and was perceived to offer the best possible chance for Ellen's recovery.

Ellie's time was divided between nursing her mother and helping her father in the store. Cornelius began to feel the strain, unable to cope with the responsibilities of managing a farm, a hotel and shop in Currawang, and a shop in town – none of which earned any real money. In desperation, he listed the property in Currawang for sale. It was advertised for months but did not sell.

For two years Ellen's malaise did not get better, but it did not get worse. Cornelius's business situation did not worsen either, though it did not stabilise. For Ellie O'Leary, however, 1893 was a turning-point year.

Sometime in 1893 she met a slightly built, pensive and philosophical young man called Alexander William Bedford Sly. It cannot be known how the two met, but with the responsibility of caring full-time for her mother, it is unlikely that Ellie travelled to Sydney or elsewhere during this time. It is more likely that Alicks travelled to Goulburn at some point that year. Travel by rail to and from the town was reliable and efficient because trains exported wool and produce from the region. Goulburn was also a popular holiday destination for Sydneysiders. Groups of road cyclists, choral societies and horse riders all incorporated a trip to Goulburn by train into their adventures. For those travelling to and from Goulburn to Sydney on business, the train could offer a 'comfortable railway carriage' for six hours and a 'good supper' to those travelling on business.

Although not a lot of information is available about this period in Alicks's life, or his courtship with Ellie, some fragments remain. He was a hardworking and committed man who exhibited an obsessive focus in fighting for the causes that mattered to him. Alicks was heavily involved in the union activities of the tailors and pressers in Sydney at the time. He was a member of the executive committee of the Pressers' Union of NSW and he was one of only six senior members who signed the historic industrial agreement between the Sydney Clothing Manufacturers' Association and the Industrial Union of Employers on behalf of its membership.

The work to draft this industrial document was painstaking, as it sets out the costing profile for every single item that might comprise a presser's work log. Everything from trousers and vests to coats is described, in every possible style of fabric, and with every button, band, lining and trimming taken into account in the pricing protocols. All of these features informed the notion of fair payment, because they conveyed the level of skill required by the presser to iron and prepare a garment. Women's clothing does not feature in the agreement; on one hand it might be said this was because the work process for many women's garments did not require the same pressing process as men's attire at the time. On the other hand, it

might be said that it reflected the very culture of the pressers'
union at the time.

The pressers did not concern themselves with women's
affairs. They were being denied work, they said, because
cheaper female labour was being used to press, trim and
cut, in outwork settings known at the time as slop shops
and sweat dens. In the process, it was argued, men were
being cut out of the industry entirely. Even by union standards of the time, which were overwhelmingly concerned with
the interests of men, the pressers' unions were particularly
vocal and active in maintaining their work as a male bastion.
As Bradon Ellem, Professor of Employment Relations at the
University of Sydney Business School noted in one of the most
comprehensive accounts of clothing and allied trades unions
in this country, 'the pressers retained greater control of the
industry than tailors did. Their labour was probably of more
strategic significance and less easily replaced.'

Alicks was one of the men who had been directly involved
in itemising an entire area of commerce and craft – but only
for men workers, and only for men's garments. The agreement which Alicks helped assemble reflects these interests: it
is concerned only with men's work, done by men, for their
male employers, to be sold to their male customers.

He was also interested in the key issues that faced his
society: the price of progress, the loss of ethics, and the desire
to preserve order and respectability. He belonged to a local
literary society, one of hundreds across New South Wales.
Such societies offered men the opportunity to gather and

socialise while discussing the issues of the day. Reflecting the segregated nature of Victorian society, women and non-white men were not allowed to join these clubs, which were also formed along class, cultural and often religious lines.

James Padley, a founding pioneer and high-profile citizen of Lithgow who was active in the community, government and economic progress of the Nepean region, came to know Alicks through mutual membership of a literary association. They read essays together, debated the state of the world, and puffed on cigars in smoke-filled community halls. The two men bemoaned the crumbling civilisation around them, but emboldened themselves with the belief that society's problems could most logically be solved through sharing wit with men who were mirror images of themselves. Padley spoke of Alicks in the highest terms as a close friend and intellectual sparring partner, claiming that his friendship with Alicks had renewed his interest in literary and philosophical pursuits.

•

When Alicks and Ellie met in Goulburn, each in their own way was ripe for the picking. Alicks was estranged from his father, and no doubt finding it difficult to spend time with his sisters and mother. As a youth who had been raised in a household of women, perhaps he was immediately drawn to Ellie and her country charms. From her point of view, Alicks's reticence to discuss his past, or any matters pertaining to family, must have added intrigue to the neatly waistcoated, conscientious and thoughtful gentleman.

Ellie was possibly caught up in a romantic dream. The writings of Stella Miles Franklin corroborate that escapism ran strong in the veins of Goulburn girls around this time; her vivid stories are notionally about growing up, but on a deeper level they are about getting away. In her reminiscences of Goulburn, she said, 'I used to feel it, the base of all travel-beginning and romance long ago.' Goulburn girls sought recognition from the wider world for their artistic and musical achievements. Raised to value, pursue and appreciate art, music and dance, Ellie would have been drawn to the city as a place of high culture with museums, art galleries and concert halls. When she met Alicks in 1893, she had been caring for her mother in their small town for close to two years. It is easy to imagine Ellie being swept up very quickly in a rescue fantasy.

The courtship was short, and in almost every way – with one exception – it was respectable. Alicks was polite. He did not drink or swear. He represented a figure of manhood that seemed less rough and brutal than what the hard country life often produced in men. Though not physically strong, he was willing to intellectually spar over issues of importance. He also seemed a good match for Ellie.

There was only one problem. Unfortunately, it was a big one. Alicks was not Catholic.

Of all the tragedies Cornelius faced in his lifetime, it is not hyperbolic to suggest that Ellie's courtship with Alicks was among the greatest. To understand the significance of this tragedy, it is necessary to understand how deeply divided the country was along religious lines.

The separation between Catholic and Protestant families in Australia at the turn of the century has been described as 'a low-level apartheid'. Segregation was particularly pronounced in regional areas like Goulburn. While no laws prevented Catholics from marrying Anglicans, families showed dogmatically unforgiving attitudes to relatives who married outside their religion. In some parts of Australia, this socially enforced segregation persisted into the 1970s. While the O'Leary family would not have approved of Alicks as a non-Catholic husband, it is also possible that he had been brought up to think of Ellie as 'an ethnic' because she was Irish.

The year 1894 began dreadfully for the O'Learys: Ellen succumbed (using Victorian vernacular) to her affliction. In February she joined Jerry at Kenmore Cemetery, her name chiselled into his tombstone.

Six weeks later, Ellie and Alicks were married in Goulburn.

That Cornelius afforded more attention and expense to Jerry's funeral and burial than Ellie's wedding is not surprising. The Victorian-era obsession with mourning rituals is well documented. Wedding services were typically short and often received less attention than funerals, which involved hearses, carriages, official invitations and processions. However, at the time of Ellie's wedding her family did not recognise or celebrate it at all, which certainly suggests that Cornelius firmly disapproved of it.

In the second half of the nineteenth century, Goulburn weddings were celebrated even among less well-to-do families. Although these events were not as large and expensive as they often are today, they were still important milestones. Their details were shared in the local paper, a tradition that was partly a formal recognition and a thank you to the guests, and partly a shameless way to show off. It was not unusual for a wedding announcement to list every guest and carefully itemise every gift: from the silver tea service, biscuit barrel, silver teaspoons, custard glasses, cruet set and Mountmellick pillow sham (an ornamental cover), right through to the silver sardine dish, toast rack and vases. A 'good' marriage – the pairing of two young people from respectable families – enhanced the status of their relatives, so it was important to acknowledge exactly who had given what. On reading these guest and gift lists stripped of their social context, it is hard not to interpret them somewhat cynically. They were presented with all the connubial joy of a stocktake at a homeware importer's store.

Ellie O'Leary and her mother often feature as guests and gift givers in these inventories. Ellie's wedding, however, did not unfold in this way. She did not marry under the conditions of a Catholic service, which to some local Irish Catholics would have been the equivalent of not marrying at all.

Many Presbyterian families elected to marry at home, but Cornelius did not provide this option for Ellie. Instead, Alicks and Ellie were married at the reverend's residence attached to St Andrew's Church. No one from the O'Leary family bore witness to the union.

This marriage was out of step with every tradition associated with weddings in Goulburn since the settlement of its Irish community. Because the town aspired to have an air of charm and grace, its wedding ceremonies reflected this, underpinned by a practical and resourceful survivalist ethic. In 1890s Goulburn, fashionable wedding gowns were made from grey or green cashmere with guipure lace trimming, teamed with chiffon-trimmed straw hats. All of this was painstakingly hand-stitched by mothers, aunts and sisters, with fabric supplied by the O'Learys. After the ceremony, rose petals and silk confetti were tossed in the air to gently rain down on the bride and groom. While this practice sounds opulent, it actually reflected the ingenuity of Goulburn mothers – the confetti was the unusable and torn trimmings from the ends of silk zephyrs, snipped into tiny and shiny pieces of splendour. The O'Learys had supplied these roll ends too.

But Ellie's wedding had none of these things. She also had no mother to oversee the rituals with a matronly attitude, and no sisters with whom to share the occasion. Her father did not give his blessing. The wedding was not publicly announced. As it took place in autumn, there were no bridal wreaths heady with the fragrance of apple blossoms freshly picked from family orchards, and no snowball-shaped hydrangea bouquets.

It seems that Cornelius O'Leary felt a great degree of shame and anger about Ellie's marriage. She was his only daughter; this wedding was his only opportunity to play the role of father of the bride, yet he still did not perceive it as a cause for celebration. The O'Learys were a proud Irish Catholic family, and to see his only daughter turn away from the faith that he held so dear was surely experienced as a personal betrayal and perhaps even viewed as a decision that placed her immortal soul in jeopardy.

Mysteriously, the only public acknowledgement of the wedding occurred seven months after the event. For reasons that are unclear, a one-line announcement was made in the *Goulburn Evening Penny Post*. Who wrote and paid for this advertisement remains unknown.

As the only daughter, Ellie had been responsible for caring for her ailing mother right up until her death. Had Ellie waited to get married as an act of generosity, sparing Ellen disappointment and shame? Or did the timing reflect much more practical considerations? Whatever the case, Ellie was finally free. Alicks, no doubt disillusioned with family life because of his father's desertion, perhaps felt restored now that he had found love.

As soon as the wedding was over, Alicks and Ellie Sly left. It is not possible to know what the newlyweds felt as they boarded the train for Sydney. There was probably some fear and trepidation as they took in the magnitude of what they had done. Estranged from their families, they were in a contradictory position. They shared a feeling of togetherness; they were in love and had each other. Yet, they were alone as they had never been before.

Or perhaps it all felt natural, like the changing of the seasons. Alicks and Ellie left in April, a time in the Southern

Tablelands when the crisp early morning air heralds the coming of winter. In Goulburn, a farming town to its heart, this was the time when locals pruned their apple trees hardest to ensure new growth in the spring.

8

MOTHER'S SAD MISTAKE

WHEN NEWLYWED ELLIE SLY STEPPED OFF THE TRAIN FRESH from clean country Goulburn into the dirty city of Sydney, she must have felt like a migrant arriving in a new country. After life in her close-knit home town, where everyone with whom she closely associated was Irish and Catholic, Sydney could only have been a shock.

Goulburn was sleepy. The town had a vigilant Early Closing Association that ensured businesses adhered to restricted retail opening and closing times. Travellers to the Southern Tablelands noted that for long periods each day the main streets of Goulburn were dead. All shops were closed at 1.00 p.m. at the very latest on Saturday, and not a soul could be seen until opening hours resumed on Monday.

Sydney never slept. Unlike the O'Leary store in Goulburn, shops in the city stayed open well after dark. Particularly in vibrant commercial havens like Newtown and Glebe, shop-keepers agitated against new legislation designed to enforce early closing. Stores were open until or even after midnight, at the discretion of their owners, and this drew customers from their homes. The city streets were never entirely empty of people.

In the early years of their marriage, the Slys had plenty to fear. The atmosphere in Sydney was infectious – quite literally. Bubonic plague arrived on Australian shores in 1900, and patient zero was traced to Sydney. Even daily household tasks like feeding children were fraught with danger. Milk, in particular, could be deadly. In the same year the Slys settled in Sydney, a milkman from their area faced criminal charges; he had provided typhoid-contaminated product to 145 families who were found to have contracted the disease.

Fears grew about diphtheria. News spread that the disease lived in the throat long after a sufferer had seemingly recovered. It was a terrifying thought – avoiding the ill was no longer enough, as even those who appeared well could be a threat. Throats should be flushed with antiseptic fluid, said the medical recommendation. The common practice of students cleaning their school slates with a saliva-coated finger was stopped, leading to the introduction of tiny inkwells of water on students' desks.

The Board of Health took radical preventative measures by distributing large amounts of poison to citizens for eradication of disease-carrying rats. As one official statement noted: 'the Premier has approved of the gratuitous distribution of rat poison to responsible householders with a view to encouraging more general active and persistent effort to destroy rats'. The government also agreed to pay rat collectors.

The Sly family had financial difficulties like many Sydney families at the time. Alicks was trained as a tailor's presser but he struggled to find consistent work in the sector. He took whatever jobs he could.

At first he settled the family in south Sydney. He may have made this decision because he perceived the area to be cleaner than the inner city. The decision may also have been driven by commercial realities: it may have been the only location where he could find work.

Alicks took a job as a dairyman. Dairies were scattered across Sydney, and it was a labour-intense industry always in need of workers. He would have milked cows, bottled product, delivered it door to door by horse and cart, and then assumed responsibility for driving the herds back and forth to grazing land at different locations across the city. A day labourer with no stake in the enterprise, Alicks would have been hired to do the hardest physical work that farmers and owners did not want to do. Dairies hired unskilled men to 'shoo', which was akin to cow crowd control. Farmers always needed workers for herding tasks, as the cows grazed freely on pastures across the south Sydney area.

The early years of the Sly marriage appear to have been free of the deep anxieties that would plague the couple a decade later. There were no police reports of disturbances in their home. No complaints were made to police about local larrikins harassing the family. No assault charges were made against Alicks – although if he perpetrated violence in the home, it likely went unrecorded because reporting domestic abuse was not the custom.

Mainstream Sydney society would have deemed the Slys to have a successful marriage because there was issue from it. Ellie had five babies in seven years, the first four within five. John Bedford was born in October 1896, and Basil Cornelius within twelve months in 1897. The next two were born in a similar pattern: Mervyn in June 1899 and Olive Clotilde in July the following year. Non-Catholics might have called them 'Irish twins': a racial slur implying that Irish Catholics were poor, simple-minded and interested in little other than breeding. The observation had no basis in statistical fact. The other main denominational group, Anglicans, also had large families, often with many children close together. Alicks's mother had birthed nine in eleven years.

For seven straight Januarys, Ellie Sly was pregnant or still wet-nursing a small child. It could only have been a relentless and tiring seven years for her. Washing, cooking, cleaning, caring and nursing so many children without the aid of mechanised devices for managing a household would have made the physical demands of mothering intense. In a world defined by a gendered demarcation of labour, it is unlikely that Alicks would have considered housework or child care as part of his responsibilities.

Sometime around the birth of Bedford, letters were exchanged between Goulburn and Sydney. The words that passed between father and daughter must have been amicable, because within a short period Cornelius relocated permanently to Sydney. For forty-five years, Goulburn had been the only home he had known. As the turn of the century approached so too did his seventieth birthday, and his health began to fail. Frail and in pain after years of farm work, he was no longer able to properly care for himself.

The reconciliation had significant implications for Ellie: she would care for her young children and her father at the same time.

Ellie's older brother, J. J., almost thirty and still unmarried, moved in with the Sly family as well. From around 1896 through to 1902, the family comprised Alicks and Ellie, J. J., Cornelius and four children.

In *Cruelty and Companionship: Conflict in Nineteenth-Century Married Life*, feminist academic A. James Hammerton argues that the notion of 'compulsory motherhood' underpinned attitudes about women at the time. It was an expectation that no woman could escape, even if she had no desire to bear or raise children. While society believed that motherhood was the only natural pursuit for women, those like Ellie faced a tricky predicament. As a youngest child, she had not been conscripted to care for younger siblings; she had therefore been afforded little opportunity to develop mothering skills. Whether she embraced the task of motherhood early on is unclear; what is known is that at the time of the Slys' deaths, their children were suffering terribly from neglect.

Important fragments of evidence appear to show that events in 1902 represent ground zero for the panic-laden final two years of the Slys' lives.

The year 1902 was particularly bad for all of Sydney. There was the return of a plague that had terrorised the city two years before. Initially the infection appeared to have been tracked to a man in Rushcutters Bay, an enclave a little away from the city centre. This would have been a relief. However, other information suggested the principal case of plague was a resident in the centre of a densely populated pocket of the city. Yet another case was located in the inner suburb of Alexandria. In February 1902, Her Majesty's Theatre was closed after a boy selling fruit and programmes to theatregoers was found to have contracted the plague and died.

The city was quickly gripped by panic. Health inspectors engaged by the state advised residents that stormwater drains created preconditions favourable for disease. While residents were enjoying the benefits of a growing transport system and the conveniences of a modern city, so too were the rats – they were using the sewer system like a subway. This was a frightening prospect, allowing infection to spread rapidly between boroughs and making containment close to impossible. Extreme measures were required to prevent a potential public health disaster. Workers used blowing machines to fumigate the old sewers with toxic gas, but this was not considered to be nearly enough of an effort.

Newspapers across Sydney provided public service announcements designed to spread terror – and so keep residents on high alert to signs of the disease, increasing the chance of early detection. The city councils argued they did not have the power to take the protective measures necessary to ensure streets and homes remained clean enough to prevent the spread of plague. The ports were put on high alert to prevent plague-infected rats arriving on our shores at all. One newspaper outlined how the fear was felt not just in Sydney, but was quickly spreading like a disease across the state. 'Sydney, being the root of all evil in regard to plague for the whole of NSW naturally invites criticism on this matter from every newspaper in the State. What is endangering to the capital also endangers every district having intercommunication with it.'

Fear also escalated in the Sly household. The troubles started with the death of Cornelius, which occurred around the same time as the birth of Ellie and Alicks's fifth child. They gave him the Christian name of Norman, and the middle name of Bede, meaning prayer.

•

After Cornelius died, the stability of the family seemed to crumble. J. J. had regular work in the department store Grace Bros as a draper, but it was poorly paid. Alicks still struggled to find work. The family relinquished their lease on their Burwood home and moved to cheaper Campsie, but only briefly. They ended up in Glebe. The suburb sits on the edge of the city, with water views. It was affordable, convenient – and utterly abhorrent.

While all roads in Glebe terminated at the bay, so too did most of Sydney's livestock. It was estimated that every month about six to seven thousand head of cattle, seventy-five thousand sheep and lambs, fifteen hundred calves and five to six thousand pigs were slaughtered at the local abattoir. The bay was said to percolate with blood. A large saltwater storage pump drained the water from the harbour, pumped it across the killing floor, and then flushed the slurry of fat, flesh, sinew, blood and waste straight back into the sea. The smell was notorious and the Slys were now living in one of the least desirable areas of the inner city.

The Slys' lives worsened. Alicks and Ellie seemed to struggle with the responsibility of caring for five young offspring. The children, even as toddlers, seemed to spend a lot of time unsupervised in the street. Neighbours began to report that the Slys were making strange complaints about the house, along with complaints about the Push and intruders.

Then things got a lot worse. When Norman reached six months of age, he suddenly became gravely ill. After five days of diarrhoea and vomiting, he died. There are three possible explanations for this.

THEORY 1:
NORMAN DIED FROM A BACTERIAL INFECTION CONTRACTED FROM CONTAMINATED MILK

Without proper refrigeration, milk vendors often struggled to keep the product fresh. The Slys purchased their milk from

Edward McGee, who also lived on Mitchell Road in Glebe. In July 1902, McGee was charged with selling 'adulterated milk'. When tested, it was found to contain boracic acid, a disinfectant used to mask a rotten taste. Both tainted milk and boracic acid were known to cause the symptoms that Norman experienced. It is possible that his death was nothing more than the sad consequence of consuming contaminated food.

At six months, Norman was in the statistical bracket identified to be at highest risk of death: zero to two years. Examinations of the available data on mortality in this period note that lower life expectancy was deeply connected to the higher level of mortality amongst children in their first year of life. The doctor who was called to assess Norman's death wrote 'gastroenteritis' as the official cause, but there would have been no further exploration by medical staff. No stool samples would have been taken for further testing, and no blood screening could have provided an answer. The early twentieth century was a dangerous time to be a child, and it might be argued that families and doctors had become more or less resigned to this.

THEORY 2:
NORMAN WAS ACCIDENTALLY POISONED

Household kitchens were arranged and used differently in 1902. There was a risk of poisoning because of the way these rooms were used not only for cooking, but also as clinics for frontline triaging of ill family members. Hospitals were often an option of last resort because they were expensive, and doctors were not generally trusted.

In 1902, before the twentieth-century categorisation of products for consumption, cosmetic or pharmaceutical use, mothers approached the mixing of both poison and food with a casualness that would be feared today. A poultice – commonly prepared to draw pus from skin abscesses or treat ingrown toenails – contained items from the larder (oats, molasses) and the cleaning shelf (grated soap), and kerosene used to light lamps. Carbolic scrubs were mixed within the home to clean the walls and floors, but also the human body: as a caustic, used neat; for a lotion, mixed with water; for a dressing, suspended in olive or almond oil. Many children died from drinking carbolic acid, either because they had reached for the bottle or a mother had.

Before the regulation of warning labels, poisoning was so common that newspapers regularly printed lists of poisons, alongside antidotes that might also be mixed at home. In the early 1900s, poisons were more readily available in New South Wales than in any other state. The means through which accidental poisoning deaths might occur were also diverse. Poor families were at greatest risk because their households were the most frugal. Door-to-door salesmen who travelled with bulk barrels on carts were popular in poor neighbourhoods because the product was affordable; vendors kept costs low by selling only the fluid, extract or powder, not the container. This meant that empty bottles from home were scavenged to decant poisonous liquids. Families were sensible enough not to repurpose poison bottles for non-poisonous fluids – however, many families were budget-conscious enough to use bottles that had previously contained harmless substances. Magnesia bottles were in many homes because magnesium hydroxide was kept in almost every home. Commercially labelled 'milk of magnesia', the product was used to treat a wide variety of ailments including upset stomachs and constipation. Repurposing these bottles was a sensible austerity measure, but children often paid the price.

Nellie Neely, the fourteen-year-old daughter of a Glebe greengrocer, drank what she thought was liquid magnesia for a headache. When she found a magnesia bottle hidden on the top of the cupboard, she assumed it had been placed out of reach of her younger siblings. But her parents had refilled the bottle with an acid soak used to clean the electroplated silver cutlery: a particularly aggressive composition of nitric acid and mercury. She died a very painful death shortly after.

In another case, a mother spooned what she thought was milk of magnesia into her baby's mouth, to ease an upset stomach. She mistook the baby's resistance to drinking as fussiness from cramps. Only after the baby smacked away the spoon did the mother realise it was not magnesia but ammonia; she claimed to have decanted the cleaning fluid without thinking. Another parent claimed to have mistaken acid for castor oil. A toddler, seeking to emulate her mother brushing her teeth, took a toothbrush and accidentally dipped it in an abrasive household pesticide and not tooth powder or paste. The child had filled her mouth with cyanide of potassium and died shortly afterwards. In an unusual child-poisoning case, a seven-year-old boy was participating in a break and enter with a gang of young thieves when he took a cheeky swig from what he thought was a bottle of Worcestershire sauce. Only after the second swig did he realise smoke was issuing from his mouth – the home owners had filled the bottle with sulphuric acid.

Even everyday household items such as matches could kill. In one case, a two-year-old died a day after sucking the wax from the tips of phosphorus matches. When a four-year-old died after bouts of vomiting and diarrhoea, in the absence of any other explanation it was conjectured that the child had used an old bug poison tin as a water canteen.

Strychnine, often an antidote for unwanted alley cats, was also identified in poisoning cases involving children. Commercially sold as grains or crystals in a delightfully pretty pink, it was irresistible to the eyes of children. In one of the less ambiguous poisoning cases of the time, a two-year-old was found close to death after tasting the magically coloured grains of sand he had found in a tin. One child died by drinking liquid of opium. A parent claimed their child had gathered grains of arsenic after it had been scattered for rats.

Some items deemed safe for consumption were ultimately found not to be – and this was often discovered only after a spate of deaths in an area. Consumption of tinned salmon that had spoilt after being opened in the heat was known to be a common cause of ptomaine poisoning. In 1901, after many children were admitted to hospital with particularly aggressive gastric complaints and abdominal pains, salmon was initially assumed to be the cause. It was not until many more children were poisoned, some who did not eat fish, that health officials began to wonder about the true nature of the public health challenge they were grappling with. Using rudimentary epidemiological techniques, which seek to track the patterns associated with exposure to a contaminant leading up to an outbreak, analysis identified an unusual source. Not all of the victims had eaten salmon, but they had all drunk the turn-of-the-century equivalent of Tang. Fruit-flavoured powders were popular drink mixers for children, and on closer examination were found to contain not just lemon juice, citric acid and sugar, but also copper, salts of potassium and lead. Unbeknown to the manufacturer, the vessels used for evaporation and crystallisation of the acid liquids had created a chemical reaction; even standard food-processing procedures could turn something as harmless as lemonade into a lethal treat. The city health department at the time had no laboratory to routinely test foods for toxicity.

Lollies could kill children too. In 1903, a confectioner in the city was charged with selling lozenges designed to be pleasant to taste but also able to ease a sore throat. Chloroform was found in the sweets, and tests discovered that consuming half a dozen or so in a row would be sufficient to kill a child. This was a remarkably similar explanation to the one offered by the Slys only a few months later, when Olive became gravely ill: they claimed it had been caused by a stranger giving her white lollies.

Though the circumstances of many accidental poisonings seem on reflection to be dubious, they did not spark the interest of investigators at the time. If parents appeared to have a coherent explanation, doctors and police were likely to accept accidental poisoning as a plausible cause of death, disinclined to investigate further. One newspaper even coined a term for the all-too-commonplace occurrence of parents poisoning their children: 'Mother's sad mistake' was the headline.

THEORY 3:
NORMAN WAS DELIBERATELY POISONED

It is possible that by October 1902 the Sly household had become contaminated – not by the plague, but by paranoia. The family were living in what was one of the most notorious parts of Sydney. They had no income, five dependants, and were led by an increasingly agitated father with spiritual interests that heretically conflicted with the mother's Catholic faith. Both Alicks and Ellie had every reason to feel scared.

As fear of the plague grew across the city, often much faster than the infection itself, councils responded with a widespread distribution of poison. The Board of Health reminded the public about the most deadly way to administer the free two-pound tin of arsenic that had been issued to residents in the inner-city boroughs. While these tips were practical, they also read a bit like a recipe. The arsenic, which came in granulated form, needed a little culinary magic in order to ensure it was ingested properly by pests. It would dissolve easily when stirred into a warm liquid like oatmeal or milk. With marketing finesse, the health department suggested the poison that was 'rough on rats' could simply be 'spread on bread'; mixing the grains with butter was an excellent way to ensure it would be irresistible, officials claimed.

Is it possible that other ideas began to spread like an infection, multiplying in the minds of some parents across Sydney? The council had, quite inadvertently, provided all the information that a mother or father might need to understand the quantity required and the best method to administer a lethal dose. Had the Sly parents followed this advice in order to rid themselves of unwanted pests in their home?

A miasma of fear seemed to blanket Sydney, just as Alicks's fear was intensifying. By 1903 his situation had become desperate, as it had for many unemployed people across the city. Unemployment was identified to be at a crisis point in Sydney, with hairdressing and tailoring roles named as occupations that had been doing it toughest in the previous year. With no social welfare support and no work, Alicks and his family were destitute.

Norman had been violently sick with diarrhoea, stomach cramps and vomiting for five days straight before he died on Saturday, 25 October 1902. His symptoms were consistent with gastroenteritis, but also broadly consistent with the effects of arsenic poisoning.

Is it possible that Monday, 20 October 1902 was the morning when Ellie Sly woke to the realisation that she, like many women in Sydney at the time, had made a very sad mistake? Or perhaps it was Alicks who had drawn this conclusion.

9

TRAGEDY UNFOLDS

INVESTIGATING THE CRIME AT 49 WATKIN STREET REQUIRED Sergeant Agnew to learn new techniques. As an experienced metropolitan officer he could manage the mechanics of law and order: process forms, prepare affidavits and charge suspects. But for this case he knew this would not be enough. In order to understand what had occurred and put forward a viable theory for consideration by the coroner, he needed to apply different skills. His analysis would focus exclusively on the most important pieces of evidence collected at the scene: the two letters. The sergeant would have to become a linguist and a code breaker.

Agnew did not have much time. Today's coronial investigations can span weeks or even months; at the beginning of the twentieth century this was not the case. Inquests conducted at the time of the Newtown Tragedy progressed with remarkable speed, sometimes with less than twenty-four hours between the discovery of an unexplained death and an inquest ruling by the coroner and a coronial jury.

What investigators and decision-makers had to work with in terms of hard scientific evidence was also more limited. Contemporary forensic science is now a vast field from which coroners can draw. Large-scale fingerprint databases exist. Injury patterns produced by a range of stab wounds are quite well understood. Bloodstains and splatters have been codified. Strict protocols to screen biological samples for poisons are well developed. In 1904, forensic science remained a fledgling field.

Investigators knew that suicides could be staged, yet proving this was not always easy. Coroners at the turn of the century faced significant challenges in deciphering evidence. When a victim was found shot, for example, the killer only needed to leave the gun at the scene to create an impression of a suicide. The discovery of letters played a vital corroborating role in concert with other physical evidence. If they could be found in a notebook or a diary, in a carefully folded page in a jacket pocket, or in a sealed envelope in a bedside drawer, the last words of the suicide victim carried immense weight. For the police and the coroner, these letters were used as a scientific way of understanding and capturing the psychological state of the victim at the time of death.

By January 1904, NSW police prioritised the importance of understanding a person's character and their capabilities.

This philosophy had underpinned police work dating back to the Bertillon method: an identification system of criminals that was based on the belief that character could be revealed through anthropometry – the measurement of body parts, skull, face and phalanges. At inquests, however, police used other means to assess character because most people who suicided were not career criminals. Investigators would use the only thing they had available – the written words of the dead – to develop a profile.

There was an increasing body of data surrounding expressions of suicidal intent. Suicide letters, like forensic evidence, were analysed for patterns. Expressions of suicidal intent took many forms, and the early twentieth century heralded the start of attempts to understand and organise them. It was a growing body of knowledge amongst Sydney police which had been accumulating slowly over the course of the previous thirty years of state policing.

•

If a letter, any letter, was found next to a dead body, somewhere among the dead's personal possessions or in their home, it was considered highly significant. When an unexplained death had occurred, and the general arrangement of the scene suggested suicide, police often hunted for qualitative insights on the dead person's state of mind in order to establish motive.

The idea that a relative may have suicided carried enormous stigma for those left behind. Although the legal and social mores surrounding suicide were slowly changing, and the longstanding felo-de-se (or 'felon of self') principle was under-going revision in the legal system, in 1904 suicide remained a crime. A note left by those who attempted it was tantamount to a signed confession, and helped to confirm something that no one really wanted to admit unless they had to.

Key phrases piqued the interest of police and were construed to indicate a suicidal narrative. If any such phrases were present in a piece of writing by the person under investigation, it was marked as evidence and treated as 'a suicide note'. In the minds of officers this was a well-reasoned investigative method – a science of a sort.

In order to understand how police interpreted the Sly notes, it is important to consider similar suicide investigations that occurred around the same time.

I TRIED

For a piece of writing to be declared a suicide note, it did not need to contain a firm declaration of intent to commit the act. Police looked for a reference to failure, an utterance of disappointment or a sense of surrender, and they took this to be sound evidence to present to a coroner.

When the body of local hairdresser Morris Cohen was pulled from a tidal inlet known as Farm Cove, suicide was not the first possibility considered by police. Farm Cove is a small bay that falls away from the adjacent city Botanic Gardens, a popular area for both locals and tourists to stroll as they appreciated the beauty of the gardens while enjoying a fresh sea breeze. Initially, police conjectured that Cohen's death was most likely an accidental drowning. It appeared he had been unlucky enough to fall in the water in winter while wearing a heavy woollen coat that had prevented buoyancy and therefore dog paddle. Alcohol had also most likely been involved, police said, though they could not conclusively establish this. The incident was redefined as something else entirely, however, when a folded note was retrieved somewhat miraculously from inside the soaking coat. The letter made no direct reference to suicide, but as far as police were concerned it passed the test. Cohen had tried and failed, and his letter represented a kind of confession to this end. He admitted that he was surrendering to a weakness within him, and that he did not have the inner fortitude to endure: 'I have had no food to eat since 3rd June, being out of employment. I could not get it. I have been sleeping out on the streets since 6th June. Cannot get work of any kind. Have tried hard. It is terrible.'

The case of Thomas Viedman, found in the water just near the shoreline, presented police with a similar scenario. Viedman's death appeared to be accidental. Steep cliffs surround most of the eastern suburbs beaches at Coogee, Bondi and Bronte, and falls were common. Viedman was a strong and healthy older man, and a skilled gasfitter and plumber well known about the area. He had often been seen walking the coastline. A letter, however, changed the preliminary conclusion drawn by police. They discovered it during their search of a room he was renting in Surry Hills.

When a man turns grey he might as well put himself away as be starved to death. I have honestly tried to get work of any description and have failed. Oh what a crime it is to get old! Many will say he was 'off his head' but I can most honestly say that I'm in the best of health. This day I have been walking until I am footsore, with the same reply from all 'We are quite full'. But I know the reason. It is because I look too old. I have lived to the age of 54 and I believe if I could get a living I would make a very old man, but I have seen enough of life this last two years. If I was a drunkard or a lazy man, I could understand it, but I am neither.

The end of the letter documented Viedman's suicidal intent in a much more direct way. He had tried and failed to buy poison. Jumping from a cliff at Coogee had been his last resort: '11.15am Wednesday I have been trying to get poison, but I have failed; so now there is nothing for me but to jump off the rocks at either Coogee or Bondi. May God forgive me.'

Lieutenant John Ellis was found dead with the nerves and blood vessels on his forearm slashed down to the bone. His death presented police with a different kind of challenge. He wrote a lot, so they had to make a difficult decision: which letter should be taken as an accurate representation of his state of mind? In one of many letters found after his death, police discovered a confession about his perceived failure: 'I hope you will not expose the name of the woman that has driven me to this, but for God's sake telegraph to her the moment . . . I have only one thing to accuse myself of, that is

I allowed her to support me. The world may judge harshly for it, but it has not been my fault. I have tried to get anything.'

In 1903, 77-year-old Thomas Cross left a letter addressed to the landlady of the Millers Point boarding house where he was living. The letter explained why he was found shot in the head at the premises. He had tried but failed to cope with the infernal bugs in Sydney, and this seemed a reasonable motive for suicide, police stated. 'I am fairly disgusted with Sydney with its mosquitoes, bedbugs, fleas etc and I will be going to some place where I will not be annoyed by them. So here goes! – T. C. Cross'.

FORGIVE ME

Notes that asked for absolution and included pleas to God immediately suggested suicide, according to police. Requests for the forgiveness of family, even if the dead person had not mentioned what they needed to be forgiven for, were perceived to be evidence in support of a suicide verdict.

A case from Melbourne highlights just how compelling written evidence was considered in this context. In one of the most unusual cases faced by Melbourne police, the occurrence of suicide was determined without the discovery of a body. Found in a neatly folded pile of clothes on a Yarra River jetty was a note. It was in the pocket of a coat, left with a hat. The note kindly provided the name and address of the author, and simply said, 'May God forgive me for what I am going to do.'

A note in Sydney, found on the body of a man on the Sydenham train line, shifted the mindset of investigators from accident to suicide. 'Forgive me for what I am about to do,' it said, addressed to a mother in England.

Some suicide letters, like the one left by Will Squire, sought absolution. His body was found on a beach with a revolver and empty cartridge shells nearby, and his note was taken to be a comprehensive explanation for the event. 'I cannot face my innocent wife and children and mother . . . forget my evil. Remember only my good. Forgive me all.'

In an attempted murder-suicide, coincidentally also in Newtown, a note left by Ernest Russell confirmed his suicidal intent for investigators. He had just killed his wife and was proceeding to kill himself when the neighbours, disturbed by gunshots, ran to the house to help. In the note found in his pocket, Russell asked for forgiveness and also wrote: 'Dear Ruby. I leave everything to you. Hoping you will be all right. The ring is for my mother.' Ruby was his pet name for his wife, who now lay dead on their lounge suite.

When Annie Chapman was found dead in the regional town of Bathurst in western New South Wales, no post-mortem could reveal what had happened as convincingly as her final note: 'Dear Mother. I am leaving these few lines behind me for you and I am sure it will break your heart when you read this, but I hope you will forgive me, for it is trouble that has driven me to this end. The pound you sent me I paid my debts with. Dear mother will you take poor Stella home. It breaks my heart to leave her behind. I thought it would be cruel to poison the poor child.' This led police to conduct further investigation into the type of poison involved. It was discovered not through chemical testing but via an interview with a local chemist who remembered selling vermin killer to Chapman.

In Tom Goodman's case, a letter fulfilled several of the criteria associated with a suicide note: 'God forgive my sins, and receive my soul, and let me be at peace. Adieu to the world, I am quite tired of my life.'

When John Edward Collins, only nineteen years old, was found dead in the early hours of a February morning in 1902, police did not need ballistic evidence to prove suicide. He had been shot in University Park, just near busy Newtown and bustling Glebe, and within walking distance of his father's residence on Parramatta Road. In his letter Collins disclosed a number of reasons for his decision to kill himself, none of which the family had any prior knowledge of. Collins had got a girl pregnant. He had sought to procure an abortion, but the operation had been botched, badly. She died shortly after. He admitted he had much to beg forgiveness for.

THE 'TO DO' LIST

If the deceased left instructions for loved ones, this too was taken to be a key indicator of suicidal intent. The investigation of the death of John Urban Vigors shows how important the police considered such a letter to be. Vigors was fifty-two years old and a well-respected mail guard on the Great Northern Line. He had been shot through the head in the middle of Lake Macquarie Road, with his mailbag dropped beside him. A revolver was found near the body as well.

Police initially assumed that Vigors had been robbed while alone and vulnerable on an early morning shift. It happened to rail guards and mail coaches often. Perhaps he had been shot by a jittery highwayman who had dropped the gun in fear and run. If it was a suicide, it was an unusual place to do so – right in the middle of a main road outside Newcastle. Very quickly, however, police discovered the evidence that permitted them to submit a brief to the coroner which could confirm the death as a suicide beyond a shadow of doubt.

A search of Vigors's mailbag produced a letter. Signed by Vigors, it mentioned his disappointment that a local police officer had accused him of a crime – he was innocent, he said. When the letter included a long list of instructions both to police and to his wife, it was considered a confession of his intent to kill himself.

You must, my best beloved wife, write to my sister, my son and daughter also my step-sister Fanny. I have no doubt they will assist and provide for you and my two beloved children . . . The Postmaster-General will no doubt pay you eighteen days' pay due me. Mr Saunders may have a small balance of mine in his hands; he will pay you if I am correct. Give the musket to the police and tell them Mr Todd, boot-maker, has the other which Mr Levinge left in my charge.

The tragic death of George Goldthorpe, only seventeen years old, had police raising questions. Suicide was common among the old and the very ill, but Victorian society found it difficult to understand when the deceased was in the prime of life. Goldthorpe was found in the front room of his father's house with a gun beside him. It seemed unthinkable that the boy, with his life ahead of him and having secured work as a servant with a reputable family, would choose to die.

A search of the father's home revealed a declaration of innocence: a note stating that Goldthorpe's grandfather had accused the boy of stealing twelve pounds from him, only a few weeks earlier. The unfairness of it was cruel, Goldthorpe claimed. He spoke sadly of the betrayal he felt when even his own father had not believed him. His 'to do' list was deeply emotional and bitter; he left instructions about how his family should feel as well as what they should do after he was gone: 'I want you all to forget me when I am buried. Go to no expense for me, for I have cost you enough already.' Goldthorpe went on to explain how he would like his effects divided. He made a special point of mentioning that the gun which he had purchased to kill himself had been bought with his own hard-earned wages.

Police found something a little more unusual to justify their conclusion that Frank Bradford had committed suicide. The 'to do' list elements were present. However, Bradford's final reflections were less suicide note and more diary and daily planner, with detailed instructions about how his affairs should be managed after he was gone. He wrote one section of the memorandum book for his wife, while other pages described how his personal effects should be distributed, including who should receive what and how some items should be sold.

The case of Fred Quintell included perhaps the quintessential final 'to do' list. His letter was not, like many suicide notes, addressed to a spouse or parents, or even to God, but to 'the Coroner'. It opened with the line: 'To save trouble of inquiry I have written this.' Quintell included all of the necessary details: 'I am a miner and bush worker, last from Queensland, 37 years of age, and a native of Portsmouth England. No people in this country. My brother's address is J E Quintell 3 St Paul's Church, London. The sum of ten pounds is to my credit in the Oxford Street Savings Bank. I desire the balance after burial expenses to be given to Mr Pratt for the Sick Children's Hospital. My effects are at 309 Crown street. I have no debts.' The note was found signed and folded in his pocket.

TIRED . . . OF LIFE

If the deceased referred in their missive to being tired, police made special note of this. Becoming 'tired of life' was an eventuality to which only certain individuals were prone, or so it was generally believed. This belief was informed by understandings of human nature that were commonly held at the time. To become tired of life suggested some constitutional weakness and inherent mental frailty that clearly placed one at higher risk of suicide.

The inquest of Thomas Plunkett highlights not only how much influence the expression 'tired of life' carried in shaping verdicts of suicide, but also the shame carried by the family left behind after one was acknowledged to have occurred. When Plunkett was found dead in Centennial Park with no suicide note, the coroner faced a challenge. It was not enough that he had been found with a deadly bottle of prussic acid in his pocket.

Described as 'an extract of bitter almonds', prussic acid was taken in very small amounts to strengthen the nerves. It was also, however, a deadly poison (cyanide) which killed quickly if a sufficient dose was taken. The name prussic acid became popular because hydrogen cyanide was first isolated from Prussian blue dye in the late 1700s.

The coroner interviewed Plunkett's sister, most likely with a view to garnering some understanding of the man's predisposition for suicide. What the coroner received were guarded and protective answers from a sister who had no interest in discussing insanity but seemed more than willing to talk about her brother's indigestion. 'He was tired of dyspepsia, but he never stated he was tired of life,' she said, during the course of the inquest. In the end it was a labourer, entirely unknown to Plunkett, who presented pivotal testimony. He had been building a road through Centennial Park on the day of the death, working in the very early morning, and testified that he had noticed Plunkett wandering through the park because it had been an unusual time to see visitors there. Plunkett had stopped, the labourer said, removed a bottle from his jacket and taken a heavy swig. In the absence of compelling words left in the form of a note, the police turned to alternative evidence to compile their brief for the coroner.

In contrast, the phrase 'tired of life' was found during the investigation into Charles Huffington Bowman's death in 1892. Bowman was a ledger keeper who appeared to have shot himself moments after arriving at his job at Parramatta's Commercial Bank. From the perspective of police, his note comprehensively included the hallmarks of suicidal intent.

> I am tired of life and have been suffering melancholia for some time. I have come to the conclusion that I am a decided failure in this world . . . My father whom I dearly love, I leave all my worldly possessions to and I beg his forgiveness for this last act of mine . . . There is ten pounds to me credit in the Commercial Bank of Australia, also some at the Commercial Bank at Sydney, which my father is to get. All I owe is the price of a suit of clothes at Peapes and Co's in Sydney and board and lodging to Mrs Neild.

For Francis Price, a journalist found dead at his Balmain home, suicide was determined by post-mortem (which identified cyanide of potassium) and by a compelling letter to his wife. Out of respect for a journalist colleague, some content was withheld from the public. The note was discreetly para-phrased, however: 'The deceased left a letter to his wife, intimating that he was tired of life.'

•

On the day of the Sly tragedy, Sergeant Agnew was back at his desk when he pulled the two letters from where they had been safely folded in his pocket. One appeared to have been written by the dead man, Alicks. It was addressed to his mother, Barbara. The other was written by the dead woman, Ellie – Agnew confirmed this by matching the handwriting in the family Bible. Ellie's letter was addressed to her brother, J. J.

Agnew would have opened Alicks's letter looking for indicators of suicidal intent in order to resolve mysteries surrounding the case. Unfortunately, Alicks's letter only created more.

Agnew found a page of symbols and letters that were incomprehensible to him. For this reason the letter was almost wholly discounted, though it was used to help establish that Alicks Sly had been of weak intellect. The verbatim content is unfortunately lost to us, with one exception. In large capitals, a few words were written in red at the bottom of the page, and it was generally believed they were an afterthought or post-script. Agnew had secured what he believed to be Alicks Sly's final words: 'I AM DYING. MY BODY IS DEAD.' While this was anything but a suicide note as defined by police at the time, it was sufficient evidence for them to extrapolate. As one newspaper wrote: 'it shows evidence the terrible act was premeditated'. Agnew had not, however, found the syntax of suicide, at least not in the place where he had expected it to be.

Next he turned to Ellie's letter. It was here that he found, to his surprise, some evidence of suicidal intent. The letter contained no reference to being tired of life. It did not ask for forgiveness. Ellie's letter was a considered 'to do' list, typical of suicide notes and certainly a heartfelt example of one. The words suggested a woman desperate to have the comfort and reassurance of knowing her brother would love and care for her children after she was gone. It also provided insight on the depth of fear the Sly couple were living with, and the sense of persecution they shared. Ellie also vehemently defended her husband's reputation to the very end.

Dear Jack.
Just a few lines to ask you to come and see me at once.
I am dying and my baby is dead. Poor girlie! Oh how
they the doctors and nurses at Prince Alfred hospital
tortured her. Alick is innocent of all their charges against
him. He never interfered with his daughter or his sons,
and I never interfered with my sons or my daughter as
they say. Oh Jack, the vendetta has taken a horrible
revenge. They all came and kicked me and Alick with
their cruelty. Jack, take charge of everything and the
men who interfered with [girlie] were Tony Redmond
and a man in a brown felt hat, a blue coat and vest, grey
pants. He was of medium height, rather thin, clean face
and brown eyes. He has been the cause of my death. Oh

Jack! Alick never kicked that boy Martin. So goodbye
dear brother. The Push were unjust to us. I kiss Jackie-
Bedford, Basil Cornelius and Merv for you. I will not
want the suit now. Oh Jack why did you leave us to these
cruel wretches?

Nell E G Sly.

The tone of the letter was consistent with what the sergeant
had observed within the Sly home. There was confusion at
the scene, and this letter too was confused. Ellie had no
defensive wounds on her arms, the way victims typically do
after seeking to stop an attack. It might at first have seemed
unbelievable to Agnew that she had not fought what had
happened to her. Whether this was because she had not been
conscious, he could not guess. He knew from experience
that a post-mortem doctor would be unable to determine
this either.

The letter raised other questions as well. Ellie seemed to
have so many facts wrong. Alicks had definitely attacked a
youth in Glebe. The Slys' daughter, Olive, was sick but not
dead; in fact, the toddler seemed to be recovering steadily
at the hospital. And there was no evidence whatsoever that
the Glebe Push had any involvement in her illness. Agnew
dismissed Ellie's accusations against the Push; the inner-city
gangs were dangerous, but sticks and stones were more their
style, definitely not razors. The gangs were also strictly territorial, and there was no evidence they even knew where the
Slys lived in Newtown. Agnew knew one thing for certain:

if members of the Push had been loitering around Watkin Street, Mrs Shaw would have known about it.

Most concerning of all, the letter conveyed that a very sad collusion had occurred between husband and wife. Alicks's letter, or at least the only fragment available for analysis a century later, even mirrors a portion of his wife's: 'I am dying and my baby is dead,' wrote Ellie; 'I am dying and my body is dead,' wrote Alicks.

Agnew was left with a bigger and even more perplexing question: under what circumstances would a person who had clearly been murdered write what could be construed as a suicide note?

While Agnew may have initially thought that the letters of Alicks and Ellie Sly would solve the mystery of what had occurred, there was another document which would shed the most light on this dark tragedy. This paper was found in the pocket of the suit Alicks Sly wore the day he died.

To this day, that document remains sealed in an estate file stored in the NSW state archives. A rusty pin with a heavy and flat top fixes the waxy piece of paper into a large legal file. Fragile, Bible-paper thin and brittle to touch, it is a pawn ticket from Mont De Piete Deposit and Investment Company in Castlereagh Street, Sydney.

This document communicates much about Alicks's desperate state of mind in the week preceding his death. It tells the story of this tragedy with all the emotion of a musical lament. Alicks pawned an instrument known to produce the most mournful of tones: the violin. He used the money to pay the moving expenses associated with relocation to Newtown and as a down payment on the first two weeks of rent. It is perhaps not even what is written *in* this document but what still remains *on* it that most accurately captures the fullness of this tragedy. More than a century later, the face of the pawn ticket is streaked with long rivers of blood. The fold lines of the yellowed sheet are marked with powdery blood dust.

The violin, belonging to Ellie, must have been of significant quality, as stringed instruments could retail at the time from as little as a few shillings up to around twenty pounds when new. Alicks had secured a cash advance of ten pounds, but it had been insufficient to clear his debts.

Agnew remained at Newtown police station until late that evening, preparing evidence for the inquest. As he sat in the hot and cramped office, known for being the most unbearable of Sydney police stations in summer, at the somewhat cooler stone morgue on George Street a doctor finalised his post-mortems of the two bodies.

What of the other parts of this tragedy yet to unfold? Four children now required a home. If the letters did little else, they at least revealed the names of the next of kin. Ellie's parents, Cornelius and Ellen, were deceased, but Alicks's were alive and well, living only a short distance away in the eastern suburbs. Agnew dispatched two constables. One was sent to a residential address in Darlinghurst, the home of William and Barbara Sly. The other went to a rented room in the Agincourt Hotel on George Street where J. J. O'Leary was living.

While Ellie Sly's final words did not offer the answers Agnew must have hoped for, she had made one point abundantly clear. Her final wish was that her brother assume care for his nephews and niece.

10

THE INQUEST

On Tuesday evening, local women had gathered on Watkin Street to share stories and consider theories about Alicks and Ellie Sly. On Wednesday morning, men of law and order gathered on George Street in The Rocks to do the same – these discussions, however, would be formally transcribed and recorded as a legal ruling.

As the group of suited men waited outside the Lloyd Hotel, they looked like any other hotel patrons who had come to smoke, drink and fraternise with men of their class. But these men were different. They had assembled to attend the coronial inquest into the unnatural deaths of Alexander William Bedford and Ellen Gertrude Sly. The inquest was about to occur in the back of a local pub.

Despite the informality of the setting, no one questioned the seriousness of the event. Inquest protocols required jurors and the coroner to visually inspect the bodies before their deliberations, and the Lloyd had proven to be an ideal location because the morgue was only a short walk away. The state had charged Deputy City Coroner Robert Henry Todd and a jury of twelve with responsibility for identifying causes of the tragedy, arriving at a legal definition for what had occurred, and considering any wider consequences for the state of New South Wales. Also in attendance were two police officers (Sergeant Agnew and a Newtown constable), two witnesses (William Sly and J. J. O'Leary), court attendants, and a handful of media men who routinely reported on inquest and court proceedings on the city circuit. The Newtown Tragedy had been a sensational news story the day before, but public interest had not carried overnight. While high-profile inquest cases often attracted large crowds of public spectators, the Sly case did not. There were, however, lawyers and doctors who had come to observe proceedings because of the curious range of issues the case raised for those making determinations regarding suicide.

The Sly deaths occurred at a time when the city was especially interested in the counting and coding of fatalities. In the past several years the city had faced the danger of contagious disease outbreaks many times. The year of 1900, in particular, had been very bad. This had heightened the state's awareness of the need to count death. These calculations culminated in the production of a monthly statistical output, macabrely and somewhat elegantly called 'the death harvest'.

The Sly deaths also occurred at a time when scientists, medical doctors and sociologists had begun to weigh in directly on debates about death that had once been strictly defined by religious doctrine. In the years leading up to 1904, revolutionary thinkers had presented fresh views on suicide. Internationally acclaimed French sociologist Émile Durkheim published his book *Suicide* in 1897, and it presented many exciting and provocative new ideas on the reasons people killed themselves. In a vastly ambitious piece of research, Durkheim had sought to look at both method and cause, and draw interesting connections between the two. He found that different countries preferred different methods of suicide. The French tended to choose suffocation by carbonic acid fumes, inhaled in a closed room. Italians and the Swiss shot themselves. Hanging remained popular throughout many countries across Europe. The cut throat, however, was a tradition exclusive to the British Empire. In this respect, according to Durkheim's findings, Sydney proved itself a truly English city, keeping pace with London.

Around the world, men were found to commit suicide more often than women. They were more likely to do so in summer, and more likely to suicide around the age of thirty-five years.

Durkheim was an influential thinker, even far away in Australia. His ideas did not displace prevailing views on genetically weak people or 'degenerates' being the most likely to commit suicide. Instead, he embellished this assumption. In 1897 he wrote, 'the degenerate is more apt to commit suicide than the well man; but he does not necessarily do so because of his condition. This potentiality of his becomes effective only through the action of other factors which we must discover.' Along with the latest European theorists on labour, industry, politics, economics and history, Durkheim was recommended reading for the NSW public service exams at the turn of the twentieth century.

For Durkheim, it was all about context. For those inclined to nervous weakness, the setting, tools and means of death could be as important as tipping points. He explained it in the following way:

There is the well-known story of the fifteen patients who hung themselves in swift succession in 1772 from the same hook in a dark passage of the hospital. Once the hook was removed there was an end of the epidemic. Likewise, at the camp of Boulogne, a soldier blew out his brains in a sentry-box; in a few days others imitated him in the same place; but as soon as this was burned, the contagion stopped. All these facts show the overpowering influence of obsession, because they cease with the disappearance of the material object which evoked the idea.

In Sydney this dangerous obsession was often alcohol. According to one 1903 headline in a local newspaper: 'Leading sociologists and scientists agree that alcohol is the most frequent cause of brain disease.' In other words, alcohol could cause insanity. The hundreds of entries in the coroners' registers around this time are crosshatched with the additional note of 'no intemperance' or 'intemperance', so important was this drug considered to be as a precondition to insanity. R. H. Todd, the deputy coroner overseeing the Sly inquest, walked into the court proceedings knowing this fact. Todd was both doctor and lawyer, and a well-read man too. He would have been informed by the latest thinking on alcohol and its effects on insanity and immorality, and would have looked for signs of alcohol consumption being involved in any unexplained death. Evidence of intemperance served two purposes. First, it helped to preserve the dignity of the families. If alcohol could be proved to have affected the decision-making, then a verdict of suicide assumed a slightly less stigmatised status. Intemperance also helped explain the inexplicable. Why had a seemingly devout person killed themselves? Why would a husband kill his wife, and then himself? The answer: alcohol.

A suicide ruling was a devastating outcome for any family in 1904. For those families who were devout, the suicide of a relative was particularly problematic. In the years preceding the Sly inquest, the Catholic Church had perceived a shift in legal, medical and sociological discussions of suicide, and feared what it perceived to be a more concessional mindset developing around these matters. Only the year before the Newtown Tragedy, the Church ran a fire-and-brimstone public relations campaign to remind society that it should never go 'soft on suicide'. Catholic newspaper the *Southern Cross* said that suicide 'is the proverbial sowing of the wind, and reaping of the whirlwind, the veritable harvest of wrongdoing in the victim themselves, or an inherited evil tendency trans- mitted by ancestors'. Parishioners were reminded that as a mortal sin, suicide placed the soul of the deceased in peril. In 1903, Catholic leaders conveyed in public sermons and speeches that: 'Against this fatal and pernicious doctrine the Catholic Church set her infallible seal of condemnation; and the ministers of all the Christian sects condemn it as being a heresy of fatal import.'

As the thirteen men had departed the north morgue, they must have come across as a chilling and somewhat grim entourage. Deputy Coroner Todd, known for his severe jawline and the sharp symmetry of his facial features, would have cut a striking figure in his fitted black frockcoat – particularly so with a solemn procession of twelve dark-suited men in his wake. Filing out of the morgue, they headed towards the Lloyd Hotel. Directly across the road, on the opposite corner, was a butcher converted from an old hotel. It was customary for butchers to display as much meat as possible, hung by hooks in the windows and from the awning outside. Right after inspecting the Slys' carcasses, the men would have been confronted by cross-sectioned carcasses of meat that swayed in the street, pushed by the rough harbour breeze as it came in from the headland. It was as if the coroner had assumed the form of a grim reaper, with twelve disciples following him, engaged in the act of death harvest. Would the coroner gather a murder and a suicide on that day, or two suicides?

•

When the men entered the parlour of the Lloyd on Wednesday, 13 January 1904, they carried a contagion of new ideas.

As one newspaper had commented in 1900: 'Nowadays the average jury is in a state of trepidation that evidence will inadvertently be tendered proving beyond a doubt that the suicide was perfectly sane.' Society could clearly not eradicate the destructive and violent tendencies that caused murder or self-murder, but they could reduce factors that seemed to trigger them in people. Alcohol was universally acknowledged to be the worst, and if Todd believed it was a factor it needed to be highlighted in his findings. As one commentary on insanity noted a year later: 'Alcohol seems to be the principal cause of insanity . . . it is not so much the quantity of alcohol that a person consumes as it is the individual who consumes it that stands in casual relation to insanity. The personal equation must always be considered.'

The room in the Lloyd had been set up with as much legal formality as it was possible to achieve in a hotel parlour. The jurors were directed to sit in two rows of chairs at one end of the room; they removed their hats and took their seats. Lying on a central table were three objects pivotal to the investigation: two letters and one cut-throat razor. A chair and heavy carved desk were positioned at the other end of the room. Deputy Coroner Todd entered last; everyone in the room respectfully rose. He assumed his seat and did not waste time.

Questions and responses fired back and forth quickly.

Todd: 'Dr Jamieson. First to the matter of the deceased man, Alexander Sly. What be the results of the post-mortem assessment?'

Jamieson was equally direct. 'On the left side of the man, near the angle of the jaw, was a skin incision which after traversing the neck for some distance, suddenly became deeper, dividing all the muscles and important blood vessels and nerves. The wound passed then across the middle line, terminating about half an inch further on. The windpipe was completely divided just above the level of the vocal cord. The gullet, lying behind, was half divided. Both the deceased's hands were covered with blood, the right hand being firmly clenched, and the left hand open. There were no other wounds on the body. The wound described was of the character of a self-inflicted injury.'

Todd: 'Was it of the character of the razor here?' The coroner gestured towards the table. An attendant dutifully held up the razor, careful as he clasped it between his fingers as if fearful of contamination.

'Yes. That would produce that kind of cut.'

Todd: 'And what of the female deceased, Dr Jamieson, can you present your findings?'

'In the case of the female deceased, there was a deep wound running across the neck from the side to side. The whole of the tissues down to the spinal neck were completely divided on both sides. The wound was below the level of the vocal cords and had evidently been made by two distinct cuts. This wound had not the character of a self-inflicted injury. There was also a transverse cut across the body. There were no cuts or wounds on the hands and no evidence of resistance. Both hands were covered with blood.'

Todd: 'She did not fight or struggle, as one would when attacked?'

'No, there is no evidence of a struggle as one might find with an attack. Her hands were soaked, but this appeared to be her own blood.'

The awkwardness of this statement hung in the air. It placed the jury inside the mind of the woman just before she died. If she had somehow surrendered to the act of her husband killing her, she most certainly had not surrendered to the act of dying. At the end of it, Ellie's survival instincts had kicked in and she had thrown her hands against her neck in a desperate attempt to save herself by pressing the wounds closed. Or, was it she who had made the first cut across her abdomen, starting around the location of her womb and slicing diagonally upwards from left to right? Did this explain the blood on her hands?

The post-mortem of Ellie's body had been cursory. To conduct it, Dr Jamieson charged the standard baseline fee of one pound and one shilling. There had been a much closer and more careful inspection of Alicks; his post-mortem cost the state three pounds and three shillings.

Two witnesses were scheduled to appear, representing each family. Todd thought he knew what to expect; he had seen families at inquests. No matter what the deceased had done, their families usually defended them. At a minimum they sought to explain the insanity that may have caused the rash, violent and shameful acts their kin had committed. Todd braced himself. Looking at the jury, he hoped these twelve men would view the family members' commentaries with an appropriate measure of caution and cynicism.

Alicks's father was called first and sworn in.

Todd: 'Sir, please introduce yourself.'

'I am William Sly, an accountant. I live at number 231 Forbes Street in Darlinghurst.'

Todd: 'Please state your relationship to the deceased man.'

'I am father of the deceased man Alexander William Bedford Sly, born in Dunedin. He would have been thirty-five next April.'

Todd: 'Can you tell us something about the circumstances of Mr Alexander and Mrs Ellen Sly before their deaths?'

'No.'

The coroner was taken aback. He was accustomed to relatives wanting to protect their loved ones, and this often resulted in lengthy over-explanation, not under-explanation.

It was William who spoke next. 'I knew nothing whatsoever about them. Thirteen years has lapsed since Alexander left home. I last saw him alive over ten years ago. I have been unable to obtain any information at all about him for seven years.'

It was a cold and indifferent response, one that Todd surely did not expect. Regardless, he pressed on.

Todd: 'Was he afflicted with anything, did he have any physical ailments?'

'He lost the use of his left eye at birth. There was nothing else the matter with him. Up to thirteen years ago he was sober in his habits and had common sense.'

Todd then asked for Alicks's letter to be handed to William.

Todd: 'Do you recognise this as your son's handwriting?'

'No. I don't know. I know nothing whatsoever about it.'

Todd: 'But it is addressed to your wife, is it not?'

'Precisely, I know nothing about it. There is little I can add to any of this.'

Again, his words were cold. The coroner considered the possibility that the witness was in shock. That certainly happened at inquests, as family members struggled to cope with their mourning. But this man's reactions seemed different. Even the coroner in his position as objective arbiter could sense resentment and cruelty in the man. William was approaching the tragedy of his son's death with a dismissiveness that verged on contemptible.

The next witness was called.

Todd: 'Can you state your name, your occupation and your current place of residence?'

'My name is John James O'Leary. I am a draper, working at the store Grace Brothers. I currently reside at the Agincourt Hotel in George Street.'

Todd: 'Can you describe for the jury what your relationship is to the deceased woman, Ellen Gertrude Sly?'

'I am Ellen Sly's brother. She was born in Goulburn. Our family, the entire O'Leary family, my parents and their children, had all lived there for many years. Ellie is . . .' He stumbled over his words, looked down at the ground and shuffled his feet. 'I should say, she was about thirty years of age.' It had been less than twenty-four hours since he'd learnt of his sister's death, not enough time for him to adjust to this fact.

Todd: 'And where did they live, Alexander and Ellen Sly, as a couple? What did you know of their family?'

'Ellie and Alicks lived at Watkin Street, Newtown. They had four living children. They had only recently moved there from the Glebe. We lived in a few places across the city before that.'

Todd: 'We?'

'Yes. I lived with the family. We lived together for eight years with all of their children.'

Todd: 'And when did you see your sister last?'

'She came to see me on only this Saturday past. She seemed fine. She came in to my work to talk about a suit.'

Todd: 'And what kind of man was her husband, Alexander Sly? What would you say about him?'

'I could not say he was temperate now, I do not know that for certain. I have not been in their house for a little while now. But he was certainly temperate for the time I lived with them. He was learning tailoring. He was sober in his habits. He was healthy. He was not someone of weak intellect.'

Todd: 'When did you last see him?'

'I saw them all on Christmas Eve. We spent Christmas together in Glebe.'

Next an officer of the court handed a note to J. J.

Todd: 'Do you recognise this as belonging to Alexander Sly? Is this his handwriting?'

'I can't say for certain that is Alicks's handwriting, I don't recognise it. It doesn't make any sense at all.'

Todd: 'Do you know if the man Alexander had any trouble?'

'He was in some trouble over kicking a boy, but he was bailed out of that trouble. It was over as far as I knew. The charge was dropped. There seemed to be nothing else that should concern them as far as I could tell.'

Todd was just about to fire another question at J. J. when he saw the man pause. He was clearly looking for a way to add something further.

'He was mixed up in that case in Glebe,' J. J. said finally. 'A local boy had been throwing stones at Ellie's three boys, that is what she told me. Alicks said he didn't beat the boy up. Nothing came of it, so I don't know why they would have been concerned about it.'

Todd: 'An officer of the court is now going to read a letter to you, Mr O'Leary, and then hand you a letter, which I would like to ask you a few questions about.'

Ellie's letter, the one that Sergeant Agnew had characterised as a suicide note, was read into evidence. The officer handed the letter to J. J. He held it lightly between his fingers.

Todd: 'This letter, addressed to you, seems to indicate your sister was in a very troubled state of mind. Can you confirm that it is her handwriting?'

'That is my sister's handwriting,' was all he said.

Todd: 'Can you think of any reason why this would happen? Why would she write this? Was there any trouble between them?'

'They were married. It was a normal marriage.'

Todd: 'But how would you know this?'

'I lived with them for eight years. I only just moved out a few months before.'

Todd: 'Is there anything that you have to say about the content of the letter, Mr O'Leary? Do you think this is an indication of some trouble?'

'She seems to be concerned about that case I mentioned – the one that was withdrawn.'

Todd was approaching the issue of insanity – but tentatively. He was almost baiting J. J., offering him every opportunity to raise it.

Todd: 'Do you think this letter indicates your sister was in some sort of serious state of mind?'

'Yes, as I said, about that case, the one that was withdrawn.'

Todd went further and asked directly. 'Was your sister strange in her mind at all?'

'No.'

There was clear evidence the woman had been murdered, but there was also significant evidence to support the theory she had participated in some way. Todd remained determined to explore these issues further.

'What religion was your sister?' asked Todd.

'Roman Catholic.'

Todd considered his next question carefully. 'Had she any fancy for spiritualism or anything of that kind?'

'No,' answered J. J. firmly.

Todd: 'Had he? Was he what you would call, a spiritualist?'

It was now J. J. who considered carefully. He took a long pause before answering. 'He didn't advertise. He wasn't making any money by it. But he used to believe he could do it. He talked to me about it some time ago.'

The jurors leant forward, listening just a little more closely than before.

'But I knocked it on the head very quick and lively. He used to have this belief he could put people into trances.'

The room went silent. Many in the community perceived spiritualism to be a harmless fad. When it was introduced in this context, it assumed great significance. Had Ellie been under a strange spell, perhaps compelled to commit an act as unthinkable as suicide? The topic cast something even darker across the proceedings, and raised many more questions.

J. J. added a comment reinforcing the suggestion that a sordid collusion might have been possible between the two. 'I just don't know what they had been doing to themselves.'

Todd moved forward before anyone had time to become carried away with wild speculations.

Todd: 'Would you say he had a belief in spiritualism?'

'Yes,' J. J. said clearly.

It was an important turning point in the proceedings. There had never been any suggestion that Alicks Sly had ever been a drunk – but he had been seduced by dangerous ideas.

While Todd kept moving forward and still did not hesitate, J. J. did.

Todd: 'Did his wife, your sister, share that belief?'

'I don't know,' was the response.

Todd redirected his line of questioning towards matters of greater moral and social concern. He needed to know if spiritualism was something that the state should be concerned about.

Todd: 'What made your brother-in-law take that belief up?'

'I don't know.'

Todd: 'Did he know it was a good way to make money?'

'I don't know.'

Todd: 'Used he to attend what were known as seances?'

'I believe so.'

Todd: 'Did he ever discuss these matters with you?'

J. J.'s response was definite, on this matter at least. 'I knew that he believed these things. But it was something that I wanted no part of, and I made that clear to him. I imagine I would not be someone that he would have discussed these things with.'

The witness stepped down. Sergeant Agnew was called next. The coroner had offered him the opportunity to make his statement last, and thereby frame the deliberations of the jury.

Todd: 'When you arrived at the house on 49 Watkin Street, can you describe what you saw for the jury, please?'

'On entering the upstairs room of a house on the corner of Watkin and Wilson streets, Newtown, there were two bodies. The particular room contained little other than a small chest of drawers, a double bed, a child's cot and a mattress on the bare boards of the floor. The woman lay face up on the mattress. The man lay on the floor, but on the boards, and his head was propped atop a small box. The man and woman were separated by only a few feet. Both had their throats frightfully gashed and blood was all over the room. The man's hand firmly grasped an open razor, the case of which lay on the bed. All appearances pointed to the husband having cut his wife's throat and then his own. The violence on the woman's body was far greater than the violence on his. The woman was clothed in her nightdress but had her boots and stockings on. The man was fully clothed. I summoned Dr Levy who confirmed that death had taken place only a short time before. The bodies were subsequently removed to the morgue by Constable Osmus. Sergeant Curry and Payne took charge of the premises. I removed from the house – the razor which lies on the table here and the two letters. The woman's letter was sealed. The man's letter was stained with blood.'

Todd: 'And of the razor, Sergeant, where was it found?'

'I had to uncurl the fingers of the man's right hand, his fist was clenched still with the razor in it. I had to draw back the fingers one by one in order to even retrieve the razor, so tightly grasped was it and so covered in blood as to make it slippery to touch.'

When the court proceedings came to an end, and all the evidence was presented, the jury did not retire to consider the verdict. Instead, the men simply leant forward in a huddle. They spoke in whispered tones for a few minutes. All others in the room waited in deathly silence.

Todd: 'Do you have a finding?'

'We do, sir,' answered the lead juror.

Todd: 'Please proceed then, sir.'

'We find that the said Ellen Gertrude Sly at 49 Watkin Street, Newtown in the district of Sydney in the state aforesaid on the 12th day of January 1904 died from the effects of a wound in the throat unlawfully inflicted upon her with a razor by her husband Alexander William Bedford Sly, tailor, since deceased. On the 12th day of January 1904 in the manner and form aforesaid whilst he was in a condition of insanity feloniously and unlawfully did murder.'

The juror paused to draw a deep breath.

'And we further find that he, the said Alexander William Bedford Sly, her, the said Ellen Gertrude Sly at 49 Watkin Street, Newtown, aforesaid in the district and state aforesaid on the 12th day of January 1904 died from the effects of a wound in the throat inflicted upon himself then and there with a razor whilst he was in a condition of temporary insanity.'

The coroner nodded. He had nothing to add, nor any amendments to the verdict.

After the closure of inquest proceedings at the Lloyd Hotel, it was customary for those in attendance to stop for a meal and a drink. In fact, the hotelier actively encouraged and welcomed grieving families and post-mortem doctors because their custom was the only way he made any real money from hosting inquests. The state paid just a small fee for the exclusive use of rooms in local hotels.

The group of men who had bumped shoulders as they filed down the stairs were now very clearly divided. The coroner and jury huddled briefly; no doubt they looked towards the exit, their thoughts turning to more salubrious places to drink. Agnew and a constable spoke quietly. William Sly headed quickly for the door. What he did not anticipate was having J. J. in pursuit. 'Mr Sly! If you please, sir, may I speak with you?'

William kept walking.

J. J. followed. 'Excuse me, Mr Sly, I just wanted to introduce myself properly. We didn't get the chance to formally meet before, but I am John O'Leary.'

William appeared to be picking up speed. 'I know who you are, sure.' He threw the comment over his shoulder.

'I just wanted to talk to you about the children.'

'I don't know anything at all about them,' sniped William.

J. J. was experiencing a role reversal from the inquest – now he was doing the questioning. But in contrast to the excruciatingly slow pace of being interviewed as a witness, this felt heated, panicked and frenetic, which had much to do with the pace J. J. was forced to keep as he trailed William down the street.

'Alicks and Ellie's children, sir. They are on their own now.'

On hearing this, William seemed to pick up even more speed. 'I'm sorry, Mr O'Leary, I don't have an answer for you.' It was clear he had no time to discuss the future of his grandchildren.

'But, sir, I am not really in a position to look after them at all. I'm not married and . . .'

At this William stopped and looked menacingly into the eyes of J. J. O'Leary. 'I am sorry, sir, but I cannot help you. I know nothing whatever about it, and want nothing at all to do with it.'

With that, William Sly turned the corner and was gone.

11

MARRIAGE, MURDER AND METEOROLOGY

In January 1904, the newly formed Australian nation got its instruments of measurement ready and began listing numbers considered vital to its ongoing health and prosperity. The data collected was commonly referred to as 'the vitals', and was mentioned in a range of key government documents including the Vital Statistics Gazettes.

The data was used to measure the wellness of the nation. Weather was monitored. Both sunshine and rain were necessary for the maintenance of a healthy, growing state increasingly reliant on grain, fruit, sheep and beef for its economic security. Periods of heavy rainfall were especially important in summer for the fruit-growing regions, particularly orchards of *Malus domestica* (the table apple) and *Pyrus communis* (European pear). Days of sunshine were counted, and so too were temperature readings in both the sun and shade. Levels of humidity were measured and collated. Inches of rainfall were tallied. There was no instrument capable of counting thunder as clouds rolled across the sky, or the quantum of lightning flashes that might indicate an impending storm; instead, meteorologists noted the moment when lightning struck with a potentially deadly force.

At the state level, statisticians and politicians paid close attention to factors considered important for growth, and these were measured as well. Population was monitored closely and three factors were considered vital to the maintenance of a healthy society: births, deaths and marriages. In the production of these vitals, however, only some events in the community were subjected to close scrutiny.

Communicable diseases were counted. The incidence of pulmonary phthisis (tuberculosis), diphtheria, measles, syphilis and whooping cough were all studied closely by statisticians. Over one quarter of all people who died each month did so because of diarrhoea, so this medical condition was disaggregated into a range of subcategories. Conditions considered to compromise a person in the long term – such as rickets and cleft palate – were also of interest to the state, as well as the incidence of epilepsy, insanity and apoplexy. All of the afflicted would require extra care, and some accounting of this was required. Cases of chronic alcoholism, and the range of observable comorbidities arising from it, were labelled by the NSW statistician as 'medical conditions of intemperance'.

Data counts on all these conditions were included as vitals as well.

Some types of violence were of special interest to statisticians. Others were not. Some violent deaths, particularly unusual ones, were recorded using a remarkable level of qualitative detail for what was supposed to be a quantitative numeric tool. A very open-ended coding frame was adopted to reflect the diverse social circumstances that led to a violent death. Violent incidents at work that resulted in fatalities were counted using labels like: 'explosion of chemicals', 'injury from bullock' and 'tetanus cut'. On the Australian frontier, a sudden, violent death could be caused by 'sunstroke', 'lightning', 'poison', 'shark bite' or 'bite of insect'. Staying in hospital also had its risks, particularly if surgery was involved. Under the counts of violent deaths was a special category for those brought about by medical intervention; these used labels such as 'collapse under chloroform' or 'collapse after operation'.

The vitals report highlighted some but not all of the inherent dangers of everyday family life; for example, 'death by drinking water whilst heated', 'death by eating unripe fruit' and 'eating unwholesome tinned fish' all featured as data labels. The risk from fruit was deemed so significant that the catchphrase 'unripe fruit is the undertaker's friend' became popular, and the education department issued a public warning about it because children in particular were deemed to be at risk.

Readers of the Vital Statistics Gazettes were also provided with an evocative set of data labels to describe the varied ways in which a person might kill themselves. Suicide featured as a subcategory of violent death, and the varied pursuits of 'gunshot', 'hanging', 'drowning' and 'cutting' all featured as data labels; so too did the quiet 'suffocation by gas', the more pedestrian 'going in front of a railway engine', the spectacular 'jumping from a great height', and the thorough and determined notion of going out with a bang: 'suicide by dynamite'.

Statistics were important because they were increasingly being used by governments to inform policy. For example, did an outbreak of diphtheria suggest a need for the Board of Health to take extra steps to prevent its spread? Should the state be concerned about growth in 'diseases of the organs of generation' because these could directly compromise fertility and therefore population growth? In this regard, statisticians closely observed data on diseases of the uterus and vagina, but close to no data was collected on male reproductive efficiencies.

Maintaining strong population growth was considered vital, and one measure was seen as important above all others: the marriage metric. This was perceived to be the foundation of 'good' population growth. Divorce, more than any disease of the female reproductive organs, was considered the biggest threat to population growth. As a 1902 editorial in the religious newspaper *Freeman's Journal* notes, the way in which society talked about and measured divorce had power; if discussed in the wrong way, the idea could become contagious, and no one wanted it catching on. 'We have refrained in this article from entering into the statistics of divorce, but it is known to everyone that they are becoming more alarming every year . . . There are evils many and terrible in the world; there are disease, pain, poverty . . . but the destructive power of all combined seems trifling in comparison with that which is summed up in the awful word "Divorce" . . . Pity that our best public men would not strive to check this evil.'

Monitoring the number of births that occurred outside of marriage was considered vital too. The state's statistician cross-tabulated this data so that the government could not only identify how many illegitimate children had been born in that month or that year, but also which suburbs they were born in. The age at marriage, religious denominations of couples, and the suburbs in which they were wed were matters of interest as well. But other aspects of marriage were not recorded by data analysts.

Wives who faced dangerous marital storm fronts were in a precarious position in 1904. Though statisticians did not look at domestic violence and abuse, a vast amount of contextual evidence suggests they existed for many as part of the climate of marriage. In one of the most comprehensive studies of historical hospital data ever undertaken in Australia, archivists made a number of remarkable discoveries about marital brutality in the late nineteenth century. The data, drawn from the doctors' ward notes of Melbourne Hospital over a fifty-year period from 1856 to 1905, reveals that women endured an extraordinary amount of this brutality – yet it was considered fairly normal according to values of the time. As Carolyn Webb, a member of the Genealogical Society of

Victoria, notes, 'domestic violence was rife'. The reasons for this are complex and deeply tied to the intractable belief that marriage, no matter how bad, was a contract 'till death us do part'.

As a columnist for the *Sunday Times* noted in 1899, society had a high tolerance for violence within marriage, despite the fact that legal measures were in place, theoretically at least, to sanction perpetrators. In an article entitled 'Wife Beating', the writer asks, 'When a man treats his wife like a dog, surely she is no longer bound to "love, honour and obey"?' A similar observation had been made by a popular columnist in Sydney thirty years before: 'If a larrikin were to assault a man with one-half the brutality men assault their wives, there would be a general outcry.' Legal changes in the 1890s had acknowledged that women needed an out when marriage turned bad; the introduction of the 1892 *Law of Divorce*, for example, expanded opportunities for wives to seek judicial separations. Obtaining a divorce, however, remained difficult for anyone, particularly a woman. She would have to prove habitual cruelty over a long period, or show significant evidence that her murder had been attempted. Both of these were difficult to prove in a sociocultural context that did not typically acknowledge or report when violent conditions were present within a marriage.

Women who left marriage had few places to turn. They rarely had income streams independent of their husbands, and only held limited or often no legal rights over property and business. Women were almost always the primary carers within a family as well; leaving a marriage meant providing not just for oneself but one's children too.

The legal system remained unwilling to intervene in a marriage, even when the spouses appeared to be suffering terribly. The words of one NSW judge powerfully illustrate how legal principles and social values merged to shape the rigid boundaries of marriage. In the case of Pearce in 1900, a wife sought divorce because her husband had deserted her, and she also provided a mountain of evidence to substantiate his cruel treatment of her. The judge ruled that domestic violence was not relevant to her claims: 'Marriage is marriage however miserable it turns out to be,' he said.

Though some commentators had begun to question the conflicted character of marriage, they represented a minority. The institution still offered the most viable form of financial security for women in a world where their options were limited for achieving economic independence. Many women, and indeed men, found themselves staying in frightfully unhappy marriages.

There was a longstanding awareness that the generalised tolerance for violence within marriage needed redress, yet it went on just the same. Legal historian Dr Colin James goes so far as to say that violence was not just tolerated within marriage, but also both passively and actively condoned by wider society and the courts: 'Many judges believed that the equality of women and men was a radical idea and allowed physical discipline as sometimes necessary for a man to maintain control in his family.' Whether physical force could be used by a husband on his wife was not really in question. But how much was too much? As James notes,

> only in cases where the man 'went too far' might the wife successfully complain to the police or to the divorce courts. The police could charge the husband with assault or attempted murder, but rarely did so, unless they believed that the woman's life was at risk . . . [T]he woman's decision to approach a court of law was always difficult and often dangerous, as she risked provoking her husband to further violence. At stake was not only the woman's physical well-being but, by jeopardising her marriage, her standing in the community, her financial survival, the custody of her children and sometimes her life.

James points out that an even more bitter jeopardy existed for women who chose to leave. If a wife fled, her husband could charge her with desertion. This meant she would not be entitled to maintenance and would most certainly lose custody of her children. There is evidence that some women fleeing violent marriages faced further sanction and certainly did not receive protection from law enforcement. Meanwhile, some husbands submitted applications for the restitution of conjugal rights, complaining that their marital problems were entirely due to their wives being unwilling sexual partners.

The focus of the statistics collection process in 1904 reveals much about the priorities of the nation. Rain was monitored closely so that the good health and wellbeing of agriculture could be maintained. When it came to the climate of marriage, however, the state left it to the husband to sort out. Indeed the term 'domestic violence', as it is applied today, did not exist in descriptions of family life in 1904.

The Sly inquest findings were recorded in data counts for the vitals that month: one count of murder and one of suicide. While the tragedy was generally being referred to as a murder-suicide in press reports and legal records, this was not a distinct data label in statistical reports at the time, or in the statistical gazettes that followed. Yet in terms of statistical significance, murder-suicide had one of the most powerful correlations to only one other factor: marriage. Strangers were not targeted as unwilling participants in murder-suicides, only wives. There were statistical labels for women based on their marital status: brides, widows, spinsters and even the term 'minor' brides was used (for those who wed under the legal age of adulthood, which was twenty-one). Suicide brides, however, were not counted anywhere.

It is noteworthy now, though it wasn't considered so at the time, that in matters of marriage, murder and meteorology, Ellie Sly was not the only suicide bride discovered that year, or in the years before and after. Morbid ceremonies for suicide brides were held every month of 1904 in every Australian state.

In February a Western Australian man, Richard Sparrow, had planned a moonlight ceremony for his suicide bride. In the small boarding-house room where they lived, Richard waited for his wife, Margaret, to fall asleep, then quietly crept across the room in the dark and put a gun to her head.

The cold metal on her skin woke Margaret, just in time for her to hear the words: 'We would both be better dead.' She tried to leap out of the way, but not quickly enough to avoid the gun altogether. Richard then turned it on himself. Again, he missed the mark. Their fellow boarding-house residents reported hearing Margaret's screams before the gunshots. She burst from the room into the hall, a smoking gunpowder mark in the middle of her forehead and blood running down her face. She was still screaming, but surprisingly she was not seeking help for herself. 'Save my husband!' she yelled as she ran up and down the hall. Their neighbours rushed into the room to find Richard slumped in a chair, shot through the eye but miraculously still alive.

During the police investigation, tenants admitted they had heard him threaten his wife with violence many times before, but they had never reported it. Richard Sparrow told police he was despondent because no one was willing to back his invention of a spark arrestor: a device that would prevent small sparks from engines and flames leading to explosions and fire hazards. Sparrow's solution to this crisis had been to kill his wife and then himself.

In March 1904, Fanny Pannell lived to tell of her husband Joseph's failed attempt at a murder-suicide ceremony. Joseph had planned an event that was much more hands-on. He attempted to beat and strangle his wife to death, before killing himself. Fanny, a runaway suicide bride, managed to escape with her life.

Fanny's case shocked the legal establishment not only because of the stories she told about her husband, but also because she so adamantly declared her intent to divorce him. In petitioning for a divorce, she described how he had beaten her, thrown her out of bed, punched her and torn off her clothes to humiliate her. He also psychologically tortured her. He set fire to her hairbrush and placed it under her nose while she was asleep so she would believe he had set her alight, as he had threatened to do many times. He also threatened to kill her and then himself whenever she would not agree to his wishes.

During the court proceedings, the judge's wry commentary on the wife's claims of cruelty give insight on the generalised expectations of married women at the time. Fanny described how her husband insisted she should clip his toenails; if she failed to do so, he punished her – he sliced up her shins by dragging his jagged nails up and down them while in bed. For some unknown reason the judge took interest in this issue over and above the murder-suicide attempt and the frequent beatings.

'So he cut you with the nails that you would not cut?' asked the judge.

'Yes,' she replied quietly.

'Then it would have been better for you to have cut them,' he stated with great jurisprudence and wisdom.

In April, James Horner planned a Melbourne murder-suicide for himself and his bride, Elizabeth. One newspaper account of this event used the headline: 'Wife murder and suicide: a happy home broken up'. Elizabeth was thirty years younger than her husband and had been locked inside a home in Northcote, tormented and accused of being unfaithful. When police eventually came to her aid, she was found slumped, but still upright, on the sofa. James had shot her, then laid down at her feet and shot himself. After the deaths, newspapers dubbed him the 'morbid monomaniac'. There were signs the eighty-year-old had suffered from paranoia and dementia, and all the neighbours had known about it because they heard screams coming from the home all that evening. No one had called the police.

In May, a popular month for weddings during which newspapers were crammed with lengthy marriage announcements, the murder-suicide of Joseph Riley and his wife barely rated a mention in the press. Joseph, a railway worker in Kensington, Melbourne, had lost his job during a strike and 'taken to drink'. The details of the private ceremony remain a little sketchy but seemed to include the following. There had been a disagreement over a property. His wife, Catherine, had tried to stand her ground and not give in to her husband's wishes. It all seemed fine until Joseph waited in the bushes outside their house for his wife to return. He drove a pocketknife into her neck and then stabbed himself.

In June, the violence that had taken place inside the Savages' marriage was not considered worthy of a mention in any data counts. If the assaults had occurred on the streets between men, they would have been captured by crime statistics; however, they had occurred between George and Rachel

Savage. After returning home drunk one night, George tried to take Rachel's life with a razor and his own as well. She went to the police not just because she wanted to describe the attempt on her life, but also to explain that this had not been the first time. This was an extremely unusual step for a woman in Rachel's position to take. During the divorce case, a constable who had witnessed the violence she had suffered came forward in her defence to attest that George was 'violent and sullen'.

In July, Robert Kingsley's plan to end his marriage in a murder-suicide were thwarted only because Hannah, his blushing, beaten and bruised wife, had managed to escape. He had threatened not just to kill her but himself as well. In her petition for divorce she documented a harrowing story of cross-country violence: she had endured beatings from Sydney to Broken Hill, to Trunkey Creek, on to Coolgardie and then all the way to Fremantle.

In August, in outback Bathurst, Joseph Artery's suicide bride had not suspected the surprise her husband had planned for her. She had left him, and she thought the trouble was over. When he arrived at her home one evening and offered to take her for a friendly moonlit ride in a sulky, she agreed. After shooting his wife three times out on the open road, Joseph calmly travelled three miles to his father's residence and shot himself through the head with a revolver.

In September, Joseph Duff in Melbourne attacked his wife, Mary, with an axe on a Saturday morning while she lay in bed. After leaving her for dead, he ran to Auburn train station intending to throw himself under an oncoming train. Almost unbelievably, he missed, and the train took only part of his leg. Miraculously Mary had survived, though she was beaten and blue. Joseph had survived only because medical staff had worked quickly and efficiently to amputate his leg. Unaware his wife was still alive, he stated to a constable, 'I murdered my wife and I kissed her goodbye.'

In October, a constable was stopped on a South Melbourne street and asked to attend to a suicide bride at a wooden cottage on Cromwell Street: 'A man has just cut his wife's throat. Come quick.' When the constable arrived he found a squalid home covered in blood. The wife was still alive, while her husband, Tom Wood, was sitting in a chair with a deep gash across his neck, also still alive. Adding the failure of his crime to what was clearly a long list of regrets that defined his life, his only comment to police when they arrived was, 'It's a pity I didn't finish it.'

Police took Tom to hospital. He was lucky – he had only just missed his jugular. He received twenty stitches. His wife was lucky too: the razor had been blunt, police said, and her hands were badly gashed because she had fought hard to live. Her quick reflexes had saved her life. In the journey from hospital to lock-up, police asked Tom why he had done it. With his neck heavily bandaged, he whispered that his wife's temperament or character had very little to do with it. His decision to take a suicide bride had been practical and not romantic. 'I'm too old and feeble to get work now,' he said. He could no longer support himself or his wife. In her interview with the police, Mrs Wood described her long-held fear that her husband had wanted to make her his suicide bride. 'I think my husband must be a little out of his mind for he has often threatened that he would kill himself, but would finish me first. He threatened too that he would kill himself, and leave a letter behind putting all the blame on me.'

In November, Mary O'Hara, eighteen, had been married for two years when her husband decided to make her his suicide bride. Oswald, her 26-year-old husband, slashed both her throat and his. They had placed their child in a Home in Ashfield, and Mary had already left him, twice. It was just before midnight when Oswald finally tracked her down, as she waited for a tram in Surry Hills. Both survived his attack. As Mary was being taken away in a hospital cab, Oswald pleaded with a constable at the scene, 'but let me kiss my wife . . . she is the dearest little woman in the world . . . but she has brought it on herself'.

By the end of the year, no one had been counting, so no one could prove if there had been an increase in the murders and attempted murders of wives. There was, however, a generalised understanding that something was going terribly wrong in the institution of marriage, and that little was being done to address the issue. One newspaper noted:

Several cases have been dealt with in the Criminal court, and the remainder in the lower courts. Seldom, perhaps never, within a similar period, have there been so many cases of this kind in the metropolis. The evidence given in some of the cases showed that the women were quite unfitted for matrimony, whilst in others the proof was equally strong that the men were mere animals. The thing that puzzles a civilised man is why should a man murder his wife when she has become tired of him? If every husband were to do that, the crime of murder would become more common than the vice of drunkenness.

One case, perhaps more than any other to occur that year, illustrates the culture of tolerance towards the desire of men to take suicide brides. James Minahan killed his wife, Florence, with an axe in the front yard of their home in January 1904. This murder-suicide occurred in a neighbouring suburb and only a week apart from the Sly tragedy. After he was done chopping his wife in the head, James stabbed himself with a table knife. Their eighteen-month-old baby was asleep within metres of the event, and Florence had been heavily pregnant. James tried to slash his throat, but when this didn't work he walked to Woolloomooloo Bay to drown himself. It was here that police found him.

James's admissions in court seem raw, brutal and unfathomable now – though in 1904 his statements to the legal minds of the day were more or less accepted as a reasonable excuse. James had been violently drunk and beating his wife for two weeks, and neighbours attested to having seen and heard it for themselves. None of this was considered worrying enough for them to call the police. Appearing in the torn coat he had worn during the attack, with a gash still open across his throat, James wept and shook on the stand. He freely admitted his actions, but said he could explain them fully. 'I killed my wife. It is all her fault. I hit her on the head with an axe. She drove me to it.' Before stepping down from the stand, he declared, 'I wish I could kill myself.'

At trial, intemperance was identified as a key factor in explaining James's murderous and suicidal behaviour. A string of witnesses came forward to attest to his pattern of drinking, and his lawyer claimed that he had been insane at the time of the murder and this was entirely attributable to intemperance. One neighbour commented, 'They lived on the most affectionate terms until he gave way to drink.' Another noted, 'His behaviour was nothing short of maniacal.' A third neighbour claimed, 'Mrs Minahan said a better man never broke a loaf of bread. She never complained. Though, she was afraid of her husband when he took a glass of beer.' A doctor came forward to say James Minahan was afflicted with the condition known as delirium tremens. The fact that this was usually created by alcohol withdrawal and James was drunk when captured by police was an inconsistency not raised at trial. The jury retired for fifteen minutes and returned a verdict of not guilty on the grounds of insanity.

In the compilation of murder, marriage and meteorology statistics for 1904, the records of murder-suicides were coded in a way comparable to weather events. Patterns of aggression and threats of violence were not recorded by anyone; they were simply allowed to pass over like an inclement weather front. When lightning struck and killed, however, this was regarded as a notable meteorological event. While neighbours certainly heard and saw domestic violence, they treated it much like the rumbles of thunder and flashes of lightning that signalled an impending storm. Windows were closed and shutters were drawn while neighbours simply waited it out in the safety of their homes.

The storm of the Sly marriage only differed in one key respect when compared to most of the other marital meteorological events to occur that year: Alicks had done what many other husbands had attempted but failed to do. He had successfully carried his suicide bride across the threshold, to the other side.

12

SECOND-HAND GOODS

WHEN THE THREE SLY BROTHERS ARRIVED AT THE HOME OF Hope on the evening of Tuesday, 12 January 1904, they were not welcomed. The Hope had taken them because it had to. The boys could not stay there permanently.

It was a place for women to have children but not keep them. Based on an analysis of the administrative records remaining, on average about fifty-three women and twenty-six children resided there per week. Children certainly did pass through the Hope, but they did not stay for long.

When Bedford, Basil and Mervyn arrived, they were surrounded by women who had 'fallen from virtue'. We know this because administrators asked a specific question of women when they sought to stay there: 'Have you fallen from virtue?' The admissions process was a moral inventory of sorts, and included other key questions such as: 'What is your parents' character?', 'Who is the putative father?' and 'Will any person contribute to your support while in the Home?' While some women at the Hope were pregnant out of wedlock, others were there out of sheer desperation. A great number of married women and abused women also sought refuge at the Hope because they simply had nowhere else to go; poverty and/or violence had led them to seek sanctuary, as the institutions of marriage and family were not safe places for them.

There were women about to give birth and those who just had. Some had run from violent spouses, but many returned to their husbands after delivering because they had no other way to support themselves.

There were also those in the grip of terrible fevers from failed abortions, desperate for care and compassion but even more desperate for a life-saving curette. The partial remains of the dead fetus were often left behind to rot in the woman's womb. If this was not removed, the woman was at risk of septicaemia: a very painful and feverish death.

Only two volumes of entry books have survived from the Home of Hope's twenty-one years of operation in the Newtown and Camperdown area. Every admission form within the heavily bound books tells a unique and painful story, and there is remarkable rhythm and repetition that recurs across these accounts. The verbatim excerpts have a poetic quality both startling and sad. While they remain administrative artefacts, they can also be read as a body of work, like an epic poem narrating the life-and-death struggle of maternity. The forms often include a mix of brutal and vivid accounts of the physical health challenges facing these women, but also the emotional challenges.

Ada: does not know his address.

Amelia: fallen from virtue.

Annie 1: miscarriage, criminally brought about.

Annie 2: does not know his name nor his address.

Annie 3: Baby born (female) 6.25 am 26 October. Baby died 7 November (Frances May).

Clara: widowed six months, 5 children, 4 living.

Constance: has attended Sunday school and can read and write 'a little'.

Edith: died half an hour after admission.

Ellen: he left two months ago to seek work, she has not heard from him since.

Elizabeth: cannot afford upkeep of baby.

Ethel: went insane after birth of child, sent to Callan Park.

Hannah: first child stated to be stillborn, she placed it in a box under her bed and went about her work.

Harriet: married, poor.

Lottie: does not know the father, met him on a picnic where the event occurred.

Madge: gone home to her mother.

Mary 1: gave birth to stillborn child then herself died.

Mary 2: locked up for three months, no lawful means of support.

Mary 3: came in, in labour. Delivered immediately.

Mary Ann 1: abortion then curette.

Mary Ann 2: was familiar with the lad.

Mary-Elizabeth: mentally weak.

Margaret: can pay ten shillings a week.

Mary: husband unemployed.

Nellie: brought in by her mother.

Rebecca: character of parents good.

Rose: no physical or mental weakness ... half caste girl
[scrawled at the end of the same column].

Ruby: brought by Police Sergeant from Central Criminal
Court. She had been taken by her father to a place where
an illegal operation was to be performed.

As well as providing lying-in services for women with
nowhere else to go, the Home of Hope sourced newborn
babies for desperate childless couples from across Sydney.
What compensation or payment was provided to the Hope
in exchange for the child was carefully and meticulously left
absent from documentation – but on the bottom of some
admission forms there are hand-tallied sums, quickly scribbled
in pencil, which look like back-of-the-envelope calculations.
No notes were made beside these numbers, although they are
positioned under the column: 'How was the child disposed
of?' The Hope, like many orphanages of the time, was the
architect of a kind of insider trading in human identity. The
process was seamless, and it was believed everyone would
benefit so long as everyone collaborated in a lifelong lie about
how the child had been traded. It offered infertile couples the
opportunity to erase their shame. It allowed children to be
raised without the knowledge of a genetic legacy that was
considered to be morally tainted. It offered adoptive parents

a promise: the effectiveness of their good parenting would heal and restore a child born with a shameful past. For the biological mother, this act of insider trading was considered optimal because it delivered a kind of healing to both her and the child. In the best interests of everyone's mental health – even the children who were unwitting participants in the agreement – it was considered best to commit to a forced forgetting. It was firmly believed that no one would be hurt, so long as the secret could remain hidden forever.

The first reason the Sly brothers were not welcome at the Hope was because they were not babies. The second reason pertained to the operation of the Hope as a place of women's business. The Hope was a residential facility for friendless and fallen women, but it was also a commercial laundry. One question determined an individual's eligibility to stay: 'Will any person contribute to their support while residing at the Home?' The answer for the Sly boys was 'no'. This mattered a great deal. The situation they faced could be reduced to basic accounting: debits and credits, profits and losses. Three young boys were an expense with no prospect of revenue.

Those who needed to stay and could not contribute to their keep were required to pay back their time with labour. And it was hard, *hard* work. Making lye soap on site, boiling, washing, plunging the wash, rinsing, wringing, hanging sheets and then ironing was a dawn-to-dusk operation that involved many, many hands. Desperation created economies of scale. The more desperate women, the better for the Hope; and the more desperate each woman, the better. The Hope did not claim to be a business, but it was run by a businessman. Those women who had hit a veritable rock bottom were ideal for the bottom line.

The three Sly boys were in the most vulnerable position imaginable. The eldest, Bedford, was still six years from being of use to an employer. By fourteen many boys could at least be sent to industrial school and put to work or placed in an apprenticeship, but at eight, six and four the boys were seen as little more than liabilities. They were not being quietly sponsored by a family member, and they were too small to undertake laundry work.

Bedford, Basil and Mervyn were faced with the deepest paradox: they had been deemed by 1904 society as too poor and too desperate even to receive charity.

While the boys faced uncertainty at the Home of Hope, baby Olive faced a similar predicament at Prince Alfred Hospital. As her health improved, so too did the precariousness of her situation. Many years before, Alicks Sly had been a member of the hospital. The scheme operated like a subscription service, permitting contributors and their families to access hospital services free of charge for a year. Alicks had not paid the premiums on the policy for years; Olive's hospital bills had therefore not been paid. While the hospital may have had compassion for the child's situation, like any institution it had financial limits and a ledger to keep.

•

With four children orphaned, no provision made for their future in the form of a will and no family volunteering to assist, the state stepped in to take account for their needs. And it did so meticulously. The Curator of Intestate Estates, Thomas Garrett, assumed responsibility for managing the Sly estate, as the state appointed manager of estates without a will in place to determine the distribution of assets. Since the couple had acquired no property, this included only the pitiful shambles of their household. A final figure would be determined after every sock, boot and cooking pot was sold, and after all debts owed by Alicks Sly were paid. Whatever remained would go to his heirs. The lives of the children depended on the money to be resolved from the estate; in the absence of a guardian stepping forward, this would be the only provision made for their future.

Sergeant Agnew engaged James T. Jones, a Redfern-based auctioneer, to clear the house. Jones and his team performed many contracts for the Intestate Estates office because they could offer the convenience of a full suite of services, including thorough inventory, heavy lifting, cartage and cleaning. Agnew set them to work on the Slys' goods and chattels. Saleable items were transferred to the J. T. Jones rooms and scheduled for auction. Jones complained so much about the disposal of rubbish cleared from the house, he invoiced the estate an additional muck surcharge.

As word of the tragedy spread through the borough, individuals began to emerge from the Newtown woodwork. While money had burdened Alicks to the very last moment of his life, and perhaps been a catalyst for the tragedy, it seemed it would continue to haunt him after his death.

Some bills were expected. The undertaker and embalmer submitted an invoice. The auctioneer also calculated a charge for advertising and administering the sale of property associated with the estate. The tragedy, however, also managed to bring out the best and the absolute worst in the people the Slys had once called neighbours.

Samuel Lownds, Newtown coach builder and the Slys' former landlord, claimed for two weeks of rent: one pound and six shillings. This was the same landlord who had argued so bitterly with Alicks on the doorstep of 49 Watkin and evicted him on the eve of the tragedy.

Alicks Sly had a standing order with the Great Federal Bakery in Glebe for two loaves of bread to be delivered twice a week (Tuesday and Wednesday). The bakery staff had been delivering to the family as Glebe locals for years, and would have known them well. The baker had begun deliveries to their new residence in Newtown, with their last occurring on the morning of the tragedy. Charles Vass, the owner, was one of the very first claimants to come forward, submitting documentation of invoices to the value of eight shillings and eleven pence. It was the equivalent of about a day's wage for a low-paid worker at the time, so it is hard to envisage that loss of this income would have devastated the balance sheet of a bakery – though it would have made a very big difference to the security of four orphans who needed every penny.

Wealthy Newtown businessman Marcus Clark also came forward remarkably quickly (within two days), writing to the Chamber Magistrate at Newtown Court care of Sergeant Agnew. Alicks Sly had purchased a good deal of furniture from his department store through a 'buy now pay later' scheme and had made only one payment in three months, against a considerable debt. Clark had a reputation as a shrewd entrepreneur and exploited his large Newtown window frontage with elaborate shopfront displays. Starting at 218 King Street in 1893, his business had grown rapidly enough in four years to finance leases on 220–222 King Street as well. By 1897 the company had pushed out a local bootmaker from number 224, and marched onward to claim number 226 by 1898. Every inch of the floor space was crammed with an array of mass-produced items (brooms, chairs, hats) through to customised products (suits and drapes). Marcus Clark and Co. would sell anything from a hairpin to a full bedroom suite, or, using vernacular of the time, 'a needle to an anchor'. As one newspaper noted: 'That this firm possess a keen business instinct is evinced by the fact that they have secured one of the finest shop fronts in Sydney and that their premises for imposing exterior, graceful and handsome appearance, are unsurpassed by any establishment in Sydney.'

Like everyone else in Newtown, senior management at the department store had not only read the story in the paper but also heard local gossip about the family. Immediately recognising the surname as an account holder, the company notified Newtown police that Alicks Sly was in debt to them.

Agnew would not have been surprised to receive the letter, as almost every family in the borough had an account with Marcus Clark. The sergeant no doubt readied the paperwork in anticipation of forwarding a significant claim on the estate. The content of the letter, however, was not at all what he expected. The company had not come forward to lay claim, but to relinquish both the furniture and any debt owed them. The grim reality of four orphans left destitute by a tragedy had struck a chord in the heart of the most aggressive of Edwardian capitalists.

While Clark displayed a slightly surprising response to the Sly tragedy, so too did Sergeant Agnew. With nothing to gain from doing so, he showed a remarkable ability to consider the children and foresee what they might need to make sense of the tragedy in years to come. While conducting an inventory of the Slys' possessions, the sergeant retrieved what items he could. He looked for anything that might have meaning. They had no toys, and the clothes were in such a sorry state of repair the sergeant would no doubt have felt they were beyond saving. Instead, his observant eye spied an item that would have been significant to Ellie, described as a 'workbox' in the inventory. Agnew gathered what photographs he could find and placed them in it, along with jewellery retrieved from Ellie's dead fingers. While the term 'workbox' may have referred to a small caddy for tools, perhaps used by Alicks to carry scissors, measuring tape or buttons for tailoring, it is more likely to have been a mother's workbox. The term was commonly used to describe the sewing box, an item of significance for a woman in that era. The lids of these boxes were often personalised, usually decorated with needlework. Ensuring the items were kept safe for the children, and displaying the behaviour of an ethical police officer, Agnew sent them to the curator, Thomas Garrett, for safekeeping.

The auctioneers were expecting a busy sale, and Jones was experienced at extracting maximum value from his lots. Given the tight economic conditions of the time, the market for second-hand goods was strong. Significant investments such as bedroom suites, dining settings and lounge chairs sold well. There was a market for second-hand clothing, commonly known as 'left off'.

The second-hand auction markets also traded in much more unusual items, with economic necessity overriding any aversion to the re-use of intimate and personal possessions. Bathtubs sold well, so too did half-used bottles of medicine and liniment, cosmetics, salves and used teeth. Pots of solidified kitchen fat also had buyers. Decanting render (animal fat) from roasting meat while it was still hot and in liquid form was a common kitchen practice at the time. The fat, known as dripping, was then used and re-used at every meal. Even these family dripping jars were sold to reclaim money for deceased estates. While it cannot be ruled out that what might be called heirloom lard was purchased for consumption, more likely it was used to make tallow candles. There was a cottage candle-making industry in Newtown, and local makers advertised in the classifieds of major newspapers to trade in lard. In this area too, the need for economy overtook other concerns; although tallow candles were cheap, they were also reputed to smoke terribly and smell horrendous.

The auction had been widely advertised in major newspapers, including the two with the biggest circulations: the *Evening News* and the *Sydney Morning Herald*. When the auction day arrived, the hall was crowded. Analysis of the purchases point to patterns: some buyers were monied, others were looking for a bargain, and yet others came to rubberneck at the final public chapter of the Newtown Tragedy. Local resident Mrs Sjobert, for example, bought a range of items that suggest a housewife redecorating. Her new sitting room would include a lounge suite (couch and four Austrian chairs), her table would boast a colourful plush cover and her walls would be decorated with oil paintings of Goulburn. Mr Charles Collier bought some of the most affordable items, including cutlery, boxes of household medicines, lamps and clothing; 'all moth eaten' was written as a note by the auctioneer. The large oilcloth from the front-room floor was sold; so too the perambulator parked at the back door. The same buyer purchased the *History of Ireland* as well.

One purchase in particular suggests that some attended to gawk. While most buyers purchased multiple lots suitable for setting up a new house or perhaps preparing for a new baby, a buyer listed simply as 'Harris' bid on only one item. Unlike every other lot, this one would have been completely useless to the purchaser. For a shilling, Harris bought the brass plate engraved with the words: 'Mrs E G Sly, Teacher of music and dancing'. It is hard to imagine the buyer purchased the item for any other reason than voyeurism, and it may represent Australia's first documented case of true crime 'murderabilia'.

Of the forty-seven lots, almost everything sold. A few items – including a galvanised iron tub, a washstand and a box of old clothes – were passed in. The sewing machine earned £5:5. More than 70 per cent of the money earned by the estate, however, came from the sale of a single item. The very thing Alicks had foretold would offer an income stream for the family contributed most to the children's upkeep after he was gone. Ellie's Lipp & Sohn upright piano, which she'd planned to use to provide music classes to local children, sold for the handsome sum of £38:8:2. Pianos, particularly those with beautiful craftsmanship, had a huge resale value because of the costs associated with transporting items from Europe.

The family Bible simply disappeared. It was not sold at auction. There is also no record of it being passed along to the Curator of Intestate Estates for safekeeping on behalf of the children. It is possible that it was simply disposed of by Jones the auctioneer. It was a superstition at the time – and remains so among some traders in second-hand goods to this day – that it is bad luck for a seller to trade in used Bibles.

All costs associated with the sale, including removal of rubbish from the house, advertising and the agent's commission, came to £7:6:6. With these expenses deducted, the final sale totalled £45:8:9 in credit. This was a significant amount in 1904, when a plot of land in Newtown could be purchased for twenty pounds. The estate money would have been a huge windfall for a worker on a low wage. A man like Ellie's brother J. J., for example, who was struggling on a draper's wage, would have perceived this amount as a small fortune.

•

Within days of the tragedy, in a place far from Newtown, two people made an unexpected and very different kind of claim on the estate. Margaret and Walter Ford were Goulburn locals and had been longstanding friends of the O'Learys. Margaret's sister, Mary, was even married to one: Timothy, Cornelius's brother. Walter Ford was an older man and held a respectable position in the railway. Walter and Margaret had married later in life – they had wanted but been unable to have children.

It is not clear who instigated Olive's adoption. It may have been J. J. who approached the Fords. Or, on hearing about the tragedy, perhaps the Fords came forward of their own volition to offer assistance. Three facts are known for certain. One, the Fords did not ever make an overture to adopt Bedford, Basil and Mervyn. Two, the arrangement was negotiated quickly; the boys were not afforded any opportunity to say goodbye to their little sister, nor was any importance placed on this. Three, the Fords wanted a child whose identity could be wiped clean, as did most adoptive parents at the time. It was believed to be in the best interests of all concerned if the past was erased, so Margaret and Walter set about doing just that. She was Olive Clotilde Sly when she left Prince Alfred Hospital, and when she was carried onto a train in the arms

of a woman she had never met before. By the time the little
girl toddled off the train at Goulburn, she would forever after
be known as Mollie Ford.

Just after Olive was sent away, J. J. surfaced. On the very
day that the funds of the Sly estate sale were received by the
curator, a letter arrived at the Intestate Office.

Dear Sir
I beg leave to apply for all papers, money etc in the
estate of the late Sly case. Mrs Sly was my sister and
I have taken charge of the children. The little girl is
gone to Goulburn to friends of mine and the boys will
go into one of the homes in a short time. They are all
full at present. I have promised to contribute to their
support. All the worry has been on me as Mr Sly at the
inquest would not have anything to do with the affair at
all . . . I had to guarantee everything . . . I am only getting
two pounds a week at Grace Bros Glebe and I am willing
to pay some of that towards the children. Hoping you
will look favourably on my application.
J. J. O'Leary

The letter contained a remarkable set of claims, given that
J. J. had done nothing to care for the boys. He had not even
been the one to drop them at the Home of Hope; that task
had been undertaken by Sergeant Agnew.

The curator did not and legally could not grant J. J.'s
request. While he was related to the late Ellie Sly, he had no
legal entitlement to the proceeds of the estate. The children,

by law, were the heirs. The curator's office sent a response to J. J. that did not contain what he had hoped for. As the boys' uncle, he was asked to come in to sign for and collect a box recovered from the house. This was what Sergeant Agnew had the presence of mind to set aside for the children. J. J. initialled this statement: 'Received work box and photos and hereby undertake to mind same for the children of the deceased.' What then happened to the workbox is unknown.

J. J.'s version of events does not match the paper trail of records. He had been involved in making decisions about the children's affairs because he was pressed to do so – he was the only relative willing to assume any responsibility, and the children were not under the control of protective services. As for his claim that he put money towards their upkeep, there is no documentation to substantiate it, but rather the opposite.

Scant information is provided on the administrative form pertaining to the admission of the three Sly boys to the Home of Hope. Sergeant Agnew completed this form, but for reasons that are not entirely clear, the information on the form is limited. The names of the three boys are written at the top of the page, and scrawled across it diagonally is the summary: 'Came from Watkin st Newtown brought by police. Father murdered mother and then committed suicide.' Only a few other details are provided on this form. In response to the question 'date of discharge', 9 February is included. It is also noted that on this day the boys were taken to a Home at Baulkham Hills; the convention of using capital 'H' for this Home means the boys had been delivered to another institution. In a manner of speaking, like Olive, the boys had gone to a good Catholic home; however, it was the kind of Home known more for custodial sentencing than custodial parenting. Unlike the subterfuge surrounding Olive's adoption, the boys' placement seems to have been transparent and straightforward.

A few weeks later, another letter arrived on the desk of Thomas Garrett, Curator of Intestate Estates.

Dear Sir

I would like you to consider a claim from me in the estate of the late AWB Sly. I've had the children put in the Baulkham Hills Convent. I lost a week's worth which I cannot afford as I am in delicate health. I had been saving up some money to take a holiday with. I was given to understand at the inquest that everything was to be handed over to me as his father wouldn't have anything to do with the matter and I being his wife's brother came next. I had made arrangements to keep the house as it was and to get in someone to look after the children. The affair has cost me about 4 or 5 pounds. I had to send the little girl to Goulburn and buy all the youngsters clothes and boots. I am hoping you will consider my claim. 25 March 1904

J. J. O'Leary

There is no evidence that J. J. had made any arrangements regarding the ongoing stay of the children at Watkin Street. It is also unlikely he would have considered this as a feasible plan because he worked full time and was a bachelor. Edwardian society generally took a very dim view of single men raising children, let alone four of them. The landlord Samuel Lownds, already highly agitated by the events that had occurred in the house, had taken possession of it immediately after the tragedy. There is no evidence that J. J. entered negotiations with him. It is also unlikely that Lownds would have entered into a new arrangement with someone so closely connected to a family he perceived as unstable and troublesome, and with whom he had so openly quarrelled.

J. J.'s statement regarding the boys' placement in an orphanage was true: Bedford, Basil and Mervyn had been dispatched to a Roman Catholic orphanage on the outskirts of town. However, the manner in which J. J.'s letter discusses these events, including Olive's placement with a new family, resembles a reimbursement claim. His tone of inconvenience and detachment is hard to overlook or dismiss.

•

On 9 February 1904 when the boys left the grimy streets of the inner city, they left behind every scene, every face and every place that they had ever known. They joined what was an experimental venture for the Catholic diocese in Western Sydney at the time: St Michael's Orphanage of Baulkham Hills, bought only the year before the boys were sent there.

It was believed the benefits of St Michael's could be twofold. The orphanage could provide a place for children in desperate circumstances to be given a wholesome and righteous upbringing, and the surrounding land could provide an income stream through farming. Positioned on the outskirts of Sydney at the time, and surrounded by orchardists who grew oranges and mandarins and kept plots for root vegetables, the land offered commercial potential. It could create a self-sustaining Home for boys to be kept physically and spiritually safe from the criminal temptations of the city. But the dirt roads towards St Michael's were rocky and had been poorly levelled. The orphanage was quite literally in the middle of nowhere. There was little in the way of a transport service, with the nearest train station many miles away in Parramatta. Despite St Michael's technically being in the Sydney suburbs, not even the local mail service could be relied upon. The commercial orchardists frequently complained that the costs of getting fruit to market were making businesses unviable; fruit could easily be grown out there, but without customers the orchards were struggling. This did not bode well for the St Michael's venture, as the Church needed an income stream generated by a working farm.

There were attempts to remedy the transport problems. A steam tram, connecting the hills districts to the train line, was built for the fruit to commute. This initiative proved a dismal failure when it was discovered it was not in fact legal to transport perishable food stacked up on the floor of a tram. The vehicle was redesigned as a mobile mailbox, as well as a passenger service that few locals used. Eventually the tram did little more than collect mail and deliver children to the newly opened orphanage.

St Michael's Orphanage publicly avowed a strong mission to 'care for the orphan, educate them in the knowledge of Christian truth, also to fit them for the battle of life'. In return, orphans had to service the debt now owed to the Catholic Church because it had provided the seed funding to establish their Home. The initial debt owed to the Church in 1903 was £910:10, and by the beginning of 1904 it had grown to £1274:14:4. The Church stated that the debt should be repaid through donation collection, attracting regular subscribers known as 'friends of the children', contributions from families and parents, and working the sixteen acres of orchard land the Church had purchased. Cardinal Moran, Head of the Catholic Diocese in Sydney, considered a successful orphanage to be one that could remove all vestiges of liability and sin – though which was worse, he did not clearly define. Not only were the Sisters of Mercy expected to run a righteous institution suitable for the spiritual development of boys, but they were also expected to clear the debt and become completely self-supporting. The nuns had to answer for every thimble they purchased and justify every sack of flour consumed. Indeed, the language used by the institution and the Church in promoting the cause was to 'liquidate debt' and 'solicit subscribers'. These were almost evangelical missions.

At this point, when the pressure on J. J. to provide something towards the upkeep of his nephews intensified, his relationship with them, and the Home where they now lived, ended permanently. Not even the orphanage manager could get hold of him. J. J. eventually replied, and only once.

His letter is lost, but a missive from a nun at St Michael's to the curator, Thomas Garrett, gives some insight into what J. J.'s letter might have contained, and it certainly wasn't a cheque: 'Dear Curator . . . I am have been [sic] instructed by Mr J. J. O'leary to apply to you for some payment from the property of their deceased parents for the support of John Bedford, Basil Cornelius and Mervyn James who have been in this orphanage since February. During which we have not received anything for their support.' After the estate sale, the curator, in communication with the probate judge, had set about making provision for the boys. An affidavit, drafted and signed by the curator, was submitted to the Supreme Court applying for approval that the remaining credit of the estate be spent in the upkeep of the three boys. It would be paid in instalments to the Catholic Church care of St Michael's Orphanage until it ran out.

Memoirs of people who lived in Australian institutional care at this time highlight that orphanage residents were usually made up of three groups: orphans, children with families physically or mentally unable to care for them, and those with families unwilling to do so. The Sly children were a rare mix of all three. It would be St Michael, not family, who would raise Bedford, Basil and Mervyn.

Based on the only primary source documentation left available to us, the experience of the Sly children unfolds like an accounts payable file. Reminder notices from St Michael's were sent to the curator, who politely responded with a monthly cheque. It seems J. J. felt his responsibility to the children had been fulfilled. With the boys safely in the arms of St Michael, their religious needs taken care of, perhaps J. J. felt he had done his best.

We know a few things about the Sly brothers' journey from Newtown to St Michael's. Some details were recorded on forms retained by the Home of Hope. Under the section marked 'how disposed of' is written 'collected by their Aunt (Mrs Pope) and taken to St Michael's'. We also know a little about what their journey would have been like. Mrs Pope shepherded them onto a train to Parramatta, then a steam tram to Baulkham Hills, then walked them a mile to St Michael's. This all seems unremarkable until one further discovery is made: they did not know a Mrs Pope, and did not have an aunt or great-aunt who went by that name. Indeed, Alicks Sly was so estranged from his family, it is very unlikely one of his sisters would have become involved to drop nephews whom they had never met at a Catholic Home (it was not their religion), even if they did choose to use an alias.

What is known for certain is that in February 1904, three Catholic boys, under the spiritual guidance of the Pope and his mysterious Mrs, were about to begin their new lives.

13

THE SWORD OF ST MICHAEL

As Catholics, Bedford, Basil and Mervyn Sly had been raised with a belief that St Michael would play an important spiritual role in life and an even more important one in death. Their Church taught that it was Michael – the archangel with a sword – who met the faithful in the hour of death, defeated Satan and escorted the dead safely home to God.

The St Michael Prayer was popular at the turn of the twentieth century because Pope Leo XIII himself had written it after receiving a religious vision. The prayer, often recited by children at bedtime, asked for what all children instinctively want: protection. St Michael, perhaps more than the other archangels and saints, captured the imagination of children at the time because of the heroic and theatrical overtones surrounding him. Religious artworks depict St Michael as a charismatic figure with flowing locks, assuming a warrior stance, sword gripped in hand and dressed in a skimpy gladiatorial miniskirt. St Michael was the nineteenth-century precursor to He-Man, and for children at the time he was the equivalent of a spiritual superhero. But for the Sly children, after the events of January 1904, the figure of St Michael could only have presented disturbing and upsetting theological and personal paradoxes.

If modern-day theories on trauma are to be believed, when a tragedy is experienced in early childhood it can be exceptionally damaging to the victim in the long term. The act of reminiscence for trauma survivors becomes a vivid and visceral experience as both memory and the flight-fight-freeze response are triggered simultaneously. Survivors compare trauma to a kind of haunting. Any stimulus – sight, sound or even fragrance – can prompt a cascade of physical, emotional and psychological responses. Memories can take shape as powerfully as apparitions that are beyond the person's control.

The three Sly brothers believed that St Michael had been at their mother's side in her final moments. The archangel had come to her, defeated evil and spirited her safely home. The boys knew in great detail, however, what the bloody and uncensored reality of her death had been. From their perspective, Ellie Sly had been chaperoned into death by one male figure, their father, and led towards salvation by another, St Michael. In both cases, a man had towered over her with a blade in hand. Instead of representing protection and security,

St Michael brandished a double-edged emotional sword. Had he come to save their mother, while damning their father for what he had done?

On the day after their mother's death, the children saw and felt the influence of St Michael again. This second visitation occurred at her burial. Ellie's funeral service was conducted at Rookwood Cemetery, her body buried adjacent to the chapel in the northern quadrant of what is now called the 'old Catholic' section. To this day, despite the encroachment of a more modern aesthetic in and around the cemetery grounds, St Michael still visually dominates the site. He stands tall, a striking statue atop the bell tower of the small but grim Gothic revivalist church in the centre of the graveyard. Ellie Sly remains under the archangel's watchful gaze, as she continues her eternal slumber in the shade of his wings.

On the day of Ellie's burial, there was no mention of her husband. The children did not attend his funeral, because he didn't have one.

The third visit from St Michael occurred on the day Bedford, Basil and Mervyn arrived at the orphanage, a month after the loss of their parents. As the boys crossed the threshold to their new Home, they must have noticed the statue of the archangel positioned at the entrance. It is hard to imagine the figure offering any reassurance or providing them with any sense of safety, despite what they had been conditioned to believe.

●

The personal records kept by St Michael's are no longer available. However, it is possible to glean some understanding of what life was like for the Sly boys by looking more closely at the way the Home was run.

Two themes recur in almost all oral histories from survivors of the Australian orphanage system throughout the twentieth century. First, they describe a childhood defined by constant hunger. Second, bedtime routines were frightening, and for many were the most difficult thing about adjusting to life inside an institution.

The sleep dormitories at St Michael's were filled with rows of single beds. Whether the Sly boys were permitted to sleep in the same room we cannot know, although in all likelihood they were not. It was a convention at many orphanages to separate siblings, assigning them to different rosters of chores and different dormitories, as this was believed to be the best way to reduce mischief. Because of their recent past, Bedford, Basil and Mervyn would have found adjustment to bedtime routines especially difficult. One commentator who visited the orphanage at the time the boys were living there described it as 'strikingly clean and wholesome', in large part because the nuns placed a good deal of emphasis on bleaching all linens and cottons. The rows of single beds were covered with stark white-on-white coverlets, with white snowflakes stitched across the surface of white bedcovers. They had a striking and eerie resemblance to the Mountmellick embroidery of which the boys' mother had been so fond.

The orphanage compound comprised a very large and imposing two-storey structure, surrounded by eighty-seven acres that had been purchased to make the operation as self-sufficient as possible. Run by a team of nuns headed by the Reverend Mother Michael, routines were designed to cultivate good morals and plenty of fruits and vegetables. One statement by an official representative of the institution, made at the time the boys were living there, claims St Michael's offered 'the best care and attention' and laid further claim that 'not a single child has died here at the Orphanage at Baulkham Hills'. This spoke volumes about the outcomes expected to be derived from good orphanage care – although the claim was intended to sound like a resounding endorsement, it was the equivalent of saying, 'At least we haven't managed to kill any of them.'

The pursuit of good virtue was built into the routines of the Home, but also the fittings and furnishings of the orphanage. At night, in accordance with the prevailing belief that cold fresh air helped prevent disease and eradicate bacteria, the long windows that ran along the ground and first floors of the institution were not permitted to be closed. This surely served to traumatise eight-year-old Bedford in particular. Although every window was covered with a wire panel screwed tightly in place, this would have offered little comfort to Bedford. He had been tormented with fear by the notion that strange invaders floated into his home through the windows and walked around in his family's shoes at night.

The presence of the wire at St Michael's symbolises the hypocrisies inherent to the institution. Its mission statement may have spoken with nobility, grace and glory about God's protection of children, but in reality the boys were inmates. A 1903 newspaper article on the orphanage noted that the wire was 'used to protect against nocturnal adventurers'. While perhaps the Sly boys believed the wire was there to keep out the terrifying shapes that had tormented their parents, in truth it was only there to keep the boys of St Michael's locked in. Doors had locks in St Michael's, but only from the outside. Indeed, once the boys were locked in not even the nuns slept under the same roof. Sisters of the order lived in their own separate house – a small and very basic cottage.

When St Michael's opened in 1903, forty-eight children resided there. The numbers would rise to around eighty some ten years later. By February 1905, fifty-five orphans were registered under the care of the Home. They were expected to attend classes, clean the facility, eat meals, and work under the instruction of the Sisters.

While we cannot know what level of compassion or warmth the Sisters exhibited to these children, for Bedford, Basil and Mervyn the women came to represent their only adult attachment figures. There are fragments of evidence that suggest compassion did exist at St Michael's, at least among some of the nuns. For example, at the outset of World War I about fifty ex-St Michael's boys returned to farewell the nuns in the same way that sons farewelled their mothers. This was the same cohort of boys with whom Bedford, Basil and Mervyn had passed through St Michael's.

The decision to allow Mervyn into St Michael's could also be interpreted as an act of compassion. The institution did not typically take boys as young as four, because child residents were expected to be independent and ready to submit to the regime of cleaning, work and prayer. The age of five years was considered old enough for a child to assume these respons-ibilities. It was a rule that the institution strictly enforced because the demand for residential placements was so high. Based on the records available, it appears that Mervyn Sly was the youngest child ever to be accepted by St Michael's in the roughly seventy-year history of its operation.

Two interpretations might be brought to bear in divining the impact of this decision on a four-year-old boy. On one hand it may have exposed Mervyn to strict authoritarian figures who exhibited low levels of warmth and security, which would have been woefully inappropriate for the needs of any small child. However, an alternative interpretation is also possible. Mervyn was given a gift that birth order had denied his two older brothers. In many families where parental neglect and/or abuse is a factor, older siblings often play a unique role by exhibiting an extraordinary empathy and ability to care for younger siblings. Unlike Bedford and Basil, who had lost the two older figures who represented the key attachment figures for the provision of love and security, Mervyn was still flanked by the two people who had represented stability and with whom he spent most of his time: Bedford and Basil.

Life at St Michael's was lean. At the annual general meeting, the Church financially audited the orphanage with an invasive level of attention akin to an autopsy. Under instructions from the Church, St Michael's was required to become debt free within a year. Nuns measured everything from bars of soap to portions of bread. Some prior residents have claimed that bread was cut using the measurement of a ruler – not because nuns were concerned about the equity of portions, but for reasons of economy. Nuns spent an awful lot of time darning socks and repairing holes in short pants. Clothing was required to last a long time, and families – if still alive and contributing to the child's upkeep – were expected to buy higher-cost items such as shoes outright. Most children only had one pair of (usually) ill-fitting boots. Shoes were either hand-me-downs or too large, purchased to fit a boy's feet as he grew. While waiting for their feet to grow, children stuffed the toes of shoes with rags.

One journalist claimed that the views from St Michael's were so vast, Sydney was visible in the distance 'wrapt in its pall of cloud and smoke'. While the city may have been visible from the Home, the reverse was not true. Sisters at St Michael's had to work hard to ensure the profile of the orphanage remained high among wealthier city residents. To do this, St Michael's managed a rotation of public relations events including open days, fetes and fundraisers. Alumni were also targeted long after they left, in an attempt to convert gratitude to gratuity. Annual reunions were organised to encourage old boys to contribute to the upkeep of the Home.

Based on the accounts available, such events were happier times for Bedford, Basil and Mervyn. The boys had been living there only a year when Cardinal Moran visited. This was a very important event for the institution, indicating how much the Church valued St Michael's as a flagship financial enterprise. The cardinal blessed work benches and sheds, delivered speeches, spoke to the press and gave interviews. The boys made drums decorated with red ribbons and were permitted to bang them wildly in celebration. It was a great PR success for the Home – until the heavens opened. A storm blew in so quickly that no one was prepared. A huge and unholy surge of wind picked up the marquee that had been specially erected in the yard; it was blown across the ground as if pushed by the devil himself. The sight of nuns and priests tripping over their habits to tether a tumbling rogue tent would form the basis of any good comedy sketch, regardless of the century in which it occurred.

The orphanage environment also provided a kind of cultural continuity for the boys. As a Roman Catholic institution it had a very proud connection to Ireland, with many residents from Irish families. According to all available eyewitness reports, the annual celebration of the homeland appears also to have been a happy time for the children.

Proclaimed as the festival that celebrated the 'magnificent spectacle of the living shamrock', St Patrick's Day was the biggest non-religious celebration in the St Michael's calendar. It involved a number of inter-school festival events held at Moore Park. The orphanages, along with other educational institutions from across the city, created displays, dressed up and marched through the streets draped in green. Children baked cakes, danced and sang songs from a homeland with which they shared a deep sociocultural connection. Emerald-green-clad children walked in procession from the showgrounds at Moore Park through the streets of the eastern suburbs to the city. There were pavilions exhibiting arts and crafts, carvings, knitting, netting and crochet. Competitive sporting events were all held with the celebration of Ireland in mind.

Each Catholic college across Sydney appeared to specialise in certain activities, most likely shaped by the proficiencies of the nun and priest teachers who cared for them. Catholic schools in Lewisham produced beautiful oak frames, wood and chip carvings, freehand drawings and fretwork clocks. The Christian brothers at Waverley, reflecting their beachside location, were known for their woven hammocks and deckchairs. St Martha's, a school for girls, produced exquisite lace and needlework. Prizes were awarded to students for best knitted handbag, best hammock, best woodcarving, best coloured chalks, oil paintings and watercolours. Basil, a proficient plaiter, took along a sample of his straw plaiting to display; he received high commendation for his careful work.

St Patrick's Day was designed to be good fun for the children, but also a mass public relations exercise to promote the importance of Catholic education to the state and its superiority to that of state schools. While the St Michael's children never forgot they were 'the orphanage kids', the festival was a positive event in the lives of the boys. Bedford, Basil and Mervyn participated in it every year of their childhood.

•

The Sly boys had two years together before being separated. For children who had no family, and for whom the Church had assumed legal guardianship, living arrangements followed a set pattern. When boys turned ten, they graduated from St Michael's and were transferred to an institution known as St Vincent's, about seven kilometres away. Locally it was known as the Westmead Boys' Home. Bedford moved to Westmead in 1906 (although no documentation can confirm this with certainty), closely followed by each of his brothers in 1908 and 1910.

St Vincent's produced fast-growing crops including millet, potatoes and a range of other vegetables. Boys learnt farm skills, with great emphasis placed on dairy work. Designed to be an industrial school in a rural setting, St Vincent's offered a range of trade-based training.

Training boys for rural work was believed to deliver multiple socio-economic benefits. Industrial schools were seen as an almost perfect social, economic and morally righteous welfare intervention. From a law-and-order standpoint, it was argued that industrial training provided the structure that wayward boys needed. Those who had been unfortunate enough to be born into bad families were at the greatest risk of juvenile delinquency and antisocial behaviour, or so it was argued. The regimen of learning a trade in an industrial school on the outskirts of Sydney kept these boys away from the corruption and temptation of the inner city and reduced the risk of them being lured into gang activity. The focus on rural work was also a strategic economic move. Those farming regions that were struggling with labour shortages, as young men left small towns in search of better opportunities in the city, turned to the churches and industrial schools for a pipeline of trained and compliant labour.

The Catholic Church spent vast amounts of money on St Vincent's. It included a two-storey warehouse with a covered roof and 150 feet of floor space. Downstairs there was a machining room, print machine, boot factory, washroom and storeroom. Upstairs the boys were taught bookbinding, and another section was designated for tailoring. Eventually, it was argued, the boys could be clothed head to toe in items manufactured within the walls of the Home. One journalist praised the efforts of the institution: 'Members of the society of St Vincent . . . were able to promote the various industries and to train the children in whatever art or industry they might have a special talent for.' It was a goal capable of being achieved by the Church – so long as the imaginative pursuits of the boys were confined to brooms, boots and books.

A few facts are known about the training received by Bedford, Basil and Mervyn. Basil trained in printing and tailoring. Mervyn trained in bookbinding. The records pertaining to Bedford's time at St Vincent's have long been lost, although it is most likely he trained in general farm work at least, as most boys did. In addition to trades, the boys were encouraged to participate in sports, continue with schooling, and undertake arts and crafts. Mervyn learnt to swim, most likely in a local dam, and became a keen and accomplished cricketer. Basil exhibited skills as a weaver and also excelled as a sportsman. The skills he had shown in plaiting developed into a keen interest: weaving the large fan leaves of a widely available native plant – *Livistona australis* (cabbage tree palm) – was a pursuit many boys were encouraged to undertake. The cabbage tree hat was a particularly popular weaving project for boys at the Home at the time.

St Vincent's was a Home, a farm and an industrial training school rolled into one. It also operated with a sensibility that emulated the Home of Hope charity. Making money remained a priority for the Church. Fundraising, in particular the selling of art union tickets, was a major income stream. It was a custom at the time to sell tickets in excess of the value of the prize, but this was brought under scrutiny by the attorney-general's department, which threatened the institution with fraud.

It cannot be known whether physical and emotional abuse featured as part of Bedford, Basil and Mervyn's personal experiences while in the orphanage system. Several homes and industrial schools were identified as possible risks to children at the time. St Michael's and St Vincent's have also been identified by alumni as sites where abuse took place. What is known for sure is that the Sly boys would have experienced an environment in which nurturing and the cultivation of attachment played little role.

What is also known for sure is that the working conditions were difficult at best, downright exploitative at worst. St Vincent's was 'bright with God's sunshine', wrote one journalist, and perhaps this was not hyperbole but a frighteningly accurate description. The poorly ventilated largescale shed where the boys did their trade training would have reached stifling temperatures as the relentlessly hot summer sun baked the tin roof. Ex-residents of St Vincent's have described their treatment and the work they were required to undertake as tantamount to slavery, and the stifling physical environment of the place known – with no tongue in cheek intended – as 'the hell hole'.

While personal records for Bedford, Basil and Mervyn during their time in Catholic institutional care have long since been destroyed, fragments of information can be gleaned from other sources including media, work and personal records. For example, we know that Mervyn maintained a love of the outdoors his whole life. Basil was a resourceful all-rounder. He played rugby, but enjoyed quiet and reflective activities as well, including weaving, plaiting and reading; he also had a love for poetry. When it comes to Bedford, however, a psychological portrait informed by his early experiences remains elusive. It is clear, however, that unlike his two brothers, Bedford simply failed to fit in. Whether this was due to events prior to his entry into orphanage care or as a result of being in care, or both, cannot be known. But we know he was desperately unhappy. We know this because, sometime around the age of fourteen, he ran away, leaving his brothers behind.

14

MAKING ENDS MEET

IN ORDER FOR SOMEONE TO BE FOUND, PEOPLE NEED TO KNOW they are missing. In Bedford's case, no one did. Or if they did know, they did not seem to care. It would remain this way for forty years, until he found his own way home.

After disappearing from the orphanage, Bedford did not surface again for more than a year. He reappeared in August 1912 – in police custody. But he was far from alone in facing criminal charges: new legislation had turned many young boys into criminals.

One of the first acts of parliament made by newly federated Australia introduced compulsory military training. Under the scheme, which had multiple iterations in the *Defence Acts* of 1903, 1909 and 1911, men were conscripted for military training and service from the ages of eighteen to twenty-five, and cadetship training from the ages of fourteen to eighteen. Boys were expected to be industrious during the week by attending either school or by receiving instruction in a trade, and on the weekends were required to march around parade grounds. Military researcher Dr Craig Stockings notes that the call-up to training, even among very young boys, was considered important as 'a kind of apprenticeship to the adult army' and because there was 'widespread community concern about the degeneracy of youth'. For young men living in western Sydney, regular military training was scheduled to occur every weekend at the Parramatta parade ground. It was a wide open space with a few barrack buildings that offered the boys little in the form of proper training other than marching and exercising. About sixty young men failed to show – Bedford was one of them.

Although Bedford's failure to attend training was not particularly unusual, as many young men 'dodged parade', the circumstances surrounding his failure were. Once caught and facing the fear of gaol time, most boys showed contrition and admitted guilt. Their repentance was looked on favourably by the judge, and they were usually sentenced to nothing more than additional service. In other cases, fathers appeared in court to plead on behalf of their boys. One father, for example, sought exemption because his son suffered from a nervous tension. Another said his son was so feeble-minded he could not speak. A third father begged; his boy had been struck with a deadly case of measles, he said, and months later was still convalescing. Many boys from poor families said they could not afford the train fares to the Parramatta parade ground.

Bedford's situation was more dire. He had no one to advocate for him. He was barely fifteen and had been homeless for a year, if not longer. Unlike the other boys who may have only missed a parade here or there, Bedford had not shown up for eighteen months straight. 'I have no home,' he said in court. 'I cannot attend training on Saturday because I earn more money on a Saturday than on other days.' Records do not indicate where Bedford was working. What is most likely is that he was not working but feared getting into further trouble if he admitted to having no legal means of support. Vagrancy was a conviction that could attract gaol time.

The innocence of a teenage boy, barely fifteen and completely alone in court, elicited no sympathy from the judge. He ordered an already destitute boy to pay a fine of eleven shillings, and sentenced him to twenty hours in custody. At the time Bedford had the distinctively thin and gangly physique of an unsure young man, clearly not yet ready to assume the mantle of adulthood – but somehow the state had deemed him ready to bear the label of criminal. On his release from prison, Bedford was returned to the homelessness and poverty that had led him to being locked up in the first place.

Bedford disappeared again, this time for eight years. He resurfaced in 1920 with a charge of vagrancy in Sydney

Central Police Court. While we cannot know how much time he had spent wandering in the urban wilderness, we know that he was dishevelled and beggarly when he was found.

By the 1920s, Australian society had a little more understanding about trauma than at the time of the Newtown Tragedy, but not much. Soldiers who had survived the trench warfare terrors of World War I had returned with debilitating post-traumatic stress disorder (a diagnosis that would not be in official use until 1980). In seeking to respond to the widespread crisis, medical experts had begun to explore and expand the categories used to describe mental stress and psychological injury. There was a growing awareness that when an individual experiences terrible fear, they may suffer anxiety, dissociation, detachment and a range of other physical symptoms for a long period after the source of the fear has gone. In a 1916 paper Dr W. Ernest Jones, an Australian pioneer of trauma practice, notes, 'It is already very obvious that the war will bring us many cases of little understood nervous and mental affection, not only where a definite wound has been received, but in many cases where nothing of the sort appears.' While there was a growing recognition of the bleak prognosis for those with profound psychological trauma, or what a British doctor in 1914 had dubbed 'shell shock', both the health system and families struggled to cope with how to support sufferers. There was an epidemic of homelessness among returned servicemen who failed to reintegrate and return to the homes and jobs they had prior to war. Veterans of the war had been made veterans of the road by the souvenir of trauma they carried.

Shell shock and other symptoms of panic and depression were considered to be conditions exclusive to soldiers. Society was still a long way from understanding the complex trauma that Bedford undoubtedly carried.

•

The next records available on Bedford date from 1928. Now thirty-two, he travelled to one of the most remote places in the country, to a point on the Australian map as far as land transport could carry him from Sydney. He also picked a destination where he did not know a living soul.

Bedford's journey has all the epic vestiges of an idealised swaggie adventure. He travelled with a bed-roll roped to his back. His coat was crumpled by the damp. His sagging felt hat was tipped low and to one side, shading one eye from the sun while the other eye remained firmly fixed on the road ahead.

The Trans-Australian Railway connected South Australia to the far west. Known as the 'tea and sugar', the train travelled from Port Augusta to Kalgoorlie across the Nullarbor plain. Colloquially the 'tea and sugar' was so named because the train provided more than supplies: it also gave comfort and care to those in remote areas. The train offered the warmth and hospitality of a rolling country town. It is not clear how Bedford got from Sydney to South Australia, but he stowed away on the train at Port Augusta and miraculously slipped off at Kalgoorlie undetected. It was a testament to the man's ingenuity: carriages were accessed at every point along the route to unload vital supplies.

Unlike most train routes, the tea and sugar did not really have stations, as there were no local towns. The train simply stopped at designated points in the middle of the desert. There it would unload, and locals could jump on the carriages to shop or perhaps collect their pay. It was a rolling pay office for the railway; it was also a post office, a bakery, a butcher and a grocer for the workers and their families who lived along the line. Sometimes it contained a carriage fitted out as a child health clinic; at others a carriage functioned as a makeshift movie theatre with projectionist and seats. The butcher's car was set up not just to transport the meat but for butchering as well. The tea and sugar carried the only fresh water available across the 1700 kilometres of its passage through the desert. Hundreds of workers and their families jumped on and off its carriages during the course of its long voyage.

Did Bedford crouch between the drums of water being freighted west? Did he stand and sway between animal carcasses swinging from hooks in the coolroom? Or did he do what some swaggies claimed to have done to avoid detection when riding the rails, and crawl inside a coffin box because station guards never searched them?

When Bedford disembarked in Kalgoorlie, it was not what he had expected. But he made do, as he always had. For about three months he lived even rougher than he had on the streets and in public parks in Sydney. His appearance became more unkempt. His skin became dry and dusty, desiccated by the arid air. His hair grew wild and greasy.

Housewives eventually began to complain to the authorities about a long-haired ghoulish bushie with powdery complexion and pale blue eyes who always seemed to be hanging around. When hunger overwhelmed him, he begged for food at their doors. It was as if all the distance and years between Watkin Street and Kalgoorlie meant nothing. Some part of Bedford still seemed to be eight years old, still living in Newtown, still begging the neighbours for scraps of bread. Athough in Kalgoorlie he sometimes offered to chop wood in return for food.

For a while the police seemed content to turn a blind eye – until Bedford was caught trying the back door of a local home. When police found him, he spoke plainly about what he was doing. During the day he scavenged in town, while at night he retreated to an open cutting near the Devon Consols Mine. The goldmining operation had been abandoned the previous year, and the site was a ghost town.

Bedford used an innocent and unvarnished turn of phrase to explain his situation to the judge: 'I came to South Australia but I do not like mining work. I want to work on a farm.' If Bedford had selected Kalgoorlie as a place to call home, it was an odd place to look for farm work. Much of the land was barren of agriculture, and since the late nineteenth century the area had maintained a national profile as a gold town, and for the timber and firewood train line that passed through it. Surely this would have been known to Bedford, given his knowledge of the tea and sugar train journey. One constable offered his impression of how Bedford lived: 'He wandered around the country from place to place with no particular object in view.'

It is possible that Bedford had chosen this isolated place to be his ideal home. There were no walls and no roof, yet the abandoned goldmine burrow offered more protection than what he had become accustomed to. There were no doors, and certainly none with locks only on the outside. There were no windows with prison-like grilles to block the light. Lying out in the darkness, he could gaze at the milky dustings of stars that glowed softly and offered the certainty of a light that never dims. His own celestial body stretched atop a chaff-bag bed, there was no one to bother him, and he bothered no one. He was free to be himself.

Only six photographs of Bedford were ever taken, and all were by police photographers. Three were taken in the 1930s, and a further three a decade later. Over the course of ten years, great changes wrote their story on the surface of his skin. His face became weathered by dirt and exposure; his hair became an oily snarl. What did not change was his expression. His mouth still gaped a little and turned down at the corners. His forehead was heavily wrinkled, and his eyes seemed intensely sad – the eyes of a lost child. Bedford still looked every bit the boy in the grip of witnessing a tragedy. It is as if he was emotionally frozen in time.

In addition to the mug shots, processing forms required officers to note further identifying information such as 'any descriptive marks including scars, tattoo marks, physical deformities and other peculiarities'. An officer entered 'NIL' because police could not find a mark on him.

But there were marks.

We now know that trauma alters brainwave patterns. Bessel van der Kolk, MD, neuroscientist and Professor of Psychiatry at Boston University Medical School, is one of the leading international experts on trauma and has highlighted that trauma alters not just the brain, but the body. Trauma shapes behaviour and identity, and our reality. It shapes how we act, who we are, and what we feel and see when we experience the world. Trauma creates mental and emotional habits and physiological responses that make the search for safety paramount. Early childhood trauma, particularly exposure to abuse and neglect, not only increases a person's chance of becoming homeless but also their likelihood of establishing a pattern of homelessness early in life, most commonly in the teenage years. Bedford certainly had marks and scars, just none that could be seen.

Arrested for vagrancy out at the goldmine, Bedford was placed in the Kalgoorlie lock-up. While this is an experience that no one would care for, Bedford disliked it more than most. No record remains to explain how he managed to engineer it, but he escaped. Rather than retreat to his gold-mine, he started walking, and just kept going.

While a fugitive from one vagrancy charge, he was arrested as a vagrant again at an even smaller town, Kurrawang, about twenty kilometres south of Kalgoorlie. He was remanded for eight days on a further charge of escaping from legal custody. In the end, a Kalgoorlie magistrate simply let him walk. At the time this was considered the most effective way of dealing with a ne'er-do-well like Bedford. His problems were believed to be innate; it was considered best just to move him on.

After his release from prison, he walked for three years. He walked so far, he ended up back in Sydney.

•

Many economic historians consider 1932 to be the most difficult year of the Great Depression in Sydney. The year was also a turning point for Bedford – for the worse.

In the 1930s, a large tract of land known as Carss Bush Park was about seventeen kilometres from the CBD. Comprising a mix of wild dense bush and recreational park, it embodied the economic extremes of life in Sydney during the Depression. On one hand there was mass poverty, and many in the city were unemployed and living rough. Natural spaces like Carss Park and the shallow caves of the coastline were converted by the city's poorest into shantytowns. Families brought all of their worldly possessions and chose to squat in the most Sydney of ways, choosing places that were iconic to the city: the harbour foreshore and the bush. Sheltered by the cliffs overhanging the harbour, families set up bassinets, bookshelves and beds to create little studio apartments by the sea. With only minimal social welfare (food ration cards) and no family to support him, Bedford settled on his own piece of nature's real estate: Carss Park.

At the same time, a burgeoning middle class was also claiming natural areas, but for recreational use. For those families lucky enough to have a breadwinner still in employment, life went on almost undisturbed by the poverty surrounding them.

Bordering the newly forming suburb of Blakehurst on one side and Kogarah Bay on the other, Carss Park attracted many local families seeking to explore the raw beauty of Sydney. While Bedford slept, cocooned and protected in his little forest oasis, nearby the park was being covered in landfill so it might be flattened for more affluent families to stroll with their small children. Paths were constructed to encourage nature walks. During winter, families visited to fell trees for firewood; in summer, the same families came to dump their grass clippings from the mowed lawns of the expanding suburban development. As one local council engineer at the time noted of the Carss bushland area, it allowed families to 'view beauties of nature which at present pass unobserved'.

On an afternoon in June 1933, one local family was strolling through the bush when they got to see more naked beauty than they had bargained for. Passing through a dense part of the forest, the parents allowed their children to run ahead and explore the next pocket of raw and untamed wilderness. Just when they were out of sight of their parents, a child was heard to shriek. The parents rushed forward. They found

Bedford bent over, bush and gumnuts on display, performing his morning ablutions with a dirty rag and a billy of water.

The shocked parents marched straight to the police station where they reported the incident. It culminated in a serious charge. A conviction of vagrancy alone could attract gaol time, but with the much more sordid charge of indecency there was a risk of significant gaol time. When police came looking for Bedford, he ran. He had good reason to.

Bedford would not have been defined as the survivor of trauma and perhaps in need of proper mental health care. According to the authorities of the time he was a malingerer, and they would not have been interested in exploring alternative explanations such as poverty or mental illness. Society had deemed Bedford a monster – and there was little recognition that society may have played some role in his creation.

As Bedford ran from the police, he threw a bag into the bushes. This added to their suspicion that they were dealing with a calculating criminal in the act of trying to destroy evidence.

After Bedford was taken to await trial at Kogarah court, police took an inventory of his possessions. The task was not onerous: with the exception of the mysterious bag he had piffed into the dense scrub, he was wearing everything he owned. It was a pitiful inventory: three pairs of trousers, three shirts, two vests (one suit waistcoat style, one knitted), a jacket and two hats (both of which he was wearing).

Perhaps compared to any other criminal charge at the time, vagrancy offered judges the greatest latitude with regard to sentencing. And the perceived moral measure of the man was seemingly the most important factor in these judgements. Alex Steel, a professor of law at the University of New South Wales, argues that while vagrancy statutes have a law-and-order function they have also historically operated as instruments of power rather than protection for the community. As Steel notes, 'it is also possible to see the laws as a reaction to moral panics about undesirables'.

On that morning in June 1933, a magistrate was assigned to Bedford's case. Herbert H. Macdougal was well known for serving up both sentence and sermon, and he had vagrants firmly in his sights.

To those he saw as deserving, he showed mercy. In the previous year, his only official question for one accused vagrant was, 'Will you stop if I let you go?' To the arresting police waiting in the wings, Macdougal simply said, 'And do see if you can get that poor beggar a feed.' When nineteen-year-old Norman Abbott appeared before Macdougal because he was found to be taking food relief from police with falsified documentation, he could have been charged with fraud or theft as well as vagrancy. Macdougal showed a similar level of mercy. Rather than doling out a sentence of hard labour in gaol, he seemed visibly shaken by the boy's circumstances. 'I'm sure I don't want to send this boy to gaol. Is there no one to take charge of him?' Macdougal directed the police to liaise with a charity organisation, the Prisoners Aid Society, to see if they could provide employment assistance. In 1930, Macdougal had seemed eager to offer compassion to another accused vagrant: 'I am not going to punish men who are out of work in these hard times. The country is going through a serious period and many men are out of work who are only prepared to do it.'

Then there were the other times, when Macdougal showed an immense level of cruelty in his judgements. He used vagrancy charges, in particular, as a moral platform from which to deliver soapbox sermons. He would not tolerate perversion, and he deemed many people to be perverts.

Only two years before, an Anglo woman named Olive Hill was found to be living with a Chinese man, a market gardener in Manly. Local police believed that no white woman could live willingly with a Chinese man but were unable to find any evidence to sustain a criminal charge against him. While the man tended to the garden and sold vegetables, Olive tended to the house. Police wanted to charge her with soliciting, but there was no evidence of that activity either. Instead, they charged her with vagrancy because she was unmarried and could not possibly be living as a de facto wife to a Chinese man. Rather than being intimidated by the proceedings, Olive asked for Macdougal's permission to marry. This only enraged the magistrate, and his judgement appears to have little to do with vagrancy. 'If they think I am going to be a party to a white woman marrying a Chinaman they will find I am not. I would not dream of being party to such a thing. I hope this White Australia never comes down to such a state of affairs as that. I sentence her to four months' hard labour.'

A year later, Macdougal expressed similar wrath towards another white woman. Violet Young was also found to be living in sin with a Chinese man. The couple had seven children together out of wedlock. Macdougal again used the charge of vagrancy with great latitude. He very bluntly confessed his determination to teach Violet a lesson. Speaking to her directly, he said, 'You understand what this means, don't you? I'll have to send you to gaol . . . Why do you go with these Chinese?'

Even by 1930s standards of morality and respectability, and even for a magistrate whose job was to pass judgement, Macdougal was opinionated and didactic. He had a reputation for applying sentencing standards far beyond the norm. At one point, more of his sentences were overturned on appeal than upheld.

About to appear before a judge capable of showing immense kindness to one homeless person but an equal level of cruelty towards the next, Bedford was in a vulnerable position indeed.

When it came to homelessness, certain factors immediately attracted the attention of judges. If homeless people were found with dice or a deck of cards, this meant they were street swindlers, cheats and gamblers. If they possessed property that appeared new or could not be explained, this was clear evidence of theft. One item found with Bedford's possessions caught Macdougal's attention.

When police eventually found the bag that Bedford had suspiciously discarded, at first they were surprised to see it only contained clothes. As they sorted through the items, they put one aside to bring to the attention of the magistrate: a pair of ladies' long satin opera gloves with a glossy white sheen. When police pressed Bedford to admit he had stolen them, he emphatically refused. His explanation was straightforward and practical; the gloves were handy, he said, because he used them on cold nights when he was sleeping on rocks. This description is vivid, conjuring mental images of a vagrant curled beneath eucalyptus trees like an adorable Snugglepot, his gloved hands formed into a luxuriously soft pillow.

But Macdougal was infuriated, always quick to take the moral measure of those who appeared in court before him. He viewed Bedford's explanation as defiant and belligerent.

Bedford was sentenced to six months' hard labour for obscenity, and three months' imprisonment for stolen goods. It was a severe penalty, even for the time, and the longest sentence Bedford had ever been given. He appealed. The appellate judge confirmed the conviction to be appropriate; however, he instructed that the sentences would be served concurrently. Bedford was sent to a bigger gaol in Bathurst.

This was not the only time he challenged the charges or the verdicts against him. He appealed some sentences but was rarely successful. Between 1932 and 1933, he faced six convictions and served five terms in prison, emerging from charges in Central Sydney, North Sydney, Burwood and Kogarah.

On his release from Bathurst prison, Bedford disappeared for yet another eight years.

•

In 1941, Bedford materialised in Newcastle, emerging from the fog suspended across the saltwater lagoon known as Lake Macquarie. Police found him with a new towel, which they believed could not possibly be the property of such a destitute and dishevelled-looking man. He was charged with theft and vagrancy. However, a different magistrate (Mr C. G. Carr-Boyd) in a different city produced a different result. He showed Bedford mercy, dismissing the charges as unfounded and releasing him. However, he still did not avoid a public shaming: the magistrate reprimanded him for his slovenly lifestyle.

From Newcastle, Bedford travelled to Liverpool in far-west Sydney, then to Hornsby in far-north Sydney. He was charged with failing to enlist during World War II, as required by the *Defence Act*. Vagrancy charges soon followed, at Katoomba, Liverpool and Goulburn.

Bedford remained homeless for the next fourteen years. He had no contact with any family members. Indeed, it appears that after he ran from the orphanage, he just kept running. If any family ever went to look for him, they did not find him. While some might describe his situation as 'living on the streets', in truth the streets rarely had anything to do with his lifestyle. His preference was always to make homes in quiet parks, isolated places on the fringe of the city or wide-open remote spaces.

From the mid-1940s, Bedford's life was propelled forward with an almost circular motion. His existence began to turn in on itself.

In 1946, he surfaced in his mother's home town of Goulburn, though it was not to reunite with family. There is no doubt that he would have understood the connection his mother, uncle and grandfather had to the place. However, his connection to family members who still lived there, including first cousins, had been severed more than forty years before.

When police picked him up for living in an abandoned building at the racecourse, he had not had a haircut for five years (the last having been given to him by a Newcastle policeman). 'He has been living in filthy conditions. He has eked out an existence by demanding food from residents . . . but otherwise his behaviour has been generally good,' said one Goulburn police officer. The magistrate handed down a sentence of three months' gaol time. Thirty-five shillings was found wrapped in a dirty strip of paper in Bedford's pocket, but there is no evidence he was interested in spending any of it.

After his release from Goulburn gaol, Bedford's life followed the pattern it always had. As soon as he was free, he took off, away from the gaol as fast as he could go on foot. Next he turned up in Cootamundra, where he again served a one-month gaol sentence.

For the next few years Bedford stayed close to the Cootamundra train line, travelling back and forth between Junee, Illabo and Cootamundra. He walked and camped, and was caught. He walked and camped, and was caught again. Across his police files, the term 'insufficient lawful means of support' was used over and over. It was standard police terminology to describe a vagrancy charge in this way, but these words also poignantly describe the lonely man's situation. Genuine and ongoing support was what Bedford had needed his whole life, but never received.

In 1950, Bedford went bush again. He did not know it at the time but he was, with every step, heading closer to home.

Bedford took his last-ever train trip on a line incorporating an unusual architectural design: the physical representation of a loop. The rail line between Cootamundra and Junee is unique, as it includes a remarkable and somewhat eccentric feature known as the Bethungra Spiral. Between the two remote towns lies a mountain impassable to trains using conventional rail building approaches. They could not go over or under it, so the only option was to build a rail spiral. There are very few in the world. On the Bethungra Spiral, the train moves forward but at the same time is always travelling backwards. As the train coils around the mountain, the traveller is confronted with visions of the track already travelled. A spiral is, in fact, the only way to cross a treacherously steep mountain safely. In engineering terms, spirals mean safety. Some people might characterise trauma in the same way. By revisiting the past, a trauma survivor might hope to access a greater level of understanding and insight that will help them move forward.

When imagining Bedford's life in the bush, it is easy to colour it with nostalgic motifs reminiscent of 'Waltzing Matilda'. It is hard not to romanticise the freedom of a swagman. Bedford built makeshift homes. He used long branches of gum trees as tent props. He fashioned a roof from an old canvas tarp. He boiled tea in a billy with a gumleaf thrown in for flavour. He bunked down at night with the crackling of a low fire to keep him company. He moved often; he knew that lingering meant being noticed and soon being defined a nuisance. He stayed free by continually moving.

In either 1952 or 1953, Bedford emerged from the wilderness. He finally got to work on a farm, a desire he had expressed many years before to a Kalgoorlie magistrate. Bedford worked as a labourer at a large station, Tilbaroo, just outside of Illabo. It is not known how this arrangement began – perhaps he came knocking on the door to beg for food. It was a habit that had defined his life.

Bedford seemed to tick through the day with a sense of habit: he rose at dawn, ate about the same time every day, but there was still little order to the man. He wore a dishevelled and holey suit and canvas shoes, as he always had. He did not discuss his past. He developed a friendship with a station hand, Tommy Smith. Tommy was kind to him, though he had little understanding of the strange man who had blown into town kicking up dust. Tommy had no reason to be kind to Bedford and nothing to gain from it. He was kind because he wanted to be.

It was in this place that Bedford finally found home.

•

When Bedford went missing for the last time, it was the middle of summer. Tommy's words expressed a sadness and pity for the eccentric man in his fifties who, in reality, he barely knew. 'I worried for him,' Tommy said. 'He did not come for lunch.' Tommy added, 'I saw him at about 9am . . . He did not return to my place for his midday meal which was his usual custom.'

Tommy checked the sheds and the wood chop. He checked the shaded areas of the farm. He thought the old man might have retreated there, like the dogs did on a hot day. Bedford had done it before.

It was when Tommy began walking back up to the homestead that he stumbled upon the old man.

Bedford was flat on his back, face up in the garden just near the house. His feet were slightly apart, his eyes open and cast towards the heavens.

Bedford died in that bleached light for which the Australian outback is known, where the air close to the Earth's dry crust shimmers and distorts to make the horizon look like a mirage. Bedford's skin was heavily blistered by the time Tommy discovered him; he had obviously been in the same position for the better part of the day.

Although the symbolic significance of the scene would have meant nothing to the kindly station hand, its similarity to the event that had been so pivotal to Bedford's life cannot be overlooked. His body was posed in a way that eerily resembled the body of his mother. A garden hose was lying on him, awkwardly positioned like a long transverse cut across his abdomen. When Tommy found him at the end of the working day, the hose was gushing with the intensity of a severed artery. A deep pool had formed around his body, in the manner of a puddle of blood.

Tommy ran to get help. He stopped at the edge of the homestead yard and motioned frantically to catch the attention of a fellow worker across the field.

The two men lifted Bedford up and out of the water. They carried him into the shade of the verandah.

Those on the property knew him as Jack. When police became involved, his fingerprints were taken and sent to Sydney. Given his long criminal record, authorities quickly identified him.

Not much else could be done. No one at the property knew anything of his family history. As a result, his death certificate contains very little personal information. In the sections marked 'Mother' and 'Father', there is only a series of dashes and empty space.

The post-mortem calculated many facts about the cause and manner of death. He died midmorning. He died of a heart attack. The hose and the running water that surrounded him seemed unusual, but were quickly explained by Tommy. When thirsty, Bedford would never drink from a canteen or go to the homestead to ask for a glass of water. His preference was to drink from the end of the garden hose at the corner of the property.

Bedford had never discussed his past, though Tommy recalled him once mentioning he was Catholic. McCarthy, the owner at Tilbaroo, assumed responsibility for the burial expenses and organised an unmarked plot in the Catholic section of the Illabo cemetery. For many people this was preferable to the shame of a pauper's funeral, in which bodies were buried together in a manner deemed cheapest by the state.

Although Bedford's life could not have been more different from his father's, their deaths were similar in a number of ways. After death there is a gathering. People come together to talk about the deceased and share memories of them. This happened for Bedford, but like most of the events in his life it assumed a strange form. Neither Alicks Sly nor Bedford had a funeral service, but both had an autopsy. In the place of a wake attended by family, each had a coronial inquest held in their honour. People gathered to share reminiscences about the deceased in order to give evidence, not grieve. To this day, Bedford lies in an unmarked grave. Like father, like son.

One fact was passed over as unimportant by everyone involved. This is not surprising, as it would have held no significance to anyone other than Bedford.

The eldest son of Alicks and Ellie Sly died at the same time of day as his parents, midmorning, on the anniversary of their deaths, 12 January 1955.

For Bedford, the struggle to make ends meet was over. The loop of trauma that had defined much of his life quietly closed. He may have died alone, but he died with his face finally turned away from the darkness. As he lay staring into the sky, the blinding sunlight surely would not have bothered him because he was leaving for the last time. He would no longer need to bear the heavy weight of the swag across his body, or dip his hat to shield his eyes from the glare.

Bedford's pilgrimage that day would have felt like the lightest journey of all, because he was heading home. And with the amniotic softness of warm water on his skin, he must surely have felt like he was being born.

15

A HAPPY DEATH

In 1904 when Uncle J. J. O'Leary arranged for the placement of the three boys into a Catholic institution, he must
have reassured himself that while he may not have been
providing for their material life, he was ensuring their souls
would be saved. This decision altered the trajectory of their
lives. Though he did not realise it at the time, J. J.'s life would
be altered too.

J. J. believed that the spiritual teachings and strict discipline
of the orphanage would produce good Catholics and good
men. In the case of Basil Sly, both would be true.

Basil's life presents a somewhat alternative view of
orphanage history. Many who experienced the orphanage
system in Australia describe sadness and torment, cold treatment and abuse. Some move forward by trying to forget,

often struggling to do so. Some reject the religion in which they were raised, forever associating it with the institutions that made their lives miserable. From the evidence available, this is not how Basil felt.

He attended the annual reunions and fetes of St Vincent's and St Michael's, and became a regular benefactor to the Home. While he was a teenager and still earning very little as a farmhand, Basil's donations amounted to a few shillings. When he began working as an adult, his donations scaled up to pounds. He was the only one of the three Sly brothers to make donations to the Home. Uncle J. J. also never made any direct contribution to the upkeep of the boys or the Home.

After leaving St Vincent's, Basil went to work at a farm at Camden called The Oaks, about seventy kilometres south-west of Sydney. Although he had no real interest in farm life, or in working with dairy cows, he appreciated the sense of family and community that the opportunity afforded him. Basil was sent there as an adolescent and is documented as still living there in 1917. During this time he attended social evenings organised by the Red Cross to fundraise for the war, held in the School of Arts building. Locals gathered to waltz, play euchre, and perform plays and skits written about country life and family. The local school choir sang. Farmers jigged to the heel-and-toe polka. Wives baked cakes and sweets. The vicar shared his favourite limericks.

Recitations known as bush scribblers were a favoured entertainment of these evenings. The performance scribbler is a unique combination of comedy, verse and slang, celebrating but also lampooning the Australian identity. One Camden local got up to perform a poem called 'Not Too Bad' by popular turn-of-the-century bush poet Thomas E. Spencer; written in slang sometimes referred to as 'dingo lingo', it seeks to capture not just the phrasing but also the flat phonetics of the Australian accent. Recitations of C. J. Dennis were also popular. *The Songs of a Sentimental Bloke* had been published in one volume only two years before, and country families adored the quaint simplicity and hilarity of the courtship and settling down of Bill and Doreen. The verse novel had been serialised in *The Bulletin* for years and was always a crowd favourite at social evenings in the district.

Basil selected a much more ambitious and dignified ballad for his recitation. While 'Clancy of the Overflow' had always been popular with country people because it celebrates the rough freedom of rural life and the yearning of city men for where 'the bush hath friends to meet him', Basil had a fondness for another of Banjo Paterson's works. Basil was fascinated by the tale of heroic horsemanship set in the glorious Snowy Mountains, and it is easy to imagine that the adrenalin of the poem attracted the young man. 'The Man from Snowy River' gathers momentum and gallops like brumbies when passionately read aloud. But it is also easy to imagine that the story appealed to young Basil because it celebrates the efforts of an ordinary man, a nobody, who triumphs through honest hard work and determination alone. It is a long poem, and Basil had memorised every word. He delivered it like a song. For his efforts, he won a fruitcake donated by local woman Mrs Dunk.

Basil stayed at the farm until the end of World War I and then moved out past Goulburn for a while. This was not because he had connections to extended family there – Basil had no family with the exception of his brother Mervyn. He moved out there to work on a farm in the small town of Pomeroy. His love of poetry blossomed. He attended fundraising socials, held in the parlours of private residences, and performed his recitations there too.

By the end of the 1920s, it was becoming harder for Basil to find work in the area. He was also getting older. He returned to the city to apply the trade in which he had been trained: printing. He worked as a printer for a while, and also as a barman. By the 1930s he had found work at the Lyceum Theatre as a doorman and usher.

In 1930, at thirty-three, Basil met and married the love of his life, Bondi girl Ellen Kathleen Lonergan. They married in the most iconic Catholic church in all of Sydney, St Mary's Cathedral.

•

In the same year that Basil was experiencing one of the happiest times of his life, another member of the Sly family was wandering the streets of Randwick alone and frightened. Without knowing it, the two men were only a few streets from each other.

Police stopped the man because they assumed he was a drunk vagrant. He was dishevelled and seemed confused; he couldn't provide details like his home address. Officers assumed he was inebriated, but there was no smell of alcohol on his breath or his clothes. He had clearly been living rough, though, as police detected the distinctively ashy and sour smell of one who has been living on the street. After briefly questioning him, the police reconsidered their assumptions: he was not drunk but senile. They picked him up, put him in the police van and dropped him at the local Catholic charity run by an order called the Little Sisters of the Poor.

The Little Sisters had opened a Home in Randwick in 1887 with a very special religious calling in mind. The order specifically committed to the care of elderly people who were both destitute and alone in the world. As part of the admissions procedure, the wandering man was required to declare and surrender any possessions. A senior sister recorded these details in a columned admissions book. It was not a long entry: three shirts, one pair of trousers, two singlets and one pair of pyjamas. The man was confused about other details, but he could remember his name: J. J. O'Leary.

While more detailed records outlining the circumstances of J. J.'s admittance to the Home have long since been destroyed, it is likely that the police negotiated with the Catholic nuns. The Little Sisters were known to take the absolutely desperate, even criminals. The order's community in Adelaide, for example, housed abortionist Annie Vogg; they agreed to have her live out her remaining years there, so she would not go to prison. The state conceded – although authorities emphasised that if Annie ever tried to leave, she would be sent straight to gaol. Annie had committed acts that both the state and the

Church considered abhorrent, yet the Church took her in. The Little Sisters said they were acting in deliverance of a holy commitment: every Catholic should be able to die in a state of grace with their moral ledger balanced before meeting the Lord. Some Catholics refer to this as a happy death.

In the early twentieth century, the Little Sisters played an important spiritual role for poverty-stricken Catholics who were without family. The order provided a place for them to be loved and cared for while seeking absolution before the hour of death came. According to the 1930s mission statement of the Little Sisters, they cared for those suffering 'the livery of old age and poverty' and 'feebleness' to 'give them time to occupy themselves with the spiritual interests of their souls and thus prepare them for a happy death'. The order also played a vital social welfare role in Sydney because it provided an exclusively aged-care facility for the poor – a rarity at the time.

Almost thirty years after the deaths of his sister and brother-in-law, and after J. J. had relinquished his niece to adoption and nephews to the Catholic Church, he was now utterly alone. As a Senior Sister of the Order described it: 'John was typical of those who sought admission to the Home in those years before pensions would allow them to support themselves.'

•

Although Basil no doubt carried traumatic memories, loneliness and loss from childhood, he also built a beautiful life for himself and his wife during the 1930s. The elements of tragedy were still there but did not overshadow him, and he redefined them with moments of light. The love of Basil's life shared his mother's name, Ellen, and they gave it to one of their daughters as a middle name. They lived in a modest but cosy home in Randwick.

Basil had eight happy years. The Sly family of Basil, Ellen, Elizabeth and Valma lived just a few streets from Bondi Beach. They also lived only a few streets from where J. J. was being cared for by the Little Sisters of the Poor. Basil, however, knew nothing about this and had nothing to do with it.

J. J. and Basil remained the most devout and observant Roman Catholics in the family. Within a few short years, both men faced one of the most important milestones for any Catholic: the achievement of a happy death.

For Basil, this moment came in 1938. In the winter of that year, Sydney was struck down with what was generically described as an epidemic of pneumonia. Along with hundreds of residents, Basil's wife fell ill. Ellen Kathleen fought the illness for weeks before surrendering to it. She died on 30 August 1938 at St Vincent's Private Hospital. The prolonged nature of her illness had allowed her to participate in the most precious of Catholic rituals: the sacrament of the dying. Her death was tragic – she was young and left behind two little children. Her death was also beautiful – she died in the state of grace Roman Catholics pray for their entire lives.

Basil lived for another thirty-six years but never remarried. He raised his two daughters alone, despite immense pressure from doctors, friends and extended family to relinquish them for adoption. His connection to the Catholic orphanage in which he was raised supplied him with a loyal and lifelong friend through these difficult years. Tom Purcell was a fellow alumnus who had worked hard to become a solicitor. He assisted Basil in purchasing the only house he would ever own.

While Ellen lay dying, so too did Basil's estranged uncle. J. J.'s death, however, dragged on for years. It also presented a spiritual conundrum to those seeking to assist the man in achieving a state of Catholic grace.

J. J. spent his last few years with very little knowledge of who or where he was. He still wandered, but now it was through the seven acres bordering Centennial Park that constituted the Little Sisters compound.

In the last stage of his life, J. J. was bedridden. He suffered heart trouble as well as dementia.

As his death drew closer, Sister Clotilde nursed him physically but there was little she could do to help him mentally or metaphysically. At seventy-two, J. J. died without the spiritual closure most Roman Catholics seek. The rosary was placed in his hands, in keeping with the sacrament of the anointing of the sick. However, the sacrament of confession is vital in order for the dying person to receive absolution, and it must be taken with a truthful, lucid and contrite heart. For this, one needs memories.

On 12 November 1944, after a long battle, J. J. finally passed away. Sister Clotilde was with him. She may have been the only person he could call family. But while she coincidentally shared a name with his niece, in truth she hardly knew him.

Doctors recorded J. J.'s heart condition as the first cause of death, with senility noted as a secondary cause. A happy death eluded him. Dementia had taken his memories, but it did not take his life. Using medical terminology of the day, J. J. died of chronic myocarditis. In layman's terms, he died of a sickness in his heart.

16

VICTORY IN THE PACIFIC

AFTER LEAVING THE ORPHANAGE SYSTEM, MERVYN STRUGGLED to stay afloat. Carried by the currents of the labour market, he drifted.

For a short time he joined Basil at the farm in Camden. Farming placements were a kind of finishing school for ex-St Vincent's boys. Farmers did not have to pay very much, and lads from the Home had a reputation for working hard because they had always been required to do so. The lads were in that precarious period of transition between boy and man, and farms provided them with on-the-job skills but more importantly somewhere to live while they decided how they would make their way in the world alone.

Mervyn did not stay on the farm long. He returned to the city, moving to a house on Myrtle Street in the inner city which he shared with other young working men. Without conscious design, Mervyn had returned to the street where his family had once lived. A baby at the time, he would have had no memory of it. The grocer Beth Bowden still lived only a few doors down. Mervyn's residence, on the corner of Rose and Myrtle streets, was within line of sight of the woman who had walked that lonely pilgrimage to Watkin Street on the day of the tragedy. Mrs Bowden had seen Mervyn as a baby in the arms of his mother; she saw him again over a decade later when she served him as his local grocer. Neither recognised each other.

While living on Myrtle Street, Mervyn was employed as a bookbinder, but he clearly did not care for it as he did not stay in this occupation or location for long.

For men who entered adulthood in Australia between 1910 and 1920, the outbreak of war deeply shaped their coming-of-age experiences. In 1916, Mervyn was seventeen and wanted to fight. He wanted to fight so badly he claimed to be nineteen on his application forms, believing this would improve his chance of being accepted. In order to understand why Mervyn's compulsion to join the war was so strong, it is important to note what was occurring in Australia at the time. Jeffrey Grey, an Australian military historian, argues there was 'near unanimity of viewpoint within the Australian community which regarded the war as just, and service in it as both obligation and privilege'. Signing up for the war effort assumed the status of an essential rite of passage for young men like Mervyn.

In 1915, the government held a war census to count how many fit men of military age, without dependants, existed in the population. The total was determined to be 215 000. On this basis, targets to supply 9500 men per month were established, with an additional supplementary pool of fifty thousand identified to be needed as well. The recruitment campaign to source these men was as masterful as any modern-day marketing offensive. It was Australia's official policy to pledge troops to Britain, but now this had to be made real inside family homes across the nation. The federal government tapped the psychology of the two key demographic groups pivotal to young men signing up: the young men themselves and their mothers. It was not enough for young men to believe in their patriotic responsibility to fight – their mothers needed to believe in it too. The war effort therefore used catchphrases of guilt to work on the psychology of mothers and sons. Public spaces were coated in poster advertisements with images of mothers dutifully offering up their sons, and of virile and brave young men willingly signing up. In Mervyn's case it was not his mother encouraging him to fight but the long psychological shadow of one. While he no longer had a mother, this did not mean he would ever abandon the notion that one day, if he tried hard enough, he could be a good son. He carried the kind of longings that only other orphans could understand.

Mervyn tried twice to enlist early in World War I, in different locations, and failed both times. Lying about his age did not help. 'Physique below standard' was the official comment on his application form. Measured to be five foot and three inches tall, Mervyn was considered too short and therefore medically unfit for service.

A year into the military campaign, and the position of the Australian Imperial Forces (AIF) changed. Having lost thousands of young men in a devastating series of engagements on the Western Front, the AIF relaxed their criteria. Mervyn's stature was now not considered a problem, so he again tried to sign up. But after he told them he was under twenty-one, enlistment officers struggled to obtain the necessary approval from a parent or guardian. On the enlistment form are the handwritten words 'parents both died' and 'consent to be obtained'. It never was.

The enlistment experience left Mervyn shamed twice. First, he was told he did not measure up as a man. Then he was told something he had no doubt felt his whole life: he was not like other young men because he was raised in an orphanage. Both were facts that he could not change, no matter how hard he tried.

By the end of the war, Australia had enlisted 416 809 men and 80 per cent served overseas; close to 20 per cent were killed and 45 per cent wounded. Mervyn's rejection probably saved his life.

•

When Mervyn could not prove himself on the beaches of Anzac Cove, he retreated to a place in Sydney where many go to be restored. He sought out a harbour beach. At some point in the 1910s, Mervyn made a discovery that would change his life. He set foot in the Pacific Ocean for the first time. It altered him. After floating for so long, swept along by currents beyond his control, he finally began to swim.

From that point forward, swimming defined him. He was a pioneer surf lifesaver before the affiliated movement even existed. In the seaside suburb of Ramsgate, Mervyn was an active member of the formal lifesaving movement throughout the 1920s. He competed in high-profile competitions like the Australian Cup. This event was one of the most gruelling contests on the swimming competition circuit because it was held in open water. Many experienced swimmers were overwhelmed by an ocean competition because they were not accustomed to swells and turbulence. To win the Australian Cup, competitors could not rely on speed alone; they also needed strength and endurance to rescue a fully clothed volunteer who pretended to be drowning. Mervyn may not have been the fastest – he never won an event outright – but he was strong. In rescue competitions, he always towed his patients safely to shore.

The ritual of ocean swimming defined Mervyn's daily life for years. He swam in the early morning, a time of day when there was no one on the shoreline and the ocean felt like his alone. As he sliced through the water, his arms and legs beating down the force of the waves, his muscles were strengthened. As he walked from the water each morning, roughly flicking the salt and sand away, he was altered a little.

It was as if the trauma that had attached to him and grown so stickily within him could now be shed as easily as dead skin cells and dried sand – it simply flaked off and fell away.

In the early 1920s, Mervyn achieved a major victory that was more important than winning any competition. He won the job to manage the Ramsgate refreshment rooms and baths. It was a very proud achievement for the young man. He stayed a few years before moving a little further south to Cronulla, where he managed the baths for about eight years.

Harbour baths were an integral part of Sydney life in the early to mid-twentieth century, on both the northern and southern beaches. Coastal councils would section off a beach to create designated swimming areas for the public. The dangers of ocean swimming were reduced but not eliminated. Nets prevented sharks from entering. Cement walls vanquished rips and created the rough outline of a swimming pool using the natural rock formations. But jagged rock walls, slippery with sea slime, could still shred the skin. Sea urchins could still puncture feet. The ocean was still unpredictable, meaning people could still drown. In days with rough sea swells, children were at risk of being swept over the edge and dumped into sharp rocks. The Sydney custom of council-condoned harbour bathing is sometimes called wild swimming.

Mervyn was a wild swimmer, but he was also a careful swimmer. He seemed to have a special ability to scan the horizon for signs of danger. Testimonials about Mervyn are available to us because the local councils that employed him wanted to know they were hiring someone they could trust to protect their citizens.

'A man of the highest integrity . . . Mr Sly always appears to have a weather eye out,' wrote a banker in Pitt Street in his summation of Mervyn.

'Energetic, intelligent and a hard-working man of excellent character . . .'

'He exercises a constant vigilance,' was what one friend said of him.

'A man of good character, temperate in his habits, honest in his dealings,' wrote a father who had entrusted Mervyn with teaching his children to swim.

'He is one of the best swimming teachers for children that I have ever met,' wrote a well-respected city doctor.

'He has won the esteem and respect of the residents of this shire,' said the President of the Sutherland Council Chambers.

Mervyn seemed able to read the sky for signs of dangerous weather fronts as they swept in swiftly from the sea. He understood tidal shifts and the treacherous rips of the harbour beaches. Most people interpreted this to be due to his immense experience as an ocean swimmer. However, a condition known as hypervigilance is often a by-product of institutional care experiences. Mervyn had grown into a man who was always looking for ways to anticipate and avert danger, because he was a survivor.

•

It was during Mervyn's time as a lifesaver that Florence first saw him.

He was sitting at the top of the lifesaving tower, scanning the horizon with field glasses. A bell rested at his side, ready to warn swimmers of impending danger.

Florence was a war widow. Her first husband, John Dinnen, had returned from the war but had not lived long afterwards. Florence was one of the many World War I widows who frequented Cronulla Beach in the 1920s. Mervyn may have seen her from afar, through his field glasses. She might have been dressed in modest knee-length bathers as she waded towards the shore. Perhaps she draped herself in a colourful beach kimono, fashionable at the time, and reclined on an iconic folding beach chair with a bold stripe. Their courtship was the most iconic of Sydney romances.

They were married in the spring of 1928. We do not know if Mervyn approached the large and grand Catholic church on Gordon Street, Rozelle, with any sense of nervousness. What we do know is that he walked right past it and went on to the very plain Anglican parish just down the road. Why the couple decided to marry in the working-class peninsula of Balmain, since they neither worked nor lived in the area, is unclear. Some known facts about the wedding, however, tell us much about Mervyn's place in the world at that time: members of Florence's family were in attendance and were the only ones to act as witnesses to the event.

Mervyn managed the baths, taught swimming, sold tea and sandwiches and ice-creams, and saved lives. He continued to acquire skills to advance himself. He qualified with a certificate in merchant accounting because he was prepared to study at night, by correspondence. He was a justice of the peace. He undertook official first-aid training. He went on to become an examiner for the Royal Life Saving Society in New South Wales, and achieved chief examiner status.

Sometime between 1933 and 1934, Mervyn won the contract to manage state-of-the-art and newly renovated harbour baths in North Sydney. It was a huge personal achievement. Roseville Baths were nestled in a valley of dense forest. The caretaker's cottage overlooked the baths and the beauty of the harbour. Roseville was considered something of a bush village. When first established as a public reserve in the 1920s it was identified as a place of undeniable beauty which was sure to 'hold the visitor in amazement' with its 'curiously shaped trees, rocks and bathing pools'.

This opportunity motivated Mervyn to work even harder. He became lifesaver, teacher, financial manager, cleaner and maintenance man. He ran an ambitious schedule of swim classes, offering a personal guarantee to any student: regardless of age or ability level, he could teach anyone to swim in only eight lessons. At night he ran competitive swim events. Clubs from all over Sydney came to enjoy the Olympic-sized pool with the reputation of a stunning view. The baths were so well known and well regarded that local Roseville College, an elite private boarding school for girls, used its proximity and easy access to them as an advertised benefit of attending the school.

As caretaker, Mervyn made the most of the opportunity presented to him. He kept working hard, and locals liked and respected him. No one would have guessed how difficult life was becoming for him at home.

Florence was sick. Not only did she suffer from a chronic condition, it was one that carried a good deal of shame: a painful inflammation of her fallopian tubes and an infection in the uterus. While it cannot be known how she contracted this condition, a common source is an untreated STI. Florence struggled with it for years, at times suffering episodes of great pain. The condition also left her unable to have children.

One theory is that John, Florence's first husband, contracted a venereal disease, most likely gonorrhoea, while serving overseas. Though his war records provide no indication that he contracted an STI, these conditions were not always detected by medical personnel. It is estimated that around sixty thousand Australian soldiers could have returned home from World War I as carriers of venereal disease. Gonorrhoea was often asymptomatic, so men passed it to their wives or girlfriends completely unaware.

As the 1930s unfolded, Mervyn and Florence fought hard to maintain a sense of stability and security. They had achieved what many other couples in Sydney had failed to do: they had not only survived the challenging economic conditions brought by the Depression, but seemed to be doing financially better than they ever had.

When World War II was declared in 1939, they most likely thought that because they were a middle-aged couple, it would have little impact on the private island they had built for themselves in Roseville.

•

Mervyn showed his patriotic support for the war effort by redoubling his efforts as caretaker. Patronage of the baths went up after the outbreak of war. Community clubs and sporting associations from all over Sydney were using Roseville Baths on a regular basis.

During the day, anyone could attend the baths. At night, Mervyn wanted to make sure they were not only used, but also offered a strong community focus during the war. Swimming teams came from all over the city's north to race the 7th Field Regiment in breaststroke, and local swimming champions pitted their endurance against the 18th Brigade in a hundred metres of the front crawl. The events were specifically designed to lift the morale of both civilians and those serving. Special bon voyage swim events were organised for the boys leaving to serve overseas. Mervyn must have felt a sense of pride that he could still make a real contribution to the war effort.

But in March 1942, a dark cloud began to creep across the horizon. While Mervyn had always prided himself on his ability to anticipate danger, this time he had not seen it coming. Everything he had tried so hard to build was at risk of being washed away by one single government edict.

Two and a half years into the war, Australia was facing a military labour crisis. More men were needed to serve overseas, and those still at home needed to be engaged directly in supplying materials, products and services that would advance the Allied forces' military goals.

In April 1942, the Australian government took radical steps to address the labour crisis. A long list of occupations were identified as being vital to the war effort, and these were not affected by the new provisions. Farmers, dock workers, miners and those on the railway, for example, could carry on with the work they had done before the war started. But for many others, the war office would insist on relocation to war work. Refusal to comply could culminate in gaol time.

Mervyn tried to argue that his role as caretaker of a public bath was essential to the war effort. Royal Australian Air Force boys, learning to fly at the local training centre at Bradfield Park, came to Roseville Baths to swim when on recreational leave. Mervyn even gave them free entry.

But the Manpower office, the directorate responsible for the deployment of labour in Australia to ensure sufficient workers were available to sustain the war effort, did not accept Mervyn's argument. He would have to apply for enlistment in one of the specified job roles. The government would decide how he would be employed, where, and for how long. Mervyn and Florence may not have realised it yet, but their castle built quite literally on sand was at risk of being washed away.

The couple's situation very quickly destabilised. Florence's health deteriorated even further. There were many days when she struggled to get out of bed. She suffered shooting pains down her legs and along her back. She was not just chronically ill but also chronically anxious. Mervyn feared leaving her on her own.

The proximity of Bradfield Park to their home – only six kilometres – gave Mervyn an idea. He had seen the officers come and go from the baths. He knew some of them well, and had competed in social swimming competitions against them. They were serving their country while still maintaining close ties to the North Sydney area.

Mervyn signed up for the RAAF and was accepted into its training programme. There was just one problem he had not anticipated, and it was a big one. There were twelve RAAF flying schools all over Australia. Mervyn was not sent to a local facility, but instead over four hundred kilometres away to the remote Riverina region. Along with thousands of men, he underwent testing and training at the No. 10 Elementary Flying Training School, which took up much of the town of Temora and its surrounds.

Mervyn and Florence were in a precarious situation. They had not accumulated capital and did not own property. If they lost the lease on the Roseville Baths, Mervyn would be unemployed and the couple would be homeless.

They came up with a solution – but it was risky. Florence would assume responsibility for running the baths. It was an unusual step at the time, as a married woman was rarely named as the legal party to a lease agreement. It was also a risky strategy because her health was changeable; she had her good days, but she could also have frightfully bad days.

Managing the baths was a busy role. In summer they had an average of more than three hundred visitors every day. The six thousand adults estimated to visit in each of the summer months were almost matched by the number of children. The baths also required a huge amount of maintenance, and Mervyn had always done the bulk of it, including painting, cleaning and gardening. Under the terms of the employment contract, the kiosk was required to be open almost all the time.

Even in the context of the very diverse records held by the military archives, Mervyn's personnel and personal records are unique. A soldier's service file usually comprises a biographical profile but may also include casualty records, promotions and transfers, special commendations and accounts of medals received. Mervyn's file contains almost no information of this kind – it is instead filled with letters that might best be described as pleas for compassion. They demonstrate the depth of love Mervyn had for his wife and document his unrelenting desire to protect her.

Mervyn was engaged in battle not with a foreign enemy but with the internal war office. From his enlistment in 1942 to the end of the war he fought for the woman he loved, producing what must be among the most unusual wartime love letters ever written. They were not for his wife, but about her. Nor do they contain anything one might expect to see in a wartime love letter – there are no protestations of love, no confessions and no promises. But while the letters are not romantic, they are extremely intimate. By the end of the war, the department of labour, the director general of Manpower and the captain at Bradfield Park were all well acquainted with the reproductive health issues of Mrs Florence Sly, Roseville caretaker's cottage, Middle Harbour.

●

On enlistment, Mervyn's health was checked. His height and weight were recorded. His teeth inspected. And his photograph was taken. It is striking for two reasons. First, his rakish smile, clipped moustache and slicked Clark Gable hair suggest a playful and waggish man. Perhaps it is nothing more than the reflection of the camera flash, but he even appears to have a twinkle in his eye. Second, he bears an uncanny resemblance to his brother Bedford – although there are some striking differences. Photographs of Bedford reveal a beaten and weathered man. In contrast, Mervyn is well groomed and poised; in one photo he is even smiling. This startling piece of qualitative evidence suggests that while the two brothers had a shared orphanage history, they had their own individual experiences of trauma, and two vastly different trajectories and long-term quality of life outcomes.

After their physical inspection, RAAF potentials were given a broad range of assessments on intellectual competency and physical capabilities such as strength, speed and quickness of reflex. The RAAF was always exacting, but even more so if an applicant sought acceptance to the rank of officer. Pilots required a certain type of psychology, and the RAAF wanted to know what kind of man Mervyn was.

He failed every test across every instrument. In all categories, he scored 'weak' to 'below average' in everything from general intelligence, capacity to carry out instructions and mathematical aptitude, through to physical capabilities. The latter results appear to be particularly surprising, as strength, endurance, agility and athleticism were usually Mervyn's forte. With these scores, he would not have been eligible for any posting of great import to the war effort, and would certainly not have been sent overseas.

In one task, applicants wrote an essay about the war on a topic of their choosing. This assessment was designed to test many factors, including intelligence, attitude to the war and organisational abilities. Mervyn did not write about military strategy, battles, defeats or casualties, but about a topic very dear to his heart: the ocean. If the Allied forces could just maintain control of the sea, he said, there would surely be a victory. In red pen scrawled beneath his essay, the assessor noted: 'the spelling is weak, grammar and comprehension – only a faint knowledge of punctuation and setting out'. It was all 'rather carelessly done'.

Mervyn was assigned the rank of LAC (leading aircraftman) equipment assistant, one of the most junior ranks in the RAAF. He was responsible for taking inventory and dispensing equipment to the airmen. As an LAC, he was posted to Bradfield Park, Lindfield, only a few kilometres from Roseville Baths. Mervyn had achieved a small victory.

In July 1942, Mervyn officially began his posting. After he arrived at Bradfield and began to understand its routines, he realised that spending time at home would not be quite as easy as he had hoped. He would not be able to work as an LAC while posing as a humble baths caretaker. There were drills and long shifts, musters and paperwork, and a continual loading and unloading of equipment.

Florence struggled on alone until December, when Mervyn applied for special leave. He returned to manage the peak period over Christmas and New Year's, then went back to Bradfield. Florence coped – just.

In 1943, the conflict in the Pacific crept dangerously close to home. In May, a Japanese submarine torpedoed a ship, the *Centaur*, frighteningly close to the Queensland coast. The event shocked the nation, and not just because 264 people had died. It was a shocking reminder that the theatre of war was now in the Pacific. The enemy had drawn nearer to Australia, and wiped out those who were sick and vulnerable: the sunken vessel had been clearly marked with the large red crosses distinctive to medical and therefore non-combat ships.

While Mervyn was no doubt affected by fears in the community about the sinking of the *Centaur*, he was also preoccupied with thoughts of home. Florence's health was in decline, perhaps due to the stressful nature of her respons-ibilities at the baths. By 1943 it was clear that Mervyn and Florence were staring down the barrel of defeat. While the Allied forces were in deep water in the Pacific, the tide was also turning on the couple.

Visitors had complained to the Roseville council about the poor state of the baths. The sea wall had started to crumble.

Oysters had grown on submerged surfaces, including the floor and walls of the bath; removing them required crawling into the water and scraping them off with sharp tools. Mervyn had not been at the baths in months, and he and Florence were unable to source any other labour for this task, so the oysters were now clustered in huge numbers. Swimmers risked raking their hands and feet across the jagged and brittle shells, which resembled broken bottles. Even the tiled and concreted surfaces around the baths were hazardous; in the past, Mervyn had used a wire brush and paint scraper to peel away the slimy algae that regularly accumulated. Several visitors had lacerated their feet on oyster shells, or come down hard when they slipped over beside the pool. Once seen as somewhere to soak up the serenity of the environment, Roseville Baths was getting a dangerous reputation.

In March 1944, the situation worsened. The town clerk of Ku-ring-gai Council wrote to the commanding officer at Bradfield Park, letting him know that the council would close down Roseville Baths if the Slys could not honour the terms of their contract as caretakers. It seemed that Mervyn and Florence would lose everything, including the goodwill they had earned within their community. Far from the World War II frontline, they were still at war.

Around this time, Florence was in constant pain. She had crippling joint and back pain, and severe inflammation of the fallopian tubes. She was diagnosed with neurasthenia: a term used by medical professionals at the time to describe a range of symptoms associated with anxiety, from exhaustion through to hysteria. In the first half of 1944, Florence's doctor wrote a detailed letter to Manpower, saying, 'Mrs Sly has been suffering . . . I consider it essential for her health's sake that her husband be released from the RAAF.' Mervyn tried to explain the situation too, this time writing to the head of Manpower in Melbourne. Mervyn was frank and unguarded: 'I fear for her safety while I am away from the home.' A town clerk from the council wrote to the National Service Office and Department of Labour: 'It is necessary to have a man in charge who is a life saver. It is emphasised that without a man in attendance boys become unmanageable and endanger the lives of themselves and others.'

Within the week, the Manpower director general responded quickly and firmly: 'I appreciate the difficulties you find yourself in, in connection with a renewal of the lease, but regret that this is not a case in which I would be justified in asking for release on occupational grounds. Owing to certain decisions by the Government, such releases are being confined to men whom it is desired to employ in only the highest priority industries.'

In December 1944, Florence's condition deteriorated even further. Mervyn wrote a candid and courageous letter to his commanding officer. He spoke openly of his worries and emotions at a time when stoic notions of masculine bravery dominated interactions between men.

In September, October and December 1944, letters flew from the RAAF base to anyone within the military who might listen. In December 1944, Deputy Director General of Manpower NSW Charles Bellemore held a hard line: 'Reference is made to application submitted by abovenamed airman for release from the RAAF in order to resume civil occupation as Swimming Baths proprietor ... for your information it is advised that the matter has received careful consideration but I am unable to support the application at the present juncture.'

Florence was engaged in the battle from her sickbed in Roseville. One summer, she wrote a letter within hours of Mervyn's departure. She was frightened and alone, and there is a clear desperation in her tone. To the director of Manpower in Melbourne, with a sense of dread and portent, she wrote, 'Our lease is up ... It means to us that we have to get out of our business which we have built up over eleven years.' She appealed to the man's sympathy for junior servicemen: 'Mervyn is only an LAC equipment assistant without prospects of promotion on that account.' She appealed to the man's mercy and compassion as well: 'I feel that manpower was not created to cause such hardship.'

But the response came quickly like return fire: 'Medical grounds as stated insufficient for recommendation.' There was a discernible tone of frustration: 'Sly has already been granted in all eight months special leave without pay ...'

The baths 'needs constant attention', wrote Florence, again to the director of Manpower.

Mervyn wrote more letters as well. His language became even more dramatic – his fear is palpable and his tone is pleading. Florence could not get out of bed.

Florence's doctor sought to strengthen Mervyn's case: 'She is suffering severe neurasthenia.'

By early 1945, Mervyn and Florence were beginning to concede defeat. While the war in Europe and the Pacific was turning in favour of the Allied forces, this was not so for the middle-aged couple.

When Germany surrendered in May 1945, Mervyn again tried hard to be released from the war machine. He wrote a string of letters to the relevant officers. None were successful. Mervyn and Florence could only have been terrified. The lease on Roseville Baths expired at the end of August, and if special arrangements could not be made, it would not be renewed. Mervyn and Florence were on the brink of losing everything.

In August 1945, he wrote again to his commanding officer at Bradfield Park. He was rejected.

On 15 August 1945, after more than five years of fighting, the Allied forces declared Victory in the Pacific. The streets of Sydney flooded with people in celebration. Martin Place was crammed with relieved revellers. The war was finally over.

Hopeful this would be the turning point in his private battle, Mervyn did not celebrate but instead returned to his typewriter. He made yet another application for leave, less than a week later. He sought six months' leave to do maintenance on the baths and restore them to good working order.

To Mervyn's shock, the application was rejected, again.

It took a few more weeks for World War II to be declared officially over. All paperwork associated with the surrender of both Germany and Japan was signed on 2 September 1945.

On 3 September 1945, the RAAF finally signed the official paperwork for a very different kind of surrender. The Air Commodore, Air Officer Commanding No. 2 Training Group rejected Mervyn's final application for leave. Instead, the commodore made a counter offer – for Mervyn's official and complete discharge from the RAAF. Mervyn and Florence, after three years of gruelling battle, had finally won.

On 28 September 1945, the director general of Manpower NSW signed off on the official paperwork that would release Mervyn back to Florence for good. The director's surrender was unconditional: 'Mervyn Sly is to be replaced on retired list at own request on compassionate grounds.'

One of the last letters Mervyn wrote to the Manpower office perhaps best captures the depth and complexity of the love he had for his wife, in one line: 'I need to act as lifesaver.'

A literal interpretation suggests he was referring matter-of-factly to his role as a swimming guard. A more figurative interpretation highlights strong and empowering forces at work in Mervyn's life as he cast himself in the role of rescuer. He believed he was fighting to save his wife's life. Florence believed it too. But all the while, perhaps it was Florence's love for Mervyn that saved him.

17

IN THE SHADE OF THE OLD APPLE TREE

> *I could hear the dull buzz of the bee*
> *In the blossoms as you said to me*
> *With a heart that is true, I'll be waiting for you*
> *In the shade of the old apple tree . . .*
> *For there within my arms I gently pressed you*
> *And blushing red, you slowly turned away*
> *I can't forget the way I once caressed you*
> *I only pray we'll meet another day*
>
> Popular 1905 song, 'In the Shade of the Old Apple Tree'
> Words by Harry Williams, music by Egbert Van Alstyne

IN SYDNEY'S HISTORY, THERE ARE TWO TRAGEDIES THAT SHARE some peculiar similarities. The first occurred in 1904, in Newtown. The second occurred twenty-five years later, in a suburb called Five Dock, not far from Newtown.

It was 1 March 1929, and it was the most typical of suburban Sydney scenes. In Henry Street, Five Dock, there were double-brick homes, parks for children to play in, and well-tended gardens. Things were generally quiet along this residential road, except for those periods in the day when crowds of children headed to and from the local public school.

Alfred Debenham, local resident and proud home owner, was making the most of the very last of the warm summer weather. He had spent the morning outdoors, weeding, pruning and watering his garden. Now, in the early afternoon, he had begun laying fresh buffalo turf in his front yard. On the first day of autumn, Alfred's only goal was to have a new lawn planted and watered by sunset.

When he heard the click of a woman's heels in the distance, moving up Henry Street, nothing seemed out of the ordinary. As the end of the school day approached, people gathered in this area of the street to wait for their children. Five Dock public school was just a few doors down.

Kneeling on the ground and shielded by the short picket fence, Alfred pressed the carefully cut sections of turf into the soft soil. It took a few moments for him to realise the woman on the street was not alone. Unlike her noisy wooden heels, the man's leather boots had been silent as they tracked alongside her. Alfred only knew the man was there when he spoke. 'Come on!' he mumbled through gritted teeth.

When Alfred heard the woman give a short and startled scream, he popped his head above the fence line – just long enough to see the man cuff the woman by the arm and drag her forward. He assumed from the close way in which the two were speaking and the intensity of their voices that they must be husband and wife. Alfred was momentarily concerned for the woman, but then he saw the man slip his arm around her waist possessively. Alfred looked away, respectfully conscious of the need to afford a married couple privacy. When police interviewed him later, he described what he had witnessed in the following way: 'I saw the man with his arm around the woman. He was saying "Come on! Come on!" He repeated this and I thought the woman may have been ill or hysterical, and her companion was merely helping her along.'

Events then moved quickly, giving Alfred little time to think. The sounds of a struggle were now unmistakable, and there was a coarse tone to the man's voice. The commotion in the street had quietly begun to draw neighbours from their homes. A resident living across the road opened his door and peered from the safety of his portico. Alfred's married daughter, Mrs Speyer, emerged from the family home to ask her father what was wrong. Everyone seemed to sense that something was about to happen, but also seemed powerless to stop it. Eerily, a bell tolled at the school, heralding the end of classes for the day.

Though what happened next may have been building for a while, it only lasted seconds. Alfred saw the man grab the woman roughly around the throat and throw her up against the picket fence.

Alfred dropped his trowel in shock.

The woman was completely trapped by the size and strength of the man's body when – and Alfred could scarcely believe what was unfolding right before his eyes – the man removed a cut-throat razor from inside his jacket. The man sliced the woman's throat in one swift and fluid motion. It took less than ten seconds.

Alfred bolted from the safety of his garden and entered the bloody scene. Other neighbours mobilised too; charged with adrenalin, they moved quickly and precisely.

The victim pressed one hand to her throat, desperately trying to stem the blood cascading down the front of her dress. With the other hand, she grabbed the picket fence to steady herself.

Alfred made it across the street just in time to scoop her up and keep her from falling. He called for his daughter to fetch bandages and towels. Mrs Speyer returned not just with blankets and towels but also pencil and paper. At first Alfred could not understand why, but then his daughter asked, 'Can she write?' Almost unbelievably, the dying woman took the pencil and tried to write as Alfred's daughter held the paper stiffly in front of her. The writing was scrawled, indecipherable, but one person present thought they read one word: 'SLY'.

For a few moments everyone seemed frozen in shock. The attack had occurred so quickly, even the woman who owned the picket fence was unaware of it until it was over. When she eventually saw the commotion in the street through her front window, she assumed that a child had been run over. When she discovered that a woman had been attacked, she ran back inside her home; a few seconds later she returned, a large foam mattress bouncing out from under her arm. She had some idea that the dying woman might be laid atop it, to provide her a little comfort.

'Call for an ambulance!' was heard from several directions.

'Mum, there was a man on the corner pulling a lady about,' yelled the fifteen-year-old son of the Keen family on Scott Street. 'I saw something gleaming in his hand.' Mr Keen immediately ran up the road to give aid.

As chaos unfolded around the victim, the attacker tried to skulk off, razor still in hand.

It was Alfred who saw the man creeping away. 'Stop him! Catch him!' Alfred yelled. He still held the woman in his arms. His shirt was now a colourful timeline of the morning's horror: muddy brown dirt, the haze of a green turf stain and a soaked patch of vivid red.

At first, the attacker did not run. He had clearly done what he had set out to do, and initially he showed no hesitation. He turned the corner and was gone.

The attack had occurred in the most public of places, in front of a group of witnesses. And its horror was about to escalate even further. Hundreds of children had just been released from Five Dock public school, and they flooded out across the street. They scattered in groups, walked alone, and circled on scooters towards the scene.

When Andrew Wilson heard panicked voices and yelling, he ran from the back of his property and pursued the attacker. He had almost caught up to him when the man turned on him suddenly, razor in hand.

The attacker brandished the blade at Wilson's eyes. 'Back off or I'll slice your throat too,' he threatened.

Wilson backed away but yelled to a bystander further down the road, 'I'm not going to stop him with a razor in his hand! Go for the police! Now!'

The fugitive picked up speed, and now everyone in the neighbourhood seemed aware that something truly horrible was occurring in their usually quiet suburb. Edward May, who was delivering ice to a customer on the corner of Henry and Elizabeth streets, stared at the attacker as he brushed right past.

'Stop him!' yelled Wilson. 'He's cut a woman's throat up the street!'

May tried to grab him but failed as well.

The fugitive, razor in hand, just kept running.

An unnamed boy on a scooter saw the man turn into Harris Street and then disappear into a small back street salaciously nicknamed Lovers Lane by locals. The boy waited with his scooter and watched. When police finally arrived, the boy pointed in the direction of the man's escape.

Now trapped between housing on one side and the Parramatta River on the other, the fugitive jumped into a section of the river known as Hen and Chicken Bay.

He sat crouched in the water for a good while. His eyes were just above the waterline, crocodile-like. Bystanders who had watched the pursuit assisted police by pointing out the strange figure amid the mangroves, submerged up to his neck in the slimy water of the Parramatta. Police called to the man from the shore. At this point, witness statements present slightly conflicting accounts. One claimed to have heard defiance in the man: 'She is better off now, nobody knows what she has done to me.' Another claimed the man's words were repentant: 'She is better off now. Nobody knows what I have done to her.'

For some time, it was a stand-off. The man could not swim further into the river, because it was too far to the opposite shore. His only option was to come ashore where police were poised to arrest him. But the man simply sat and waited. Police waded out to talk to him.

'She had me up at children's court this morning. She had an order made against me,' were the first words he offered up to police as an explanation.

'What's your name, sir?' asked one officer.

'Frederick Sly.'

'Come out of the water, Frederick Sly, or the sharks will get you,' said another officer.

Despite the ferocious energy of his flight, to the surprise of law enforcement the man surrendered. He waded back. As he came closer, officers saw why he wished to leave the water so soon. The man had slashed his throat and wrists while lying in the green-tinged Parramatta. The blood mixed with the water, running freely in thin bright-red streaks from his neck and arms. The notion that he was bleeding into the water, like shark bait, had frightened him to the shore. He was still firmly grasping the open cut-throat razor.

Back on Henry Street the ambulance had arrived, but the woman was dead. She had managed to scrawl one legible world onto a piece of paper: 'Sly'. Those present assumed it was her own name.

This assumption was soon confirmed as fact, to the utter dismay of those present, by a five-year-old student of Five Dock public. The woman was his mother, Hazel Sly. He had arrived at the corner where he usually met her after school, only to find her lying on a bloody mattress surrounded by horrified faces.

Frederick Sly died shortly after being taken into police custody.

•

Over the coming days, the investigation and subsequent inquest revealed much more about Frederick Sly than police had ever imagined.

The story of the Sly family tree had begun on the Apple Isle with two branches and two brothers: John and James. In 1904, the constabulary of Sydney would meet one of their descendants: Alicks Sly, grandson of James. Twenty-five years later, they would become well acquainted with Frederick Sly, grandson of John.

At the Burwood court inquest into the deaths of Hazel and Frederick Sly, District Coroner Mr H. Richardson-Clark noted, 'it seems to me on the whole a blessing in disguise that this unfortunate man has died after committing this inhuman crime'.

Only after the murder-suicide did the dark pattern of violence leading up to it come to light. Witnesses reported hearing Frederick threaten to cut his wife's throat while the couple lived together in a Moore Park flat. Their married life had followed a pattern. Hazel left. She returned. She left again. Then returned again. The final home they shared was a flat in Darlinghurst. Neighbours there had witnessed things too. In January of that year, Frederick had attacked his wife with a flat iron. She had been admitted to St Vincent's Hospital; according to the staff there, he turned up and again threatened to slash his wife's throat.

One witness noted that Frederick, although not usually an intemperate man, had been drinking when they last saw him, a few weeks before the murder-suicide.

On the morning of the tragedy, Frederick and Hazel had an appointment at the children's court. Hazel had set in motion a maintenance order against her husband, from whom she had separated. At the last minute, she told an officer of the court that she did not want to proceed. He was not surprised: this occurred regularly at the children's court.

The next time the husband and wife were seen together was in Five Dock, as they headed towards their son's school.

After Hazel's death, police discovered much more about Frederick Sly. Hazel had not been his first wife. And she had not been the first wife he had tried to kill.

•

Frederick was born and raised in Melbourne. His father, William Charles Sly, had settled there soon after leaving Hobart.

Frederick met Lillian while they were working in the Eastern Arcade, just off Russell Street in the centre of Melbourne. Lillian was born in Cope Cope, about 140 kilometres west of Bendigo, and had moved to Melbourne in search of better job opportunities. She worked as a waitress in a refreshment room; Frederick worked as a photographer. He was eleven years older than Lillian, who was eighteen. She was mature for her age, and a long way from being a naive teenager, but she was still immediately drawn to the confident older man who seemed to have a touch of the devil in him. When caught out telling a lie, he had been known to say, 'But I am like George Washington. I have never told a lie in my life.' In personality, Frederick bore little resemblance to his second cousin Alicks. While Alicks was quiet, withdrawn and reflective, Frederick was cocky, overconfident and impulsive.

In 1913, Lillian and Frederick married in a Church of England service. Five children soon followed, one lost early in childhood. Frederick continued his work as a photographer for a while, but then dropped this to take up an illegal gambling scam at the racetrack. He left the family home for weeks at a time, leaving his wife with only a few shillings to pay the bills.

There was violence too. He beat her, he drank, he tried to smother their five-week-old baby. Frederick had used his fists to beat Lillian on one occasion, cracking her across the jaw and in the stomach. He had put his hands in a pincer grip around her throat and pushed her up against a wall. She also described how her husband had cracked her on the side of the head with a flat iron. There had never been a police report filed, nor had a neighbour ever offered help to her when these beatings occurred.

In 1922, while Lillian was recuperating from the birth of her daughter at a small private hospital, Frederick came to visit. He punched her squarely in the face. Her explanation of the event is strange, at best: 'He was so drunk he began to show me how he could fight.' A nurse intervened and threw him out; he was barred from the hospital thereafter. Two weeks after Lillian came home, he almost choked her to death. While drunk he slobbered and wept and begged for a divorce; when sober he walked around her, ignoring her as if he could not see her at all.

This is an astonishing amount of violence for anyone to live with, made even more astonishing by the fact that Lillian lived with a variety of in-laws over a ten-year period. All of this abuse had been going on observed by Frederick's family – and no one had done anything. 'He got worse during the period of time we were living with his mother,' said Lillian.

Eventually, Frederick spent more and more time away from the home. Lillian felt relieved, except she had no money. When he eventually came home, he was paralytically drunk. 'His mother put him to bed,' Lillian said.

In September 1922, Lillian came to fully understand her circumstances. Frederick, out of the blue, mentioned that he hated hospitals. When she tried to press him on what on earth he was talking about, she was told 'never mind'. Then came a string of curious questions about doctors and hospitals. 'Does a water break before a baby is born?' he asked.

Late one night, he arrived home drunk and passed out. When he woke the next morning he was confrontational and arrogant. He commanded Lillian to fetch his jacket, which was hanging on the back of a chair. He told her to go through its pockets.

Inside she found letters addressed to a man called Frederick Gordon. They were signed by a woman who called herself 'your loving wife Hazel'. The letters were on hospital paper.

Frederick then laid out the facts to his wife. He used the alias of Gordon to engage in illegal gambling. But he had not been travelling to the country race meetings; instead, he had been living in a hotel with a girl. 'She is the most passionate woman I have ever met. I have had a naughty from her several times and can always get one from her whenever I want it.'

To Lillian's utter dismay, it worsened still.

'I am broken-hearted,' he said. 'Hazel has gone through an operation for me and I cannot give her up. She is the most passionate woman I have ever met and I intend to stop with her tonight.'

Hazel was recovering in hospital from an abortion. She had been six months pregnant when she had undergone the procedure. Frederick had just spoken to a nurse, not so much to inquire after Hazel's safety but rather to ask if he would be up for manslaughter. Despite his new willingness to be transparent, at this point he again became secretive with Lillian. He would not go into the details, he said, but his main concern seemed to be that he now owed the Women's Hospital forty pounds.

Lillian told him it was over.

She went to a solicitor. She took her children and left. She took out a summons for maintenance against her husband.

At the Collingwood court of petty sessions, the bench ordered Frederick to provide for his wife but refused to take steps to end the marriage. The couple needed more time, the court advised. Marriages should always be saved, if possible, lawyers said.

The legal proceedings focused on preserving the institution of marriage at any cost. Lillian, in particular, was judged harshly for her pursuit of a divorce.

The discussion between Mr Vale (speaking on behalf of Lillian) and Mr Doria (representing Frederick) reveals much about the values surrounding divorce at the time.

'I didn't want him to come home telling me all about the other woman,' said Lillian.

Mr Vale, her legal representative, confirmed this by adding, 'He had boasted to his better half that he had got a woman into trouble.'

Lillian introduced a photograph of Hazel, along with some samples of the letters her husband had used to torment her. She produced these documents as evidence it was not her decision to end the marriage but her husband's. His attentions were clearly elsewhere, Lillian said. One of the lawyers described Hazel as 'a very smart looking girl'. She was about twenty years younger than Frederick, and even the lawyers seemed impressed with his seduction of such an attractive younger woman.

During his appearance at the Collingwood court, Frederick would be required to explain why he had left his wife and four children without means of support. He would not be required to answer why he had used violence against his wife.

While some spouses who were petitioned for divorce in the 1920s responded defensively, hitting back at their partner with every accusation they could think of, Frederick had nothing bad to say about Lillian.

In exploring whether there were grounds for a divorce, a lawyer asked him: 'Have you anything against your wife?'

'Nothing at all,' was the reply.

'Has she conducted herself properly as a wife and mother?'

'She has.'

This significantly reduced Lillian's chances of gaining a divorce because, irrespective of her husband's behaviour, she had been too good a wife. It was a cleverly manipulative ploy on Frederick's part, making him appear a satisfied husband and Lillian a vexatious wife.

Legal representatives pursued an entirely different line of questioning with Lillian. She needed to justify why she could not tolerate her husband's behaviour. Violence was used as her reason for leaving the marriage, but the legal minds overlooked this issue and directed their attention to other matters. Mr Doria, Frederick's representative, put forward a provocative counterargument: it was indiscreet and inappropriate for Lillian to raise the issue of infidelity. There was no mention of Frederick's willingness to commit infidelity; the wife was simply hysterical and exaggerating. Mr Doria said that Frederick had not 'got a woman into trouble': 'That is not so and should not be brought out in the interests of the little children, seeing that I am trying to bring the parties together again. The bother rose out of a difference caused through an unfounded allegation being made. If this case is adjourned, the parties could come together again.'

When Frederick was presented with the photograph of a woman who was not his wife, taken from his own jacket pocket, he denied he knew her. Lillian called out in frustration, 'It's a wonder you don't drop dead in the witness box.'

Very early on in the proceedings the chairman set the tone for all of the discussion to follow. 'This bench has been very successful in many ways in disputes between husbands and wives, and this witness should not take up a foolish attitude. We are going to decide the issue, and not the wife, who is adopting the wrong attitude. We are the deciding factor in this matter.'

'Why not give the husband another chance?' asked Mr Doria.

'Not me,' replied Lillian.

'Just because he said some silly things while in drink? . . . You know it is never too late to mend, don't you?' asked Mr Doria, following up confidently with, 'If you give him this chance, you will never regret it.'

Lillian's only response to this was to answer with what she knew to be true of her husband, 'Yet it will go on just the same'.

Lawyers insisted that Lillian adhere to a cooling-off period before proceeding with any plans to divorce. They asked her to give it a month.

Three weeks later, Frederick turned up at Lillian's new residence and banged on the door, demanding that she hand over her wedding ring because it did not belong to her anymore. He needed it for Hazel.

Lillian refused, and the next day she petitioned for a divorce.

With very little money and with a court order to pay maintenance to his wife hanging over his head, Frederick disappeared. Lawyers spent a year searching for him. There were rumours that he and Hazel had fled to Brisbane and now had a child. Lawyers wrote the necessary letters to check whether any child had been registered in the name of Sly in that state. The searches produced nothing. The trail ran cold.

Again, lawyers tried to discourage Lillian from proceeding with the divorce. For her, however, the shine was well and truly off the Sly apple.

In the 1920s, it was easy for people to hide. With only paper and non-photographic forms of identification, and with little consolidation of data between the states, law enforcement found it difficult to track fugitives once they left the state. The Supreme Court subpoenaed Frederick Sly, but nothing happened. Lillian wrote to anyone she could think of, including Frederick's brother Horace. She pleaded for help: 'I am going to divorce him and I want his address to serve the papers on him.' Newspaper advertisements were placed as far away as Queensland, using the guise of the 'missing friends' column to see if this might draw her husband out. None of it worked. Frederick Sly had gone to ground.

As the years rolled on, lawyers stepped it up. They used newspapers again, this time to advise Frederick of impending legal action: 'TAKE NOTICE that Lillian Alice Sly of 27 Eastham Street North Fitzroy in the said state married woman, has instituted proceedings for divorce against you her husband on the grounds of desertion and repeated acts of adultery . . .' Frederick was given, by court order, a month to come forward. Months and months of paperwork shuffled back and forth between law offices and between states in search of Mr Sly so the divorce might proceed.

Lillian had to fight hard continually in order to ensure the divorce moved forward. Lawyers, judges and even family members continued to actively discourage her from doing so.

She was taking a big risk, they said.

Marriage is sacred, they said.

She had four children to care for, and without a husband, her life would be difficult, they said.

And there would be the shame of a failed marriage to carry forward as well, they said.

The decree absolute between Lillian and Frederick Sly was made final in October 1926.

In the four years it took for the divorce to be finalised, Lillian had time to reflect on her experiences and on the challenges that lay ahead for her. During this time, a lawyer tried to make her see reason by asking, 'But your husband admits he has made a fool of himself, don't you want to give him another chance?'

In a reflective mood after all she had been through, and perhaps made wiser by the realisation she had come perilously close to being killed by her husband many times, Lillian did not answer. Instead, she posed a question to the lawyer: 'What would my life have been worth if I went back?'

A little shocked by her audacity and quick wit, the lawyer did not know how to respond.

Lillian eventually received the answer to her question, although it took a long time. A few years later, on 1 March 1929, a congregation of dearly beloved gathered together on a street in Five Dock to witness the joining of a man and woman in holy acrimony. The groom held his wife close. He stared deeply into her eyes. He took his vows. And with a fleeting caress of her neck, a second Mrs Sly was made a suicide bride.

18

EPITAPH

The Sly suicide brides – Ellie and Hazel – were memorialised at the times of their deaths. Physical remnants of these terrible events remain as part of the landscape of Sydney to this day. Though their murders were similar, their burials were not.

In 1929 Hazel Sly's death was memorialised by her husband's family. They assumed financial responsibility for her funeral arrangements. On 4 March 1929, she was given a memorial service and laid to rest alone in a single grave in the Anglican section of Rookwood Cemetery. But Hazel did not remain on her own for long. It took a few days for Frederick Sly to die from his self-inflicted injuries. After he did, on 9 March, he too was buried at Rookwood. Frederick's family purchased the plot right beside Hazel's. Husband and wife now lie together eternally, side by side in a marital bed of rock, soil and Rookwood clay. Hazel tried many times to leave her husband, but even in death she could not achieve this goal.

In 1904, twenty-five years earlier, Ellie's death was also memorialised. It was J. J. O'Leary, however, and not a Sly, who had the final word on how both Ellie and Alicks would be remembered. J. J. ensured that Alicks was buried shallowly and anonymously, with no memorial. For his sister, J. J. ordered a headstone and asked that a personalised inscription be chipped into it. The undertaker's account was eventually paid by the state, from the couple's resolved assets.

Ellie and Alicks were laid to rest at Rookwood. Theirs is an unusual grave configuration for husband and wife. Ellie lies top to toe with her baby Norman in ground consecrated by the Roman Catholic Church. Alicks is in the outer limits of the Anglican section; the exact location is unknown because his grave was deliberately left unmarked.

Ellie's grave can still be found but it is now almost overgrown with bramble and long grass. The slab of stone that marks the site is still there, but at some point, obviously long ago, the headstone severed from the footing and fell away to one side. The tablet remains in one solid piece. Year by year it sinks slowly into the damp marsh grass that feels like a swamp underfoot.

The headstone has not fractured. Today it almost looks like a clean slate because exposure to the elements has eroded the words. If one attempts to trace the letters, the surface of the stone rolls away like grains of sand beneath one's fingers. J. J.'s parting message to his sister, in the form of an epitaph, will unfortunately never be known to us.

•

At the time of the Newtown Tragedy, some commentators attributed the tragic deaths of Ellie and Alicks Sly to hauntings and spiritualism. Travelling to the sites of both Sly tragedies today sheds no real light on the mysteries that continue to surround them.

In Sydney, two physical sites are meaningful in any retelling of the story of Ellie and Alicks Sly: a terrace in Glebe, and a house in Newtown. In her family home in Glebe, Ellie may have played a role in perpetrating a murder. In her final home, in Newtown, she became the victim of one. Both Sly family homes are still standing, though a modern streetscape now surrounds them. They have undergone restoration; many new awnings, doors and verandahs have been added over the century. The exteriors have been repainted many times. The foundations, however, remain the same. Standing before these old homes today leaves the observer with an uneasy feeling. While the façade of the inner-city streetscape has undoubtedly changed, below the surface things have not changed much at all. The substructure of the nineteenth-century family home continues to provide the foundation of the modern one.

Newtown cherishes its nineteenth-century roots, and the local councils of the area fiercely protect the legacy of the old borough and the many heritage homes within their borders.

Visiting Newtown today can feel a little like time travelling, at least when one walks along the streets untouched by apartment development. The train remains the best way to get there, although the station approach is much quieter than it was a hundred years ago. Home fires no longer blanket the air with heavy smoke. The noise of hard-working butchers, bakers and candlestick makers has gone too.

The Sly family home in Newtown still towers over its neighbours. Visual cues subconsciously suggest this could be a site of tragedy and a place one should enter with caution. Traffic signs are oddly positioned, suggesting travellers should take heed. Wilson Street, which once provided a wide turning circle for horses and bakery carts, is now a narrow one-way street with a dual carriage for bikes and cars. A large sign warns motorists that no entry is possible; the distinctive red-and-white signage, now wonky and faded, tilts as if pointing towards the home rather than the street. The urn ornament still adorns the roof. The windows and shutters remain fixed as they were when the home was originally built.

Travelling further back in time to the Glebe house only raises more questions about the Slys. Glebe has changed a lot since the Edwardian era. Mitchell Street is no longer filled with street kids, and the road no longer crunches underfoot with chipped bluestone. Large liquidambar trees now tower over even the highest terrace. Sunlight breaks through to softly dapple the painted steel roofs. The abattoir has gone from Glebe, and with it the smell. In what might be labelled foretelling, some of what Alicks predicted has come to pass.

He described invisible wires across the roof of his home, which only he could see – powerlines now crisscross the street, and electrical cables swoop and dip perilously close to roofs.

The Glebe terrace that was once the Sly family home looks out serenely on a smooth plane of asphalt, and the intersection is guarded by two metal sentries: large stop signs that demand we pay closer attention. The same wrought-iron Victorian spikes adorn the front fence. The property line has not moved, firmly separating the public realm of the street from the private life going on within the borders of the tiny terrace.

There is an eclectic mix of family life and industry here, just as there was when the Slys walked these streets. A slickly suited inner-city worker rushes across the road to avoid traffic. He holds tight to his hat just as a gentleman might have in 1900, though his outfit is now topped with a fashionable trilby rather than the round-topped derby hats common at the turn of the century. A resident passes by, homeward bound, shouldering a heavy burden of grocery bags. Two women lean over a fence line, perhaps whispering gossip about family and children just as Ellie Sly and Beth Bowden would have done. On this, a spring day in 2018, the door of the old Sly family home sits slightly and ever-so-oddly ajar, just as it would have on the day when baby Norman died within its walls.

•

Though it is tempting to travel to the sites of these tragedies, in truth such journeys can never provide answers. Any discovery regarding the Slys, and what haunted them, cannot be found here. The fixtures and fittings of the homes they left behind offer no clues, and when one leans carefully against a wall to listen for any spiritual echoes, one hears only a stony cold silence.

For houses do not keep secrets; people do. And any secrets held by Alicks and Ellie Sly died with them.

ACKNOWLEDGEMENTS

THANK YOU TO MY PUBLISHER, SOPHIE HAMLEY, AND THE TEAM at Hachette, including Fiona Hazard, Kate Goldsworthy, Karen Ward, Jenny Topham, Christa Moffitt, Daniel Pilkington, Chris Sims, Katrina Collett, Louise Sherwin-Stark, Justin Ractliffe and Klara Zak.

Thank you also to:

The National Library of Australia and the treasure that is Trove.

The State Archives NSW, Kingswood, and the wonderfully committed and helpful archivists there.

Leanne Diessel at the Wagga Wagga & District Historical Society Inc.

Margaret Suda, Royal Prince Alfred Hospital, Sydney.

Mackay Family History Society.

The Little Sisters of the Poor, Randwick.

Emeritus Professor R. Lynette Russell and Dr Jenny Blundell at the Nursing History Research Unit, Sydney Nursing School, University of Sydney.

And to the members of the Sly family I have been lucky enough to meet while on the writing journey for this book. A group of kinder and more generous people you could not hope to meet: Gail Eastaway, Gloria Jesser and Susan Peters-Smith.

ENDNOTES

AUTHOR'S NOTE: WHEREVER POSSIBLE THE DIALOGUE HAS BEEN directly cited from primary source documents. A range of sources has been used to inform this process: police gazettes, gaol records, trial transcripts (divorce, criminal, inquest proceedings), media reports, witness statements provided during legal proceedings. Due to the age of this material, and the fragmented nature of archive collections available from this period, it has not always been possible to reproduce dialogue (verbatim) which may have occurred between parties. For this reason, some small sections of dialogue have been reconstructed, often corroborated using multiple sources, in order to bring this story, and the characters within it, back to life.

CHAPTER 2: THE CALL-OUT

p. 9, 'Agnew had managed to drag': 'Sydney sensation: terrible harbour fatality', *Toowoomba Chronicle and Darling Downs Advertiser*, 28 September 1899, p. 3.

p. 9, 'weights and measures': Under the NSW *Weights and Measures Act* of 1898, members of the police force were nominated to act as inspectors.

p. 9, 'electoral roll': 'Disappointed police: electoral roll', *Sydney Morning Herald*, 5 January 1904, p. 4.

p. 10, 'his duty gear': 'A new police whistle', *Riverine Grazier*, 9 August 1884; Police Department Inspector General's Office, Report to the Colonial Secretary on the Police Regulation Act of 1862, Inspector General's Office, 1–7 June 1872; 'The Police: their training and their work', *Sydney Mail and NSW Advertiser*, 24 September 1902, p. 796.

p. 12, 'Newtown at the turn of the twentieth century': *Newtown Land Use 1862–92*, 'Chapter 2: Land Use: Housing, facilities and industry', courtesy of The Newtown Project, the City of Sydney.

p. 12, 'shopfronts on King Street': 'Marvellous business at Newtown', *Australian Paper for Australian People*, 24 June 1905, p. 15.

p. 15, 'A small cartel of landlords': Newtown rate assessment books 1863–92, Newtown Council, City of Sydney Archives.

p. 17, 'William Carlton': 'Strange suicide', *Evening News*, 2 December 1890, p. 5.

p. 17, 'Almost twenty years earlier': 'Coroner's inquest', *Sydney Morning Herald*, 18 November 1886, p. 4; 'The Newtown tragedy', *Singleton Argus*, 20 November 1886, p. 1.

p. 19, 'In the past few days': 'Mad couple in Newtown', *Truth*, 17 January 1904, p. 6.

p. 20, 'white lollies': 'Tragedy at Newtown', *Daily Telegraph*, 13 January 1904, p. 8; 'Tragedy at Newtown', *Sydney Morning Herald*, 13 January 1904, p. 7.

p. 23, The Home of Hope: 'Home of Hope', *Sydney Morning Herald*, 27 December 1895, p. 3; 'Sydney Rescue Work Society', *Maitland Daily Mercury*, 14 February 1906, p. 3; 'For the poor and needy', *Sunday Times*, 7 August 1927, p. 18.

CHAPTER 3: THE DEADLINE

p. 24, The identification of Ebenezer Furley as the journalist who drafted this article has occurred via examination of his proximity to the event at the time it occurred and his availability to write an article of this kind. He lived only a few doors away and was on the scene almost immediately after it occurred. He published regularly in the press (a regular and shipping editor at the *Daily Telegraph* responsible for the timetable of comings and goings of shipping vessels), and was a colourful character known as 'The Admiral' in his later years. There is no way of confirming that Furley reported on the Newtown Tragedy, because it was not the convention at the time to name the journalists responsible for specific articles. The journalist who undertook a stealthy investigation of the house is simply described as a 'representative'.

p. 25, 'Civic concerns': 'City dust and short lives', *Australian Newsletter*, 2 April 1904, p. 15.

p. 25, 'reporters read council minutes': 'The year's returns', *Evening News*, 11 January 1904, p. 3.

p. 26, 'Petitions to remove the abattoir': Newtown City Council meeting minutes, 18 June 1901; NSW Parliament, Hansard, Sydney abattoir construction bill (second reading speech), 17 December 1906, p. 4964.

p. 26, 'butcher etiquette': Newtown City Council meeting minutes, 25 September 1900; 'Notes of the week', *Sydney Mail & NSW Advertiser*, 15 October 1902, p. 977.

p. 27, 'almost entirely of women': 'Tragedy at Newtown', *Sydney Morning Herald*, 13 January 1904, p. 7.

p. 27, Mrs Shaw's account: 'A neighbour's story', *Evening News*, 13 January 1904, p. 3.

p. 28, contextual information about the newspaper industry at the time: V. Isaacs & R. Kirkpatrick, *Two Hundred Years of Sydney Newspapers: A short history*, Rural Press, Richmond, 2003.

p. 28, 'celluloid film recordings': 'Evidence on celluloid: film screened in court', *Evening News*, 18 May 1935, p. 7.

p. 29, 'British policing in the Victorian and Edwardian eras': H. Shpayer-Makov, *The Ascent of the Detective: Police sleuths in Victorian and Edwardian England*, Oxford University Press, Oxford, 2011, p. 154.

pp. 31–37: 'The Newtown tragedy: A ghastly sight: How the bodies were found', *Evening News*, 13 January 1904, p. 3; 'Tragedy at Newtown', *Sydney Morning Herald*, 13 January 1904, p. 7; 'Terrible domestic tragedy', *Australian Star*, 13 January 1904, p. 6.

CHAPTER 4: BLACK AND WHITE AND READ ALL OVER

p. 40, 'Alicks was held by police': 'Tragedy at Newtown', *Scrutineer and Berrima District Press*, 16 January 1904.

p. 40, 'the boots were reportedly so high': 'They wore photos on their feet', *Sydney Morning Herald*, 17 January 1953, p. 9.

p. 41, 'the Slys were aware of the Push': 'Pushes and pugs: Battle at Glebe', *Australian Star*, 19 November 1904, p. 6; 'A push row', *The Maitland Daily Mercury*, 16 January 1899, p. 3.

p. 41, 'Some claim the Liver Push': J. Clare, 'Ollie Ollie Vallely: A time and isolation study', in P. Craven (ed.), *Best Australian Essays 1999*, Black Inc., Melbourne.

p. 42, 'Gangs were dangerously unpredictable': 'Chased by the push', *Evening News*, 13 July 1893, p. 3; *The Lingo: Listening to Australian English*, G. Seal, UNSW Press, Sydney, 1999; 'Disgraceful outrage', *Telegraph*, 18 December 1893, p. 4; 'The push again at hotel wreck: police assaulted', *Evening News*, 15 August 1892, p. 4; 'Glebe larrikins', *Newcastle Morning Herald and Miners' Advocate*, 17 February 1902, p. 6; 'Larrikins at the Glebe', *Australian Star*, 15 August 1902, p. 6.

p. 42, 'Victims and witnesses of assaults': 'The Push on the warpath', *Evening News*, 12 January 1891, p. 3.

p. 42, 'One journalist called': 'Straw hat push', *Evening News*, 24 February 1899, p. 8.

p. 42, 'In 1897, the tension': 'The push and the police', *Bathurst Free Press and Mining Journal*, 9 March 1897, p. 2; 'Sydney pushes', *Maitland Weekly Mercury*, 13 March 1897, p. 14.

p. 43, 'After Alicks died': 'Tragedy at Newtown', *Scrutineer and Berrima District Press*, 16 January 1904, p. 5.

p. 43, 'Law-abiding Sydneysiders': 'The push militant', *Australian Star*, 5 June 1900, p. 4.

p. 43, 'According to newspapers': 'A domestic tragedy', *Narracoorte Herald*, 19 January 1904, p. 4.

p. 45, 'A 1908 British Royal Commission': Great Britain. Royal Commission on the Care and Control of the Feeble-Minded: *[Report]*. (London: printed for H.M. Stationery Off. by Wyman and Sons, 1908), p. 136.

p. 45, 'A century later': H. Freeman, 'Psychiatry in Britain, c. 1900', *History of Psychiatry*, vol. 21, no. 3, 2010, pp. 312–324.

p. 46, 'Editorials from this era': 'The morally insane: a child's deep-laid plot', *Mosman Mail*, 12 August 1905, p. 5.

p. 46, 'The propagation of lunatics', *Daily Telegraph*, 3 November 1894, p. 7.

p. 46, 'Tom Butler noted': T. Butler, *Mental Health, Social Policy and the Law*, Palgrave Macmillan, London, 1985, p. 77.

p. 47, 'A number of newspapers investigated': 'Murder and suicide at Newtown, *Sydney Mail*, 13 January 1904, p. 84; 'A ghastly tragedy', *Chronicle*, 16 January 1904, p. 30; 'Tragedy at Newtown', *National Advocate*, 13 January 1904, p. 2; 'A shocking tragedy', *Leader*, 16 January 1904.

p. 47, 'Spirituality': 'The Newtown tragedy', *Newcastle Morning Herald and Miners' Advocate*, 14 January 1904, p. 5.

pp. 48–49, 'Dr Alfred Gabay': A. Gabay, 'Alfred Deakin and Swedenborg: An Australian Experience', *The Journal of Religious History*, vol. 16, no. 1, June 1990, pp. 74–90.

p. 49, 'Henry Melville': H. Melville, *Sermons on Certain of the Less Prominent Facts and References in Sacred Story*, vol. 1, London, Rivingtons, 1872, pp. 57–58.

p. 49, 'He could channel messages': A. Gabay, *Messages from Beyond: Spiritualism and Spiritualists in Melbourne's Golden Age 1870–1890*, Melbourne University Press, Melbourne, 2001; 'The Newtown tragedy' *Evening News*, 13 January 1904.

p. 49, 'Alpheus': A. Alpheus, *Complete Hypnotism: Mesmerism, Mind-Reading and Spiritualism. How to Hypnotize: Being an Exhaustive and Practical System of Method, Application, and Use*, M.A Donohue & Co., Chicago, 1903.

p. 50, 'Some mediums used objects': W. Reichel, *An Occultist's Travels*, R. Fenno & Co., New York, 1908, p. 172.

p. 50, 'Edward Power': 'A believer in spirits: spooks, ventriloquism and hypnotism', *Evening News*, 21 February 1907, p. 3.

pp. 51–52, 'Police had failed': 'Mad couple in Newtown', *Truth*, 17 January 1904, p. 6.

p. 52, 'An article written two days after': 'Baptism of blood', *Singleton Argus*, 14 January 1904, p. 2.

p. 53, 'As *Truth* wrote': 'Mad couple in Newtown', *Truth*, 17 January 1904, p. 6.

p. 53, 'Perhaps, as one newspaper suggested': 'Shocking tragedy', *Clarence River Advocate*, 15 January 1904, p. 4.

CHAPTER 5: BAD APPLE

p. 55, 'Families grew and sold apples': A. McConnell & N. Servant, *The History and Heritage of the Tasmanian Apple Industry*, Queen Victoria Museum and Art Gallery, Launceston, 1999.

p. 55, 'Henry Reynolds': Henry Reynolds, 'That hated stain: the aftermath of transportation in Tasmania', *Historical Studies*, vol. 14, no. 53, 1969, p. 21.

p. 55, 'In the mid-1880s': B. Madley, 'From terror to genocide: Britain's Tasmanian penal colony and Australia's history wars', *Journal of British Studies*, vol. 47, no. 1, 2008, p. 82.

p. 56, 'John was a skilled craftsman': *Tasmanian Morning Herald*, 25 September 1866, p. 2.

p. 56, 'His boots were so impressive': 'Imports', *Colonial Times*, 23 November 1854, p. 2; *Hobart Town Courier and Van Diemen's Land Gazette*, 26 June 1840, p. 4.

p. 56, 'The brothers did not discriminate': 'Winter boots and shoes', *Hobarton Guardian*, 1 April 1854, p. 1.

p. 57, 'Loose jackets known as mantles': 'Classified advertising', *Hobart Town Daily Mercury*, 12 November 1859, p. 4; 'Classified advertising', *Hobart Town Daily Mercury*, 13 October 1859, p. 1.

p. 58, 'These deaths were harrowing': 'Deaths', *The Mercury*, 22 January 1863, p. 1.

p. 58, 'The buildings burnt to the ground': 'Tasmania', *The Argus*, 7 May 1859, p. 5.

p. 59, 'Local farming families were distressed': 'Apple Grub', *Launceston Examiner*, 21 February 1861, p. 3; 'The Codlin Moth Act', *The Mercury*, 1 March 1888, p. 4.

p. 59, 'those in remote areas': *Cornwall Chronicle*, 21 July 1876, p. 2.

p. 60–61, 'The Bridgewater murder', *The Courier*, 19 March 1859, p. 3; 'Horrible murder of a child near Bridgewater', *The Courier*, 17 March 1859, p. 3; 'The murder of Alice Hughes', *Launceston Examiner*, 5 June

1860, p. 2; 'Tasmania: the murder of Alice Hughes', *Geelong Advertiser*, 12 June 1860, p. 2; *Hobart Town Mercury*, 29 February 1860, p. 2.

pp. 62–63, 'William Charles': 'Family notices', *The Mercury*, 4 June 1881, p. 4.

p. 63, 'Only the right genetic combination': C.A. House, *Leghorn Fowls Exhibition and Utility*, Poultry World Ltd, 2015.

p. 64, 'Local newspapers were proud': 'Dunedin canary and poultry show', *The Mercury*, 8 September 1873, p. 2.

p. 65, 'The society had a reputation': 'Colonial Mutual Life Assurance Society', *Sydney Mail and NSW Advertiser*, 18 December 1886, p. 32.

CHAPTER 6: COLD COMFORT

pp. 70–71, 'a cleaning catharsis': 'Funerals & classified advertisement column', *Evening News*, 1 May 1896, p. 1.

pp. 72–73, 'Beth Bowden': 'A woman's statement', *Australian Star*, 13 January 1904, p. 6.

p. 74, 'Arnott's': 'Advertising', *Evening News*, 16 September 1905, p. 12.

p. 74, 'The coroner ruled': 'Parramatta', *Evening News*, 14 January 1890, p. 6; 'A sad case of poverty and suffering', *Cumberland Argus and Fruitgrowers Advocate*, 4 January 1890, p. 8.

pp. 74–75, 'miracle cure Zam-Buk': 'The composition of certain secret remedies – preparations for eczema', *The British Medical Journal*, vol. 1, no. 2468, 1908, pp. 942–44; 'Child's terrible eczema', *Preston Leader*, 4 April 1914, p. 4.

p. 75, 'Mrs Bowden was not afraid': 'Sunday trading', *Evening News*, 31 October 1900, p. 4; 'Police courts', *Sydney Morning Herald*, 7 July 1897, p. 10.

CHAPTER 7: LOW-HANGING FRUIT

p. 81, 'Cornelius migrated first': *Goulburn Herald and Chronicle*, 10 June 1868, p. 2.

pp. 81–82, 'one newspaper wrote of Goulburn': 'The City of Goulburn', *Sydney Mail & NSW Advertiser*, 28 July 1894, p. 179.

pp. 82–83, 'Stella Miles Franklin described Goulburn': Jill Roe, '*My Brilliant Career* and 1890s Goulburn', *Australian Literary Studies*, vol. 20, no. 4, October 2002, pp. 359–369.

p. 83, 'Almost every resident': 'American grapes and blight proof apples', *Empire*, 9 July 1874, p. 4.

p. 83, 'resilient varieties': 'Fruit at Goulburn', *Australian Town and Country Journal*, 14 April 1888, p. 45.

p. 84, 'Despite the best efforts': P. Belbin & D. Burke, *Changing Trains: A century of travel on the Sydney–Melbourne Railway*, Methuen, North Ryde, 1982, p. 21.

p. 84, Mountmellick style of needlework: Mountmellick lace article and information courtesy of Laois Heritage Society and B. Dunne.

p. 86, 'on reaching manhood': 'Country news: Goulburn deaths', *Evening News*, 22 August 1891, p. 6.

p. 86, 'Timmy, the eldest': 'St Joseph's Convent School, Windsor', *Freeman's Journal*, 30 December 1882, p. 16.

p. 87, 'The young man decided to stop over': 'Obituary', *Goulburn Herald*, 14 August 1891, p. 5.

p. 88, 'Late in the evening': 'Miraculous escape for Mr O'Leary', *Goulburn Evening Penny Post*, 18 August 1891, p. 4.

pp. 88–89, 'The funeral for Jerry': 'Country news: Goulburn deaths', *Evening News*, 22 August 1891, p. 6.

p. 89, 'a mystery illness': A. C. Peterson, 'Brain fever in nineteenth century literature: fact or fiction', *Victorian Studies*, vol. 19, no. 4, 1976, pp. 445–464.

p. 90, 'he listed the property in Currawang': 'Advertising: By order of the mortgagees and for positive sale, O'Leary's farm Currawang', *Goulburn Evening Penny Post*, 17 November 1892, p. 3.

p. 91, 'For those travelling to and from Goulburn': 'A trip to Goulburn', *Empire*, 27 June 1870, p. 3; 'Cyclists on the road', *Australian Star*, 19 January 1895, p. 8; 'Goulburn Liedertafel', *Goulburn Evening Penny Post*, 11 October 1902, p. 2.

p. 91, 'He was a member of the executive committee': 'In the court of arbitration', *Government Gazette of the State of NSW*, issue no. 382, 24 July 1903, p. 5489.

p. 92, 'They were being denied work': 'A tailor's wail', *Truth*, 15 March 1903, p. 6.

p. 92, 'Bradon Ellem': B.L. Ellem, 'The history of the clothing and allied trades union', University of Wollongong thesis, 1986, p. 80.

p. 93, 'James Padley, a founding pioneer': 'Lithgow news', *Lithgow Mercury*, 15 January 1904, p. 4.

p. 94, Stella Miles Franklin cited in J. Roe, '1890s Goulburn and *My Brilliant Career*', *Australian Literary Studies*, vol. 20, no. 4, October 2002, pp. 359–69.

p. 95, 'The separation between Catholic and Protestant families': S. A. McHugh, 'Marrying out – Catholic–Protestant unions in Australia, 1920s–70s', *Negotiating the Sacred V: Governing the family*, Arts Faculty, Monash University, Victoria, 14–15 August 2008.

p. 95, 'The year 1894 began dreadfully': 'Death', *Goulburn Herald*, 12 February 1894, p. 3; *Goulburn Evening Penny Post*, 13 February 1894, p. 2.

p. 98, 'The only public acknowledgement': 'Family notices: married', *Goulburn Evening Penny Post*, 6 October 1894, p. 2.

CHAPTER 8: MOTHER'S SAD MISTAKE

p. 100, 'Goulburn was sleepy': 'The City of Goulburn', *Sydney Mail & NSW Advertiser*, 28 July 1894, p. 179.

p. 101, 'In the early years of their marriage': 'Evening meeting', *Sydney Morning Herald*, 14 May 1894, p. 6.

p. 101, 'Diphtheria', *The Dawn*, 1 May 1897, p. 37.

pp. 101–102, 'Board of Health statement': Newtown council meeting minutes, 24 April 1900.

p. 104, 'compulsory motherhood': A. James Hammerton, *Cruelty and Companionship: Conflict in Nineteenth-Century Married Life*, Routledge, Oxford, 1992.

p. 105, 'The year 1902': 'The Plague', *Sydney Morning Herald*, 12 February 1902, p. 8; 'Plague', *Balmain Observer and Western Suburbs Advertiser*, 22 February 1902, p. 4.

p. 106, plague in Sydney: 'The plague and city council', *Australian Star*, 21 February 1902, p. 4; 'The plague and the Health Act', *Sydney Morning Herald*, 24 March 1902, p. 6; 'Bubonic plague', *Sydney Morning Herald*, 3 December 1902, p. 13; 'The plague in Sydney', *Clarence and Richmond Examiner*, 4 March 1902, p. 5.

p. 106, 'Fear also escalated': 'Death', *Goulburn Evening Penny Post*, 3 April 1902, p. 4.

p. 106, 'They ended up in Glebe': 'The gruesome mysteries of the Glebe Island abattoirs. How the offal is disposed of. Some objectionable surroundings', *Sunday Times*, 15 March 1896, p. 5.

p. 108, 'Selling adulterated milk', *Daily Telegraph*, 24 July 1902, p. 8.

p. 108, 'the available data on mortality': M.W. De Looper, 'Death registration and mortality trends in Australia 1856–1906', thesis submitted for the degree of PhD, ANU, Canberra, 2014.

p. 109, 'Many children died from drinking carbolic acid': 'Child poisoned', *Kalgoorlie Miner*, 15 March 1898, p. 8; 'A child accidentally poisoned', *Express and Telegraph*, 16 December 1905, p. 1.

pp. 110–111, Nellie Neely: Courtesy of member of Glebe Society Inc. documents: source identified as Lyn Collingwood.

pp. 111–113, cases of child poisoning: 'A sad case: accidental poisoning of a little girl', *Australian Star*, 24 October 1906, p. 4; 'Inquest on a child', *The Age*, 14 March 1892, p. 7; 'Accidental poisoning', *The Advocate*, 20 June 1890, p. 3; 'Child's strange death', *Australian Star*, 4 July 1905, p. 4; 'Accidental poisoning', *Albury Banner and Wodonga Express*, 15 October 1897, p. 28; 'Child poisoned', *Newcastle Morning Herald*, 24 March 1886, p. 5; 'Accidental poisoning with arsenic', *The Age*, 17 May 1895, p. 6; 'Poison', *Carcoar Chronicle*, 6 December 1901, p. 4; 'The public health', *Narromine News and Trangie Advocate*, 10 May 1901, p. 6; 'Death in cough lozenges', *Goulburn Evening Penny Post/ Sydney Daily Telegraph*, 5 September 1899, p. 4; 'Mother's sad mistake: Unsuspectingly poisons her child', *Evening News*, 15 October 1904, p. 6.

p. 113, 'As fear of the plague grew': 'Rat destruction', *Evening News*, 30 November 1901, p. 3.

p. 114, 'many unemployed people': 'Solving the unemployed difficulty', *Young Chronicle*, 1 July 1903, p. 2.

p. 114, 'occupations that had been doing it toughest': 'A tailor's wail', *Truth*, 15 March 1903, p. 6.

CHAPTER 9: TRAGEDY UNFOLDS

p. 120, 'Cohen had tried and failed': 'Attributed suicide to lack of work', *Sunday Times*, 19 June 1904, p. 8; 'It is terrible: a Sydney suicide', *The West Australian*, 14 June 1904, p. 4.

p. 121, 'When a man turns grey': 'Pathetic suicide', *Albury Banner and Wodonga Express*, 24 October 1902, p. 28.

pp. 121–122, Lieutenant John Ellis: 'Curious suicide', *Wagga Wagga Advertiser and Riverine Reporter*, 26 April 1871, p. 4.

p. 122, Thomas Cross: 'An Old Man's End', *Evening News*, 26 January 1903, p. 4; 'Suicide's remarkable letter', *Blayney Advocate and Carcoar Herald*, 31 January 1903, p. 4.

pp. 122–123, 'A case from Melbourne': 'Note found near the morgue', *Ballarat Star*, 24 August 1911, p. 1.

p. 123, 'A note in Sydney': 'Forgive me: man cut to pieces', *National Advocate*, 22 February 1912, p. 2.

p. 123, 'Some suicide letters': 'Suicide's note', *The Argus*, 23 January 1908, p. 4.

p. 123, 'In an attempted murder–suicide': 'Erskineville tragedy', *Sydney Morning Herald*, 15 November 1902, p. 6.

pp. 123–124, 'When Annie Chapman was found': 'Bathurst Suicide: a pathetic letter', *Australian Star*, 17 December 1896, p. 4.

p. 124, 'In Tom Goodman's case': 'Extraordinary suicide', *Maitland Mercury and Hunter River General Advertiser*, 21 November 1876, p. 3.

p. 124, 'When John Edward Collins': 'Romantic suicide', *Armidale Express and New England General Advertiser*, 28 February 1902, p. 6.

pp. 124–125, 'the death of John Urban Vigors': 'Distressing suicide: Coroner's inquest', *Newcastle Chronicle and Hunter River District News*, 23 August 1865, p. 3; 'Distressing suicide of a railway mail guard at Newcastle', *Sydney Mail*, 26 August 1865, p. 6.

p. 126, George Goldthorpe: 'Suicide by a boy', *Richmond River and Northern Districts Advertiser*, 5 June 1891, p. 4; 'Suicide by a lad', *Sydney Morning Herald*, 26 May 1891.

pp. 126–127, Frank Bradford: 'A suicide's letter: preferred death to charity', *Evening News*, 31 May 1900, p. 3.

p. 127, 'The case of Fred Quintell': 'Suicide', *Walcha Witness and Vernon County Record*, 12 January 1901, p. 2.

p. 127, 'If the deceased referred to': 'Tired of life', *Advertiser*, 23 June 1903, p. 4.

p. 128, 'prussic acid': 'Prussic acid', *Southern Argus*, 4 January 1906, p. 4.

p. 128, 'The name prussic acid became popular': D. Beasley & W. Glass, 'Cyanide poisoning: pathophysiology and treatment recommendations', *Occupational Medicine*, vol. 48, no. 7, pp. 427–431.

p. 129, 'he had noticed Plunkett wandering': 'Centennial Park suicide', *Evening News*, 1 August 1901, p. 3.

p. 129, Charles Huffington Bowman: 'Sad suicide', *Goulburn Evening Penny Post*, 7 June 1892, p. 4; 'Suicide', *Sydney Mail and New South Wales Advertiser*, 11 June 1892, p. 1358.

pp. 129–130, Francis Price: 'Suicide', *Australian Star*, 22 July 1893, p. 11.

p. 130, 'Alicks Sly's final words': 'Murder and suicide', *Newcastle Morning Herald and Miners' Advocate*, 13 January 1904, p. 5.

p. 130, 'As one newspaper wrote': 'The Sly Tragedy', *Darling Downs Gazette*, 14 January 1904, p. 3.

pp. 131–132, Ellie's letter: 'The Newtown Tragedy', *Maitland Daily Mercury*, 13 January 1904, p. 5. Author's note: The actual letters were destroyed; they appear nowhere in the files or probate documents or anything else that was found in the house. Instead what we must go with is a version – the best approximation – by cross-referencing the different reports of the letter.

p. 134, 'The violin belonging to Ellie': 'Palings Music Instruments Advertisement', *Clarence and Richmond Examiner*, 5 July 1902, p. 2.

CHAPTER 10: THE INQUEST

p. 136, accounts of the inquest: 'The inquest', *Scrutineer and Berrima District Press*, 13 January 1904, p. 2; 'Newtown sensation', *Bathurst Free and Mining Journal*, 14 January 1904, p. 3; 'The Newtown tragedy', *Sydney Morning Herald*, 14 January 1904, p. 5; 'Newtown tragedy inquest of victims', *Newcastle Morning Herald and Miners' Advocate*, 14 January 1904, p. 5; 'The Newtown tragedy', *Evening News*, 13 January 1904, p. 5; 'The Newtown tragedy', *Daily Telegraph*, 14 January 1904, p. 7; 'The inquest', *Burrowa News*, 15 January 1904, p. 3.

p. 137, 'While high-profile inquest cases': 'Crowds at the Lloyd Hotel', *Australian Star*, 25 April 1904, p. 5.

p. 137, 'the production of a monthly statistical output': 'Suicide statistics', *The Telegraph*, 12 October 1907, p. 11.

pp. 138–139, Durkheim on suicide: E. Durkheim, *Suicide*, 1897, p. 80.

p. 139, 'Durkheim was recommended reading': Government Gazette of the State of NSW, 10 July 1903, issue no. 354, p. 5093.

p. 139, 'For Durkheim, it was all about context': E. Durkheim, *Suicide*, 1897, p. 94.

p. 139, 'According to one 1903 headline': 'Suicide', *The Telegraph*, 27 June 1903, p. 6.

p. 140, 'The answer: alcohol': F. van Poppel & L. Day, 'A Test of Durkheim's Theory of Suicide – Without Committing the "Ecological Fallacy"', *American Sociological Review*, vol. 61, no. 3, June 1996, pp. 500–507.

pp. 140–141, 'In the years preceding the Sly inquest, the Catholic Church': 'The crime of suicide', *Southern Cross*, 1 March 1901, p. 7.

p. 141, 'When the men entered the parlour': 'Suicide', *Table Talk*, 28 June 1900, p. 3.

p. 142, 'As one commentary on insanity noted a year later': 'Insanity', *Clarence and Richmond Examiner*, 19 September 1905, p. 4.

p. 145, 'Alicks's father was called first': 'Newtown sensation', *Bathurst Free Press and Mining Journal*, 14 January 1904, p. 3.

pp. 151–153, 'Sergeant Agnew was called': 'Terrible domestic tragedy', *Australian Star*, 13 January 1904, p. 6.

CHAPTER 11: MARRIAGE, MURDER AND METEOROLOGY

p. 158, 'Unripe fruit undertaker's friend', *Bendigo News*, 24 October 1907, p. 3.

p. 159, 'Divorce', *Freeman's Journal*, 15 February 1902, p. 19.

p. 160, C. Webb, 'Hospital records paint bleak picture of 1800s Melbourne', *The Age*, 7 June 2010. Data drawn from Patients in Melbourne Hospital 1856–1905.

p. 161, 'As a columnist for the *Sunday Times*': 'Wife beating', *Sunday Times*, 10 December 1899, p. 10.

p. 161, 'A similar observation': 'Wife beating', *Weekly Times*, 13 September 1873, p. 8.

p. 162, 'In the case of Pearce': C. James, 'A history of cruelty in Australian divorce', *ALZLH*, 2006, p. 22.

pp. 162–163, 'Legal historian Dr Colin James': ibid.

pp. 164–165, Richard Sparrow: 'Domestic tragedy', *Ballarat Star*, 19 February 1904, p. 3; 'The bazaar terrace affair', *The Mail*, 11 April 1904, p. 4.

pp. 165–166, Fanny Pannell: 'A patient wife', *Australian Star*, 10 March 1904, p. 4.

p. 166–167, James Horner: 'Wife murder and suicide', *The Register*, 18 April 1904, p. 4.

p. 167, Joseph Riley: 'Alleged attempted murder and suicide', *Daily Telegraph*, 16 May 1904, p. 5.

pp. 167–168, George and Rachel Savage: 'Savage v. Savage', *Australian Star*, 7 June 1904, p. 5.

p. 168, Robert Kingsley: 'Doings in divorce, *Truth*, 23 July 1904, p. 3.

p. 168, Joseph Artery: 'Murder and suicide', *The Argus*, 3 August 1904, p. 5.

p. 168–169, Joseph Duff: 'Attempted wife murder', *The Argus*, 6 September 1904, p. 7; 'An unfortunate man', *Evening Journal*, 28 September 1904, p. 2.

pp. 169–170, Tom Wood: 'Domestic tragedy', *Australian Star*, 6 October 1904, p. 5; 'Attempted murder and suicide', *Record*, 8 October 1904, p. 3.

p. 170, Mary O'Hara: 'Crown street tragedy', *Sydney Mail and NSW Advertiser*, 23 November 1904, p. 1339; 'Crown street tragedy', *Australian Star*, 22 November 1904, p. 7.

pp. 170–171, 'Several cases have been dealt with': 'Wife murders', *Cobar Herald*, 10 December 1904, p. 6.

p. 171, James Minahan: *The Mercury*, 5 January 1904, p. 4; 'Fearful tragedy', *Geelong Advertiser*, 5 January 1904, p. 4; 'Horrible murder', *Kerang New Times*, 5 January 1904, p. 2; *Zeehan and Dundas Herald*, 5 January 1904, p. 3; 'Terrible wife murder', *Ovens and Murray Advertiser*, 9 January 1904, p. 4.

pp. 171–172, 'James's admissions in court': *Ballarat Star*, 5 January 1904, p. 1; Register of bodies brought to North Sydney Morgue 4 January 1904, no. 1114, p. 354.

p. 172, 'entirely attributable to intemperence': 'Waterloo tragedy', *Australian Star*, 18 February 1904, p. 6.

p. 172, 'One neighbour commented': 'Murdered with an axe', *North Eastern Ensign*, 8 January 1904, p. 3.

p. 172, 'Though she was afraid of her husband': 'Waterloo tragedy', *Evening News*, 9 January 1904, p. 6.

p. 172, 'A doctor came forward to say': 'Central criminal court', *Zeehan and Dundas Herald*, 18 February 1904, p. 2.

CHAPTER 12: SECOND-HAND GOODS

pp. 181–182, 'It was the equivalent of about a day's wage': 'Seven shillings a day', *Sydney Morning Herald*, 3 December 1900, p. 6.

p. 182, 'Marcus Clark', *Sunday Times*, 17 December 1905, p. 7.

p. 184, 'There was a market for second-hand clothing': *Sydney Morning Herald*, 22 August 1904, p. 12.

p. 185, 'trade in lard': ibid.

p. 186, 'All costs associated with the sale': Newtown rate assessment books 1863–92, Newtown Council, City of Sydney Archives.

pp. 191–193, Information about life in the Hills District in the early twentieth century drawn from *The Hills Oral History Project*, The Hills Shire Council, interviews gathered 2002–2009.

p. 193, 'St Michael's Orphanage', *Cumberland Argus and Fruit Growers Advocate*, 6 March 1918, p. 2.

p. 193, 'The initial debt owed to the Church': 'St Michael's Orphanage', *Cumberland Argus and Fruit Growers Advocate*, 18 February 1905, p. 11.

p. 193, Cardinal Moran: ibid.

p. 193, 'The nuns had to answer for every thimble': 'The cardinal at Baulkham Hills', *Freeman's Journal*, 18 February 1905, p. 25.

CHAPTER 13: THE SWORD OF ST MICHAEL

p. 199, 'One commentator who visited': 'The cardinal at Baulkham Hills', *Freeman's Journal*, 25 April 1903, p. 25.

p. 200, 'One statement by an official': 'St Michael's Orphanage, Baulkham Hills', *Sydney Morning Herald*, 14 February 1905, p. 8.

p. 201, 'A 1903 newspaper article': 'The cardinal at Baulkham Hills, Opening St Michael's orphanage', *Freeman's Journal*, 25 April 1903, p. 25.

p. 201, 'Sisters of the order lived': 'St Michael's orphanage', *Catholic Press*, 30 March 1933, p. 17.

p. 201, 'By February 1905': 'St Michael's Orphanage, Baulkham Hills', *Sydney Morning Herald*, 14 February 1905, p. 8.

p. 201, 'They were expected to attend classes': 'Baulkham Hills orphanage', *Cumberland Argus and Fruitgrowers Advocate*, 16 April 1913, p. 2.

p. 201, 'At the outset of World War I': 'Farewell to the good nuns', *Cumberland Argus and Fruitgrowers Advocate*, 31 July 1915, p. 8.

p. 203, 'One journalist claimed': 'The cardinal at Baulkham hills, Opening St Michael's orphanage', *Freeman's Journal*, 25 April 1903, p. 25.

p. 204, Cardinal Moran's visit: 'St Michael's Orphanage', *Cumberland Argus and Fruitgrowers Advocate*, 18 February 1905, p. 11.

pp. 204–205, St Patrick's Day: 'St Patrick's Day. A record celebration', *Freeman's Journal*, 24 March 1906, p. 12.

p. 206, St Vincent's: 'The cardinal at Baulkham hills, Opening St Michael's orphanage', *Freeman's Journal*, 25 April 1903, p. 25.

p. 207, description of St Vincent's: 'Progress at Westmead Home: the new workshops', *Catholic Press*, 29 November 1906, p. 22.

p. 208, 'St Vincent's was a Home': 'Boys' industrial home', *Daily Telegraph*, 3 November 1913, p. 12.

p. 208, 'threatened the institution with fraud': 'In the assembly', *Richmond River Express and Casino Kyogle Advertiser*, 25 August 1905, p. 2.

p. 209, 'bright with God's sunshine': 'Cardinal Moran at Westmead', *Daily Telegraph*, 18 November 1907, p. 4.

CHAPTER 14: MAKING ENDS MEET

pp. 211–212, 'compulsory military training': C. Stockings, 'The Great Debate: Conscription and national service 1912–1972', *Proceedings of Conference Held at Pompey Elliot Memorial Hall, Camberwell RSL*, Military History and Heritage, Victoria, 30 May 2015; 'Dodged parade. Roll Call in court. The captain and his cadets', *Cumberland Argus and Fruitgrowers Advocate*, 3 August 1912, p. 12.

p. 213, 'the innocence of a teenage boy': 'Dodged parade. Roll Call in court. The captain and his cadets', *Cumberland Argus and Fruitgrowers Advocate*, 3 August 1912, p. 12.

p. 214, 'In a 1916 paper': 'A case of shell shock: remarkable features', *Barrier Miner*, 19 March 1916, p. 4.

p. 216, 'what some swaggies claimed to have done': 'Escapee caught', *Wagga Wagga Express*, 20 February 1932, p. 12.

p. 217, 'an open cutting near the Devon Consols': 'Devon Gold Mine', *The Argus*, 12 February 1925, p. 8.

p. 219, 'We now know that trauma alters brainwave patterns': M. Mar, I. Linden, I. Torchalla, K. Li & M. Krausz, 'Are childhood abuse and neglect related to age of first homelessness episode among currently homeless adults?', *Violence and Victims*, vol. 29, no. 6, 2014, pp. 999–2013.

p. 220, 'While a fugitive from one vagrancy charge': 'Items of news', *Kalgoorlie Miner*, 21 April 1928, p. 4.

pp. 220–221, Carss Park: Municipality of Kogarah Advertisement, Kogarah Historical Society sourced in *Landscape Heritage Study for Carss Bush Park*, Kogarah Council, 2002.

p. 223, 'while vagrancy statutes have a law-and-order function': Alex Steel, 'Consorting in New South Wales: substantive offence or police power?', *University of New South Wales Law Journal*, vol. 26, no. 3, 2003, pp. 567–602.

pp. 223–224, Herbert H. Macdougal: 'Get him a feed: magistrate's pity', *Sydney Morning Herald*, 27 August 1931, p. 6; 'Kogarah Police Court', *St George Call*, 20 December 1929, p. 2; 'SM Cannot punish them', *The Labor Daily*, 9 August 1930, p. 7.

p. 224, 'Olive asked for Macdougal's permission': 'White girl and a chow found living in market gardens in Manly: SM prevents marriage', *Truth*, 24 February 1929, p. 24.

p. 225, 'Violet Young was also found': 'White girl's awful degradation', *Truth*, 5 January 1930, p. 20.

p. 225, 'Even by 1930s standards': 'Sentence varied', *Labor Daily*, 5 June 1926, p. 7; 'Quarter sessions appeals', *Sydney Morning Herald*, 6 June 1928, p. 12; 'Appeal is upheld', *Labor Daily*, 7 December 1927, p. 6.

p. 225, 'When it came to homelessness': 'Vagrant convicted', *Sydney Morning Herald*, 1 September 1933, p. 12.

p. 226, 'Bedford was sentenced to six months': 'Man sent to gaol', *The Propeller*, 30 June 1933, p. 7.

p. 227, 'In 1941, Bedford materialised': 'In court today', *Newcastle Sun*, 25 September 1942, p. 4.

p. 228, 'In 1946, he surfaced': 'Leaders wanted for Goulburn youth association', *Goulburn Evening Penny Post*, 25 August 1944, p. 1.

p. 228, 'Next he turned up in Cootamundra': 'Police Court', *Cootamundra Herald*, 22 July 1947, p. 2.

CHAPTER 15: A HAPPY DEATH

p. 236, 'He attended the annual reunions': 'St Vincent's', *The Catholic Press*, 2 January 1930, p. 15.

p. 237, 'dingo lingo': K. Richards, *The Story of Australian English*, NewSouth, NSW, 2015.

pp. 237–238, 'Basil selected a much more ambitious': 'Social and gift evening', *Camden News*, 30 August 1917, p. 1.

p. 238, 'His love of poetry blossomed': 'Pomeroy War Chest', *Goulburn Evening Penny Post*, 16 November 1918, p. 4.

p. 240, 'According to the 1930s mission statement': 'Catholic', *Freeman's Journal*, 28 November 1935, p. 7.

CHAPTER 16: VICTORY IN THE PACIFIC

p. 245, 'For men who entered adulthood': J. Gray, *A Military History of Australia*, Cambridge University Press, Melbourne, 2008, p. 88.

p. 247, 'By the end of the war': ibid., p. 91.

p. 248, 'In the seaside suburb of Ramsgate': 'Ramsgate Life saving club', *St George Call*, 15 December 1922, p. 8.

p. 248, the surf lifesaving movement: 'Life saving', *Sydney Morning Herald*, 14 September 1927, p. 16; 'Royal life saving carnival', *Arrow*, 11 March 1927, p. 7; 'Life savers', *Daily Telegraph*, 15 March 1927, p. 8.

p. 249, ocean baths: K. Rew, *Wild Swim: River, Lake, Lido and Sea: The best places to swim outdoors in Britain*, Guardian Books, London, 2008. Used by *Australian Dictionary of Biography* entry on ocean baths.

p. 252, Roseville baths: 'Roseville chase', *The Sun*, 20 August 1923, p. 3; 'Roseville swimming carnival', *Labor Daily*, 24 February 1936, p. 7.

p. 252, 'The baths were so well known': 'Roseville Girls' College', *Sydney Morning Herald*, 26 November 1940, p. 19.

p. 253, 'It is estimated that around sixty thousand': R. Dunbar, *The Secrets of the Anzacs: The untold story of venereal disease in the Australian Army 1914–19*, Scribe, Melbourne, 2014.

p. 254, 'Swimming teams came from all over': 'Big programme at Roseville', *The Sun*, 11 December 1939, p. 18.

p. 255, 'He would have to apply for enlistment': 'Air Force needs Men Now', *Daily Examiner*, 6 February 1942, p. 4.

CHAPTER 17: IN THE SHADE OF THE OLD APPLE TREE

pp. 266–267, 'It was 1 March 1929': 'Domestic tragedy', *Northern Star*, 2 March 1929, p. 9; 'Throat gashed', *The Sun*, 1 March 1929, p. 11.

p. 268, 'They must be husband and wife': 'Shocking tragedy', *Singleton Argus*, 2 March 1929, p. 2.

p. 268, 'When police interviewed him later': 'Throat slashed', *Evening News*, 1 March 1929, p. 9.

p. 271, 'the fugitive jumped into a section of the river': 'Woman murdered', *The West Australian*, 2 March 1929, p. 19.

p. 272, 'For some time, it was a stand-off': 'Tragedy at Five Dock', *Daily Advertiser*, 2 March 1929, p. 1.

p. 273, 'The woman was his mother': 'Murder in street', *Albany Advertiser*, 2 March 1929, p. 1.

p. 273, 'At the Burwood court inquest': 'Throat cut', *Evening News*, 25 March 1929, p. 10.

p. 274, 'After Hazel's death': 'Fighting husband', *The Herald*, 23 July 1926, p. 6; 'Five Dock tragedy', *Sydney Morning Herald*, 26 March 1929, p. 12.

p. 276, 'There had never been a police report': 'Shocking tragedy', *Cairns Post*, 4 March 1929, p. 5.

p. 276, 'In 1922, while Lillian was recuperating': 'Other cases', *The Age*, 26 July 1926, p. 17; Divorce index books 1926, Victorian Supreme Court.

p. 280, 'Mr Doria said that Frederick': 'The eternal triangle', *Truth*, 19 November 1922, p. 3.

ALSO BY TANYA BRETHERTON

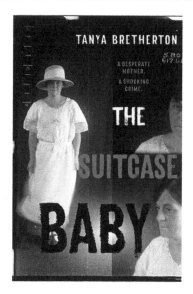

SHORTLISTED FOR

2018 Ned Kelly Award
2018 Mark & Evette Moran 'Nib' Literary Award
2018 Danger Prize

In the early hours of Saturday, 17 November 1923, a suitcase was found washed up on the shore of a small beach in Sydney. What it contained – and why – would prove to be shocking . . .

Sociologist Tanya Bretherton masterfully tells the engrossing and moving story of the crime that put Sarah Boyd and her baby at the centre of a social tragedy that still resonates through the decades.